MULTIHULLS

FOR CRUISING AND RACING

MULTIHULLS

FOR CRUISING AND RACING

Derek Harvey

INTERNATIONAL MARINE PUBLISHING COMPANY
Camden, Maine

Published by International Marine
Camden, Maine

10 9 8 7 6 5 4 3 2 1

Copyright © Derek Harvey 1991

TAB BOOKS offers software for sale. For information
and a catalog, please contact TAB Software Department,
Blue Ridge Summit, PA 17294–0850.

Questions regarding the content of this book should be
addressed to:
International Marine Publishing Company
P.O. Box 220
Camden, ME 04843

First published in Great Britain by Adlard Coles, 1990.
Printed and bound in Great Britain.

ISBN 0-87742-293-1

CONTENTS

FOREWORD

by Austin P. Farrar C. Eng., F.R.I.N.A.

It gives me great pleasure to write a foreword to this book. I have never actually owned a multihull myself, although as a designer, boatbuilder and sailmaker I have done a lot of sailing in other people's yachts, many of them multihulls whose rigs I have been involved in. So I feel able to take a truly independent view of the world of multihulls in general and fast ones in particular.

Multihull yachts, as distinct from fishing and small trading vessels, have only been with us in any numbers for about forty years, for most of which time they have been of limited interest to the cruising sailor, and experience in the arts of designing and building them in their present form has only evolved in the past couple of decades.

The recent rapid expansion of the multihull fleets in Europe, the United States and Australasia has led to an awakening of public awareness of this form of boating, tempered by a degree of mistrust engendered by some well publicized accidents and, all too often, a misunderstanding of their causes. There still seems to be a surprising scarcity of information and a vast area of ignorance surrounding these versatile craft. Literature about them has been very largely confined to magazine articles, which are necessarily somewhat ephemeral, and as far as I know to a few books concerned mainly with beach cats or big boat racing.

Here, at last, is what I for one have been waiting for – a comprehensive and well informed book covering multihulls large and small, cruising and racing, catamarans and trimarans, how they are designed and built, and how to get the best out of them. Drawing on his own considerable experience in a variety of small boats with one, two and three hulls, Derek Harvey has aimed the book at the newcomer to multihulls, while assuming that the reader is already familiar with the basic principles of sailing a monohull. But it contains so much useful information that I can foresee many an experienced sailor of either persuasion learning something more on subjects that he or she thought they already understood.

ACKNOWLEDGEMENTS

In the course of preparing this book I have often had to seek the assistance of individuals and firms in the multihull world, including several of the designers and builders of the boats in its pages. I have been encouraged by their generous response to my requests for advice and information, and I am grateful to all who helped in this way, whether or not I have directly made use of the material they supplied. Furthermore, such is the pace of multihull technology that some information will inevitably have become available too late for inclusion in this edition; I shall of course hope for the opportunity to update it in a future one.

I am especially indebted to Derek Kelsall, John Shuttleworth and Richard Woods for their expert guidance on matters of design, to Dick Newick and Phil Bolger for their innovative ideas and words of boating wisdom, and to Nico Boon for steering me through some of the complexities of the handicapping minefield. I should also like to thank those busy magazine editors, Charles Chiodi and Ava Burgess of *Multihulls* and George Taylor of *Practical Boat Owner*, for taking the time to deal with my queries; historian and keeper of sailing records D. H. 'Nobby' Clarke for casting his eagle eye over the first chapter; and my old friend and sail wizard 'Clarence' Austin Farrar for writing the foreword.

INTRODUCTION

I had been sailing for twenty years before I ever gave catamarans a second thought. So many of those I'd come across looked like floating caravans that would topple over in the first strong gust, while others seemed to be freaky contraptions held together with string. But it also happened that the mate had developed back trouble, and rather than give up sailing altogether, we were persuaded to try some upright cruising.

I'm thankful we did. For in the course of the next two years, we learned that a 9m (30ft) cruising cat can not only be safe, stable and extremely comfortable, but also deceptively fast off the wind. However, cosseted and isolated from the elements as we were inside her wheelhouse, and also hampered by a particularly insensitive wheel steering system, she felt slow and unresponsive. Indeed, her performance to windward was distinctly soggy, so we spent rather a lot of the time noisily motoring; and to crown it all, she looked a bit of an ugly duckling among the swans along the marina pontoon. In my view, there are few things more offensive to the eye than a badly proportioned yacht. I believe one should feel a sense of attachment to one's boat. Granted, this one provided what had become an essential element in our lives – being able to get out on the water. But we didn't love her.

So, when the mate's back showed signs of real improvement we lost no time in changing the cat for a fast, modern monohull, and all the old fun and sparkle came back into our sailing; we were content once more – until one day at a boat show, we condescended to take a demonstration trip in a lightweight cruiser-racer catamaran, which was labelled a 'micro-multi-hull'.

This was a new class of boat, the salesman explained, 8m (26ft) long, trailerable, with camping-style accommodation for three, and suitable for coastal sailing. Sounded interesting. We had not, we explained, the slightest intention of buying it. We knew about cats. We were simply curious to find out how this one handled.

The next half hour turned all our previous standards and convictions upside down. The little boat didn't just get under way in the normal, dignified fashion to which we were accustomed; as sheets were gathered in, it took off like some sort of waterborne rocket at speeds that were quite outside our experience, and proceeded to point as close to the wind as our racy monohull ever did. It was even more exhilarating to sail, tacking like a dinghy and skimming across shallows that would have been off limits to any keelboat.

No matter, we said, when we'd got our breath back, that the 'accommodation' on this particular boat was a bit of a joke, even by camping standards. We decided we would gladly put up with it for the sake of such performance. So we changed boats again, back to two hulls. Now, after ten more years of owning or sailing cats and trimarans of various types and sizes, we are so wedded to the concept of 'straddle stability' that we would like to spread the word to others who may not realize what they are missing.

This, then, is a book about multihulls, their evolution, how they are designed and built, how they sail and what they look like; and it examines the reasons for choosing one in preference to a conventional boat. This is not to suggest that multihulls are necessarily any better than monohulls. Horses for courses, as the old saying goes. Both have their pros and cons, and I have tried to be unbiased in discussing them. I hope that this book reflects a realistically balanced viewpoint – although I have tried to convey my enthusiasm for multihulls and to whet the appetites of those who haven't tried them – and that it may serve to clear up some of the prejudices and misconceptions that still linger about these craft.

The proven success of modern multihulls has largely overcome their earlier reputation for mishaps – some of it justified, much of it wildly exaggerated – and nowadays they are hardly more likely to capsize than monohulls are to sink. Catastrophes still occur in grand prix events, and they make sensational headlines. There is a world of difference, however, between the huge and fragile racers that can outpace an ocean liner in gale force winds, and the sensibly sailed micro. These pocket cruisers seem to put you in touch with the sea in a way no other type can (dinghies do too, of course, though sometimes too literally). In my view they offer more fun for your money, more quiet pleasure – or excitement if you prefer it – more sheer enjoyment when time as well as funds are limited, than can be found in any other form of sailing. But like most good things, they have their limitations.

A micro is undoubtedly a bit too basic and restricted in its facilities to suit all tastes. If you prefer to cruise in greater comfort and can afford to pay for it; if you want to be able to make long offshore passages and are confident your crew can handle some heavier sails, winches and ground tackle; if you are prepared for the added responsibilities that size can bring, then go for a bigger boat. How much bigger? There's a well-known maxim which defines the smallest practical cruiser as one which can sleep two, eat four and drink six. Most multihulls of 10m (33ft) and above can double these figures.

Aside from the pride of ownership, there can be no doubting the rewards from a 'big' boat, with a bridgedeck saloon as well as accommodation in the hulls – a boat you can walk around in, where you can rest in the privacy of your own cabin while someone else cooks (should you be so lucky) and the crew rattles around on deck. Unless it is designed for high performance, it will lack the micro's sensitive responses and sizzling acceleration, but it will more than make up for this in its spaciousness, steadier motion, and the increased sense of security that comes with size; there's something about the feel of a big boat's wheel.

Size plays tricks with the senses. I have often been struck by the abruptness of the transition from a micro to a bridgedeck cruising cat, from a neat little boat to a veritable liner, even though on paper one may be hardly any longer or beamier than the other. On any boat, an extra foot here or half metre there can make a quite disproportionate improvement in habitability; but somehow the difference always seems more dramatic on multihulls.

Most of what I have written concerns micros in the 6–8m (20–26ft) range, and the broad spectrum of cruising boats and cruiser-racers up to about 12m (40ft), because although there are plenty of other interesting multis, these are the two categories most likely to concern the average yachtsman. Phil Bolger, that American guru of small craft design, summed it up for me when he wrote 'The best boats are either small enough to carry home, or big enough to live on.' Taken literally, this could include day sailing beach cats, maxi cruisers, and even some of the rare and exotic racers. That's not quite what he meant; but I have included references to both because it seemed to me that since the same general information, theory and practice, and most of the basic design principles apply regardless of size, too strict a cut-off might limit the perception of what multihulls are all about. I only regret that no one seems to have thought of a generic name that's less of a mouthful.

1 IN THE BEGINNING

The origins and evolution of the multihull, and the lessons learned through trial and error

Multihulls have existed ever since man discovered he could prevent his log boat from tipping over by lashing several together to form a raft, which was not only fairly stable but could carry a larger load. Some form of raft, probably built of papyrus reeds, must have been used by the Pharaohs to float their huge granite blocks down the Nile to build the Pyramids. Others, made from balsa logs and rigged with sails, are believed to have been drifted downwind for thousands of miles across the Pacific Ocean by the first Peruvian settlers to the South Sea Islands. The feasibility of such a voyage was demonstrated by Thor Heyerdahl with his famous raft *Kon-Tiki*, although his hypothesis of a westward migration is still disputed by some experts.

Raft boats

From the basic rectangular raft, whose blunt shape took a lot of pushing through the water, there evolved two distinct forms of transitional craft, the raft boat and the log-supported raft. The raft boat was made by binding together a number of logs or bundles of reeds, shaped to nest into one another, with the longest in the middle, to produce a boat shape with a comparatively smooth outer surface that was more easily driven than the simple raft. There was no need to make it watertight because it had enough buoyancy from the natural flotation of its lightweight materials to support itself and its cargo. Such boats are still in use today for inshore fishing and transport in many parts of the world, including the West Indies and South America, and along the Coromandel Coast of India, where they are known by the Tamil word *kattumaram*, meaning literally 'tied wood'. The derivation 'catamaran' did not come into use until the end of the 17th century, and then quite wrongly, and for no reason that can be discovered, to refer to water craft of an entirely different culture, the Pacific double canoes.

Log-supported rafts and outriggers

The primitive forerunner of the Pacific double canoes is thought to have originated among the islands of Melanesia, whose fishermen found that by placing a large log under one side of a raft – which had the effect of reducing its wetted surface and hence its drag through the water – it was made much easier to paddle. But the sloping raft was uncomfortable to sit on, so the next stage of development was to add a horizontal platform above it, supported on sticks. From then on it was only a matter of time before the original raft disappeared, leaving the main log – by now a dugout, which was lighter to haul up the beach as well as providing some rudimentary accommodation space – connected by cross-poles and a cradle of connecting sticks to a slender outrigger log, the

A raft was hard to paddle...

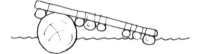

so the Melanesians propped
up one end on a log

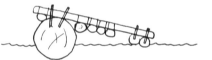

raft was later pegged to its log
floats

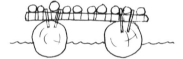

the Polynesians preferred
two logs

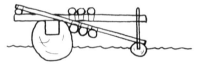

horizontal raft above existing
canoe

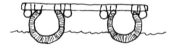

primitive double dugout

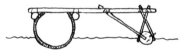

raft eventually replaced by
crossbeams

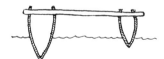

deep main hulls of Tongan 'flying
proa' minimized leeway

Hawaiian canoe with curved
crossbeams

Indo-Javanese planked hull
with double outriggers

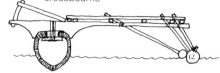

Matema Islands
Sea-going canoe with helmsman's
platform above main hull

Sulu Islands variant. Bent withies
raise crossbeams clear of the water

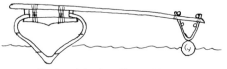

Society Islands sailing pahi
with channeled keel

Tuamotu, fishing dugout with sprung
outrigger attachments

Caroline Islands, sailing canoe.
Asymmetric hull gave lift to
windward.

Fig 1.1 *Evolution of the double canoe and Pacific
outrigger craft. A small selection of the many
geometries, crossbeam arrangements and float
connectives in use over the centuries, and in the
various regions and island groups.*

ama. This acted as both float and balance weight, and later gave the boat enough stability to carry a sail. Thus was born the outrigger canoe, or proa, which is still used by the fishermen and traders of Africa and Asia, as well as throughout the Pacific. Their general shape has changed little over the years, and crude though they may look they are highly efficient machines.

Double canoes

The early Polynesians did things differently. It is generally accepted that the majority of these people originated in Burma and Indo-China, and probably began migrating eastwards around 2000 BC through Indonesia to the far-off Pacific islands of Fiji, Samoa and Tahiti, and centuries later – between AD 300 and 1000 – to New Zealand and Hawaii. Around the time the Melanesians were propping up their sloping rafts, the Polynesians started putting pairs of logs under theirs to keep them level. Later on the logs became dugout canoes and the raft was replaced by crossbeams that were flexibly mounted so as to allow some 'give' between the two hulls as they moved with the waves. The resulting double canoe, or *pahi*, was as stable as a raft, but with its slim hulls was much faster, and easier to steer.

Some are known to have been over 30m (98ft) long; great sailing vessels with roofed shelters for their several hundreds of passengers. For the eastwards migrations to have taken place they must have been capable of sailing to windward for thousands of miles, probably using vertical 'leeboards' at various positions along the hulls to hold the bows up to the wind, and to adjust the steering trim by balancing the forces of the winds and waves.

Just before the beginning of the Christian era, and long after the Polynesians had become established in the Eastern Pacific, yet another hull configuration began to evolve, this time in Indonesia, where people were arriving from Malaya. Theirs was a more advanced culture than that of the Polynesians who had preceded them, and their boats were plank-built and shaped so as to be reasonably stable without any exterior support. But they must have discovered some of the canoes left behind by their predecessors, for they sought to improve the seaworthiness of their boats by fitting them with outrigger floats or amas. They found, however, that a single lightweight float provided insufficient ballast to be effective on a 40-footer. So, instead, the Malays made use of its buoyancy by putting one on either side, and the resulting double-outrigger is another of the watercraft still in service in some parts of the world. It is not as fast as the proa, because of the drag of its two immersed surfaces (the third one being canted up clear of the water, to windward) compared with the single hull and 'flying outrigger' of the well sailed proa.

Pacific proa

The proa relies very much, however, on the agility of its crew, who try to keep the outrigger just skimming the waves by scrambling from side to side to balance every gust. Since the Pacific proa must always present its outrigger side to the wind, tacking is achieved by sailing backwards, with the bow becoming the stern, after the tack of the sail and its supporting spars have been walked to the opposite end of the boat. Small wonder that capsizes are commonplace during this manoeuvre, but they

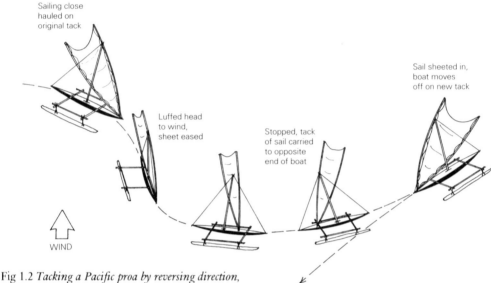

Sailing close
hauled on
original tack

Sail sheeted in,
boat moves
off on new tack

Luffed head
to wind,
sheet eased

Stopped, tack
of sail carried
to opposite
end of boat

WIND

Fig 1.2 *Tacking a Pacific proa by reversing direction, the bows becoming the stern and vice versa.*

seem to be cheerfully accepted as a normal occurrence in gusty weather, for the waters are warm and the boats remain afloat even when swamped. (Today's Atlantic proa needs no such gymnastics, because its outrigger float is nearly as big as the main hull, and is carried on the lee side. But it is nevertheless somewhat accident-prone, usually when the boat screws up into the wind after an accidental gybe and puts the float the wrong side of the main hull.)

Captain Cook

Development and refinement of the Oceanic canoe in its various forms continued over the centuries, and by the time Captain Cook arrived on the scene in 1770, during one of his historic voyages of exploration, he was surprised to come across such large and fast vessels. Drawings by his artist show that many were now built of carved planks sewn together, with a pronounced vee-bottom to their deep and narrow hulls. The majority of the big seagoing single-outrigger boats even

featured an asymmetrically shaped main hull, with more curve on the windward side than on the other, so that it generated lift in that direction to counteract the drag of the float (which was not 'flown' in the manner of the smaller boats).

Sail shapes, like the hulls, varied from one region to another, but basically they changed very little over the years. Originally made from matted pandanus leaves, and later on from woven flax, they appear quaintly primitive to our eyes, but they are deceptively efficient. Working on the principle that the wind is always stronger aloft than at sea level, where surface friction slows it down, they are set with their widest part at the top to catch the wind, and their narrow end on deck, where, incidentally, they offer the least obstruction to crew and cargo.

On the larger double canoes seen by Cook, the luff of each sail (for some were schooner rigged) was lashed to a mast – or in some cases to one side of a bipod mast mounted like a pair of sheerlegs astride the hulls – while the leech

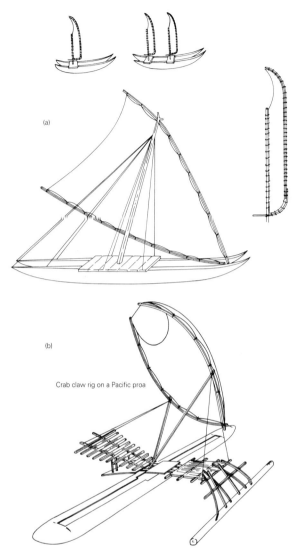

(a)

(b)

Crab claw rig on a Pacific proa

Fig 1.3 *Polynesian double canoes, with (a) the high aspect ratio boomed-leech sails, used mainly on lagoon fishing boats and (b) the Oceanic lateen (crab claw) sail, which is still the accepted rig in the Eastern Mediterranean and the Pacific.*

was attached to a lower spar lashed to the upper one at the bow, the angle and tilt of the sail being controlled by a rope at either end, so that it could almost be flown like a kite. This form of Pacific rig does in fact provide considerable lift in addition to drive, which partly accounts for the proa's speed. Indeed, recent wind tunnel tests by C. A. Marchaj for MacAllister & Partners, at Southampton University, have shown the 'crab claw' sail to be more efficient than many of our modern configurations, although it is somewhat awkward to handle.

Sir William Petty

No wonder Cook reported so enthusiastically in his journal on the performance of the double canoes; they could sail faster and closer to the wind than his own ship *Endeavour*. So, he later discovered, could the Hawaiian outrigger canoes, which his artist depicted with gracefully curved crossbeams in place of straight poles and stick connectives.

George Anson, who made his famous circumnavigation in the middle of the 18th century, even brought a double canoe back to England as deck cargo. The designers of that period were a conservative bunch, and showed little interest in such a crude native contraption, yet they must have known of the series of twin-hulled boats that had been built in Dublin 100 years earlier by one Sir William Petty. This distinguished gentleman may perhaps have learned of the existence of double canoes from the Dutch explorer Tasman, who had recently discovered New Zealand, Tonga and Fiji. If he had also heard about the shape of their sails, he made a big mistake in not trying to copy them. At any rate, Petty reinvented the

was carried aloft on a curved spar taller than the mast itself. The most widely used rig, which has survived to this day, was shaped like the claw of a crab. The top edge was laced to a long curved yard which swept diagonally upwards from the bow and past the short mast to which it was attached by a halyard. The foot principle of 'spread buoyancy' for himself, and obtained a commission from King Charles II to design the prototype of what he called a 'double-bottom' boat.

The first of these, *Simon & Jude*, consisted of a pair of cylinders 60cm (2ft) in diameter and 6m (20ft) long, bridged by a wooden deck 2.75m (9ft) wide and setting a fore-and-aft spritsail rig. Launched in 1662, she won a number of races against other boats, including the King's barge, and was timed at no less than 20 miles per hour (17 knots) by the Royal Society. A larger version, *Invention II*, followed later the same year, clinker-built of planking, and square-rigged in the big ship manner of the day. She twice made the voyage from Dublin to Holyhead, beating the regular packet ship by 15 hours on one occasion.

Two years later Petty built *The Experiment*, a 30-ton boat with a crew of 33, who perished when she went down in a storm in the Bay of Biscay; and in 1684 a still larger double-bottom ship *Saint Michael the Archangel*, which proved so unmanageable that she was scrapped after her initial trials. Petty's first little boat had been quite successful, but interest in these early European multihulls evaporated without anyone realizing that the essential but missing design ingredient was lightweight construction.

Two hundred years were to elapse before catamarans began once more to appear on the scene. These included several large passenger steamers with their paddlewheels one behind the other in tandem between the hulls, but they were heavy and uneconomical, and despite their wide beam they had an uncomfortable motion in a seaway. One, the 90m (295ft) *Calais-Douvres*, operated for 11 years as a cross-channel ferry, but was eventually withdawn because of excessive coal and maintenance costs.

Nathanael Herreshof

The first sailing catamaran of 'modern' design was built in 1868 by John Mackenzie in

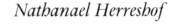

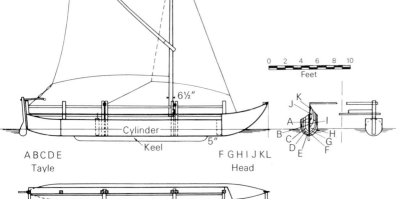

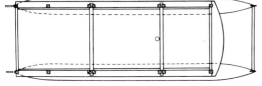

Fig 1.4 *Britain's first multihull. The 6m (20ft) Simon & Jude of 1662 was timed at 20 miles per hour (17 knots) by the Royal Society – an extraordinary performance from a boat that was smaller and heavier than most of today's micro racers.*

Belfast. She was a chunky little 6.4m (22ft) yacht, with a 3m (10ft) beam and asymmetric box-shaped hulls carrying shallow fin keels. Sturdily built and fully decked, she must have needed all of her generously proportioned gaff rig to drive her at any speed, and no more is known of her. To his credit, Mackenzie was first in the field with a multi-hulled yacht, but it fell to the American designer Nathanael Herreshof to make public history.

Herreshof's 7.6m (25ft) *Amaryllis* of 1876 was of an advanced design, with pencil-slim vee-bottomed hulls, each with a centreboard, and an overall beam of no less than 5.5m (18ft). Three crossbeams connected the hulls through an ingenious arrangement of universal joints which allowed them to pitch independently; the crew were perched in a central oval-shaped cockpit. The hulls were indeed so narrow that they were short of buoyancy, and in a strong breeze *Amaryllis* was prone to bury her lee bow and pitchpole over it in a most spectacular form of capsize. Conversely, in light airs she was disappointingly slow, due to her excessive weight. Nevertheless she easily beat the entire fleet of 33 larger boats in the New York Yacht Club's centennial regatta – and in return was promptly banned from all the club's future events. Undeterred, Herreshof went on to build several more catamarans, and the vital principles he established – of low wetted surface area, and sufficient beam to support a large sail area – were soon adopted by other designers. But after

Fig 1.5 *John Mackenzie's asymmetrically hulled catamaran of 1868 was a fully decked yacht, but her heavy construction must have prevented her from attaining much speed.*

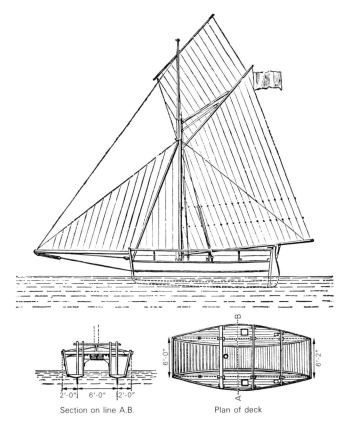

2'-0"   6'-0"   2'-0"

6'-0"   6'-2"

Section on line A.B.   Plan of deck

Fig 1.6 *In 1868, the trimaran raft* Nonpareil *sailed from New York to Southampton in 51 days. Her cylindrical hulls were made of rubber, and she had daggerboards forward and aft to help steer and heave to. Copyright* Illustrated London News

Fig 1.7 *Nathanael Herreshof's* John Gilpin *(1878). Taking his inspiration from the slender canoes of the Ladrone Islands, Herreshof built a series of racing catamarans which so outclassed their conventional competitors that they were banned from one regatta after another.*

Fig 1.8 *Victorian freak: Robert Fryer's steam driven tri-ball* Alice. *Her behaviour at sea is not recorded.*

further successes, catamarans became increasingly treated as unsporting and unwanted freaks. They were banned from one regatta after another, and as there were not enough of them to race among themselves, they gradually dropped out of the yachting scene. Then, as now, racing played an important part in yacht development and in consequence, progress on multihulls was stifled for the next fifty years. Herreshof himself returned to

monohulls, and went on to become famous for his America's Cup designs.

Apart from a few sporadic experiments, such as the racing scow *Dominion*, a monohull whose bottom was raised into a central tunnel to make her effectively a catamaran – she beat all the other scows and was immediately banned from further racing – it was not until 1936 that the next milestone in multihull history was reached.

Kaimiloa

This was the year in which the French explorer and seaman Eric de Bisschop was wrecked in his junk on the coast of Hawaii, and while recovering there, became interested in Polynesian double canoes, models of which he studied in the local museum. He and a companion then proceeded to build the 11.6m (39ft) catamaran *Kaimiloa* on Waikiki beach, rigging her as a junk because he was accustomed to this type of sail, and in March 1937 set off for France, where he arrived 14 months later. De Bisschop not only proved that a small catamaran could safely undertake ocean voyages, but his achievement undoubtedly provided an inspiration for the many French multihulls that appeared in the years following the Second World War.

Fig 1.9 Kaimiloa, *built in 1936–7 by explorer Eric de Bisschop on Waikiki beach after he had been shipwrecked, and in which he sailed back to his native France.*

Hawaiian catamarans

Among the many technological spin-offs of wartime armaments production were the resin glues and waterproof plywood sheeting developed for the construction of aircraft and gliders. These materials made it possible for the first time for amateurs to build strong, lightweight boat hulls at reasonably low cost. Among the first to recognize this was a former glider pilot, Woody Brown, who lived in Hawaii. In 1948, with the help of a skilled local boatbuilder, Alfred Kumalai, he designed and built the 11.7m (39ft) catamaran *Manu Kai*.

By using the new materials in an aircraft-type stressed skin construction, they managed to keep the weight down to an astonishing 1400kg (3100 lb) – to put this into perspective, today's state-of-the-art Formula 40 racer, admittedly an infinitely more complex machine, turns the scales at around 1800kg (4000 lb). Designed to operate straight off the beach and through the surf, *Manu Kai* had no centreboards and relied instead on deep asymmetric hulls and long shallow keels to

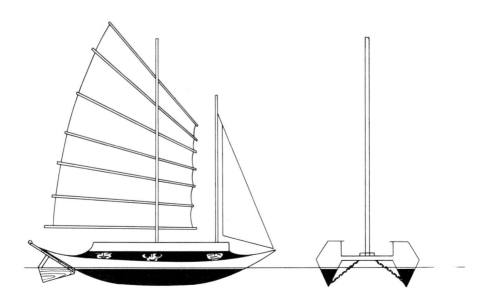

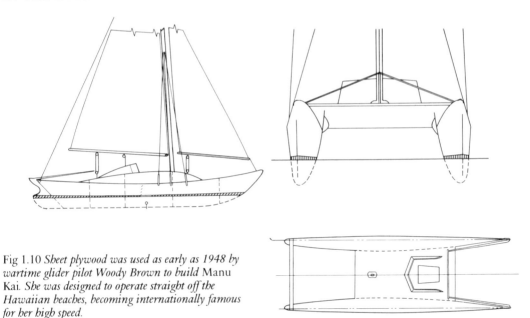

Fig 1.10 *Sheet plywood was used as early as 1948 by wartime glider pilot Woody Brown to build* Manu Kai. *She was designed to operate straight off the Hawaiian beaches, becoming internationally famous for her high speed.*

grip the water. This made her slow to tack, but she made up for this in sheer speed, and her reputation soon spread worldwide.

Kumalai was later joined by Rudy Choy and Warren Seaman, and together they formed the now famous firm of C/S/K. In the succeeding years they built many large and successful cruising catamarans, and Rudy Choy himself produced a series of highly sophisticated racers, sticking to their narrow asymmetric hull/long keel formula which suited the mostly 'downhill' tradewind races on the Pacific coast. Elsewhere, designers were also quick to realize the advantages of plywood construction, but they mostly opted for centreboards, more beam, and less wetted surface as a combination that gave a better all-round performance.

For the Cunningham brothers in Australia, this took the form of an updated Herreshof catamaran, with hard-chine symmetrical hulls and shallow canoe sterns. It was an immediate success and fleets of them, mostly about 6m

(20ft) long and home-built from Cunningham plans, were racing by the early 1950s.

The Prout brothers

Meanwhile in England the Prout brothers, working in their father's boatyard, were producing kayak canoes from moulded plywood, the rounded shape making it possible to dispense with many of the supporting frames and stringers required in hard chine, flat panel construction. As a result, the canoes were finger light. Influenced by the success of *Manu Kai*, the brothers began experimenting with pairs of canoes bridged together with a plywood deck; and by 1954 their 4.9m (16ft) 'Shearwater' cat had become Europe's first production multihull. It was, for its size, by far the fastest sailboat that money could buy, because by chance its designers had hit on the principle that the semicircular hull bottom has the least possible wetted surface area, and hence the least drag through the water.

More than 3,000 Shearwaters have now been built, and it is still among the largest of the cat racing classes in the UK. The Prouts subsequently produced the very first glassfibre cruising cat, the 8.2m (27ft) 'Ranger', from which their current boats are all descended.

The Cunningham and Prout boats started the fashion in dinghy cat racing. By 1959, the International Yacht Racing Union had formed a Multihull Committee to regulate the sport, and cat fever was spreading throughout Europe. Among other British designers to make their names were Rod Macalpine-Downie with his C-Class cats that in 1961 won the first Little America's Cup, and in the hands of Reg White successfully defended it for six years; Rodney March with the 'Tornado', which in 1976 became the first cat to attain Olympic status, with Reg White winning a Gold in the boat he himself had built and helped to develop; Bill O'Brien, an RAF flying boat pilot who built his first cat soon after the war from a pair of Sunderland wing floats and later became widely known for his 'Bobcat' and 'Oceanic' cruising cats; and Tom and Mary Lack, who produced some 500 of the roomy and dependable 'Catalacs' between 1965 and 1980. Meanwhile in America, Hubert Alter launched his famous 'Hobie' cat and in ten years produced the first 10,000 of them.

Early trimarans

The 1950s saw a wide variety of multihulls appear on the yachting scene. Notable among these, if only for its name, was a 7.3m (25ft) double-outrigger design by Victor Tchetchet, a Russian-born American, who coined for it the descriptive name 'trimaran', which we now apply to all triple-hulled craft. Developed from the prototype he had launched as early as 1945, Tchetchet built a number of these slippy little craft for his yachting friends. Bob Harris, who has since become one of Canada's leading designers, produced a successful series of small flat-bottomed cats on Long Island; and in England, Erick Manners built a number of ingenious and occasionally eccentric designs, based on his pre-war hydrofoil experiments. They included the very first car-toppable cat, and the first trailerable tri, which featured folding 'hydrowings', as Manners called them; all of them were engineered to minimize weight.

Fig 1.11 *French heavyweight. The 13m (42ft) trimaran* Ananda, *built in 1946 of mahogany planking on oak frames, displaced 8.7 tons. She somehow managed to sail 2,100 miles from the Cape Verde Islands across the Atlantic in heavy weather at an average of 4.4 knots, but her motion was so violent that her crew suffered from eyesight trouble.*

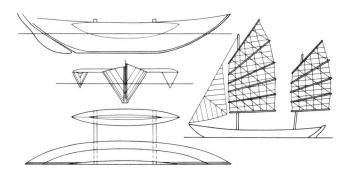

Other designers, choosing to ignore the lessons of history, reverted to building mahogany-planked or even sheet-steel cats that proved no less disappointing than their overweight predecessors. Both France and Germany produced some massive steel catamarans, which somehow managed to cross the Atlantic, despite being ponderously heavy to the point of being dangerous, while in the United States, Creger produced a range of small cats with deep fin keels. These performed quite well as picnic platforms, but most of them were overweight, narrow beamed and sluggish. He based their stability on an entirely false premise, his larger designs carrying as much as a ton of ballast in their

Fig 1.12 The all-steel 14m (46ft) Copula, launched in 1948, was not only the first ocean cruiser with asymmetric hulls: at 22 tons she must rank as the heaviest catamaran of her size ever built. She was nevertheless a good seaboat and on one long voyage, overloaded with diving equipment and a fully equipped laboratory, she covered some 9,000 miles in 90 sailing days, averaging just over 4 knots.

keels, but they were easily capsized when it blew a good breeze, and embarrassingly slow when it didn't. They provided a convincing demonstration that heavy keels and twin hulls are incompatible.

James Wharram

Then in 1955 came an achievement which must be judged as rivalling those of Woody Brown and the Prouts for its impact on multihull history, although at the time it received scant recognition. A very determined young Englishman, James Wharram, built the now famous *Tangaroa*, a distinctly utilitarian 7.2m (24ft) catamaran in the Polynesian style, and with two young German girls as crew, he sailed it to Trinidad. For the sake of cheapness and ease of construction, the hulls were parallel sided, blunt ended and flat bottomed – 'like a couple of coffins' was how some people described them – and although there was plenty of living space on the open deck, the

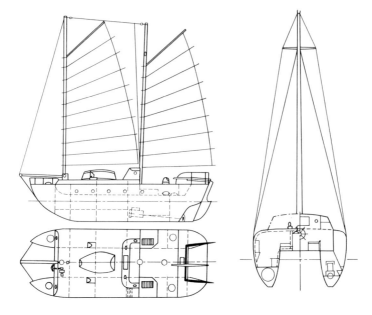

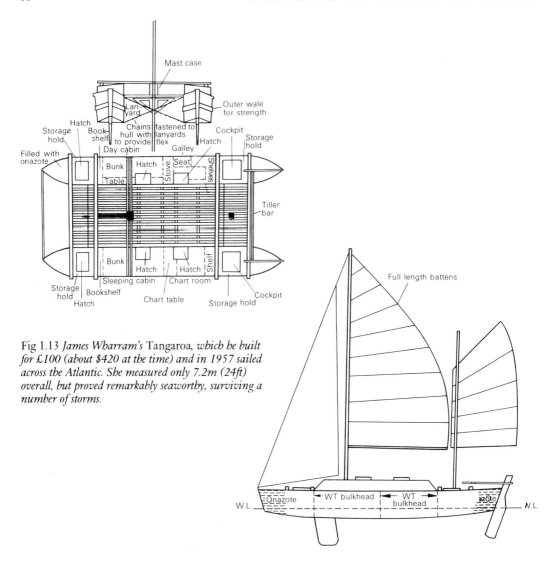

Fig 1.13 *James Wharram's* Tangaroa, *which he built for £100 (about $420 at the time) and in 1957 sailed across the Atlantic. She measured only 7.2m (24ft) overall, but proved remarkably seaworthy, surviving a number of storms.*

inside accommodation for the three of them was very cramped for such a long voyage. Nevertheless they weathered a number of gales, and their little craft proved remarkably stable and buoyant, lifting easily over the waves, with only the occasional breaking crest exploding up through the slatted decking between the hulls, and quickly draining away.

Convinced of the intrinsic safety and vice-free behaviour of this type of open-deck catamaran, Wharram immediately set about designing the next one. With the help of the girls and some friends they had made on the island, he built the 12.2m (40ft) *Rongo*, which embodied the distinctive features for which his designs have become internationally famous: narrow, vee-shaped hulls built of sheet plywood, with no centreboards, joined by flexibly mounted beams and open, slatted decks. In this they sailed back to England in 1959, making the first west–east transatlantic crossing by multihull. Four years later, Wharram began designing on a commercial basis.

The year 1955 also saw the foundation of the Amateur Yacht Research Society, by another Englishman and keen multihull sailor, Dr John Morwood. Through its meetings and booklets, it was soon to become an international forum for discussion among designers and yachtsmen, and a world authority on yacht research.

Arthur Piver

Among those to accept its advice was a go-getting Californian publisher by the name of Arthur Piver. He had built a number of unsuccessful dinghy cats, but in 1957 adopted the hull shape suggested by Morwood for a series of simple sheet-ply trimaran designs, which he sailed with gusto and promoted aggressively to home builders; he also antagonized the yachting establishment with his bull-in-a-chinashop tactics.

Best known of these designs were the 7.3m (24ft) 'Nugget' and 9.1m (30ft) 'Nimble', and when properly built they were reasonably fast and seaworthy boats with good accommodation – the first small multihulls to offer such a combination. They were especially popular in the UK, thanks to the marketing efforts of an enterprising yachtsman D. H. 'Nobby' Clarke, who had some 200 professionally built, a number of which – including 20 that were exported to America – featured floats that hinged down for trailering. These were, in fact, the world's first production micro-multihulls. In addition, Clarke supplied around 400 sets of plans to amateur builders, supplemented by his own construction notes, since Piver's drawings left much to the imagination.

Too many novices were dazzled by Piver's hot-gospelling and wild claims for ease of building. He also exaggerated their trans-ocean capabilities, although to be fair, several of Nobby Clarke's customers succeeded in making ocean crossings in their Piver boats, including the 12.2m (41ft) *Victress*, in which Nigel Tetley circumnavigated the five southernmost capes. Piver made a couple of long voyages in his own trimarans, including one in a 'Nimble' which he had entered for the Transatlantic Race of 1960. As it happened, he arrived too late for the start at Plymouth, but he returned to England in 1967 with his last and fastest ocean racer, the 10m (33ft) *Stiletto*, finishing third overall in the Crystal Trophy race. When he tragically disappeared at sea in 1968, the sailing world lost a great character.

Piver left behind him a trail of part-built boats and disillusioned hobbyists; and a worldwide fleet of successful trimarans. He had also inspired others to adopt the trimaran format; few people had previously considered multihulls as cheap ocean cruisers, for James Wharram's designs were not yet widely known.

Among the many who were fired by Piver's infectious enthusiasm was his protégé Jim Brown. But when his young friend produced suggestions for a refined design, he was promptly sacked – so Brown started his own firm selling DIY plans for a range of 'Searunner' trimarans, each backed by comprehensively documented instructions, and Brown's own highly developed sea sense. They proved popular with cruising sailors, and many hundreds have been built over the years.

Back in England, several fast cruising cats, including Macalpine-Downie's long-lived 'Iroquois', were beginning to come off the lines, and two more yachtsmen, who had been doing some sailing in Pivers, turned to design-

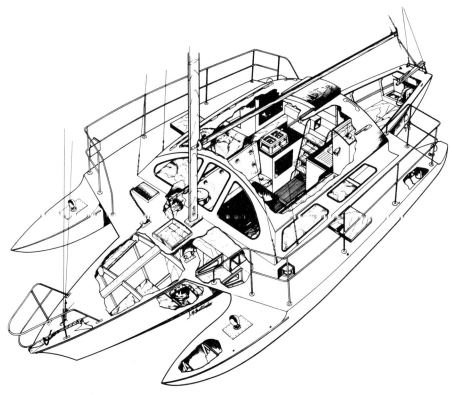

Fig 1.14 *The Piver 'Nimble' (1960). Over the years,
hundreds were home-built in the USA and elsewhere,
including Britain. They were deservedly popular for
their spacious accommodation and good performance.*
(Photo © D. H. Clarke)

ing. The first of these was Derek Kelsall, who
began by competing with his own Piver in the
1964 Single-Handed Transatlantic Race, and
two years later won the Round Britain in the
12m (40ft) trimaran *Toria*, the first of many
multihulls he designed and built himself, and
the first example of his pioneering work on the
foam sandwich method of construction in universal use today. The other was Tony Smith.
Based on his experience with a modified
'Nugget', he went into series production with
his 'Telstar' design, a roomy little trimaran
with hinged floats that is still popular many
years after the last one left the lines.

It was after a fast trip in Kelsall's *Toria* that

the legendary French yachtsman Eric Tarbarly gave up monohull racing and commissioned the building of the 21m (69ft) trimaran *Pen Duick IV*, in which he broke many ocean-crossing records. This was the first of the big multihulls with which France was later to dominate the racing world. Tarbarly became a folk hero, and his exploits, supplemented by the arrival of some Piver tris from England, were largely responsible for the rebirth of the French multihull tradition that had begun with de Bisschop thirty years previously. (A recent count, which excluded the dozens of dinghy cats, showed over 100 types of multihull on the French market – of which 30, incidentally, were micros.)

Fig 1.15 *The 27m (89ft)* William Sauran, *designed in 1979 by Derek Kelsall, reaching at 26 knots in 30 knots of wind. At this speed she would have been developing some 350 horsepower.* (GAMMA photo)

Among other notable designers of the 1960s were Americans Norman Cross and Ed Horstman, with their spacious wing-decked trimarans; the Gougeon brothers with their featherlight racers which led to the development of the Wood Epoxy Saturation Technique – the WEST system for which they were to become famous; and Hedley Nicol, a hard-driving Australian sailor in the Piver mould, who in the worst sea conditions would shout for more wind and more rain, and who died when his tri lost a float while on passage to America. And there was Dick Newick, another legendary American, whose graceful trimarans were wider and more stable than Piver's, ranging from the popular 9.4m (31ft) 'Val' to famous racers such as the 15m (50ft) *Moxie*, which won just about everything she was entered for.

Newick specialized – and still does – in

lightweight, high-performance trimarans, in contrast to Jim Brown's chunky, easy-to-build plywood cruisers. For 'accommodation' multihulls (as distinct from dinghies) these two design styles typify the divergent trends of the 1970s: on the one hand, the no-compromise racer with extreme overall beam, narrow hulls and powerful sailplan; and on the other, the more spacious, less highly stressed, and much less expensive, cruiser. The smallest of these, such as Jim Brown's 25-footer, besides appealing to the novice or the impecunious yachtsman, attracted the dinghy cat sailor who wanted to move up to a boat big enough to live aboard for a weekend, but still small enough to tow home. Another of these early 'micromultihulls', as they became known, was Australian Ian Farrier's 'Trailertri', with its ingenious float-folding geometry; while in England Richard Woods and John Shuttleworth, both of whom had worked with Derek Kelsall, began designing their own boats, Shuttleworth becoming acclaimed for his large racers and high-performance cruisers, and for the computer-aided design techniques he has developed, and Woods pioneering the micro-multihull movement in the UK.

Today's designers

A number of other Britons have made their names in recent years: Nigel Irens for his design of the record-breaking trimaran *Apricot* and her successors, including the French boats that finished first and second in the 1988 Single-Handed Transatlantic Race; Adrian

Fig 1.16 Steinlager 1 *reefed down at 30 knots in gale force winds.*

Thompson for the radical American tri *Sebago* that came fourth; David Alan-Williams, who drew the powerful *Steinlager 1* that won the 7,600 miles Round Australia race in storm-force winds the same year, finishing *five days* ahead of the next boat; and Martyn Smith, who was responsible for the number-crunching in many Irens designs, and for the successful 'Firebird' micro-cat (alas no longer produced, following a disastrous factory fire). In the USA, designers such as Kurt Hughes and Gino Morelli now rank among the leading proponents of high performance multihulls, while Denmark's Borge Quorning has become well known for his 'Dragonfly' trimarans, and Lars Oudrup for his race-winning micro-cats. But it is France, with a formidable force of designers such as Briand, Fountaine, Lerouge,

Lombard, Nivelt and Ollier, that continues to offer the widest selection of production cruising multihulls and to field the largest fleet of big racers, backed by commercial sponsorship on an unprecedented scale.

These are the boats in the news, high tech and big budget. Nevertheless, the majority of all multihulls have been home-built by amateurs – sometimes badly, it must be said, greatly to the detriment of the breed's general reputation. It so happens that their seemingly simple lightweight forms, with no heavy keel stresses to cater for, are well suited to the DIY sailor looking for ease of construction and what must be the ultimate satisfaction: setting sail in a boat he has built himself.

It is an unavoidable fact that a multihull costs more than an equivalent monohull,

Fig 1.17 'Firebird', race-winning micro of the 1980s.

because of having two – or three – hulls and their connecting structure to build. Even on a series production basis, it is admitted by many who have tried it that it is extremely difficult to pitch the price at an attractive level and still show a reasonable margin of profit. All the more credit must go to the few specialist manufacturers who have succeeded in doing so: foremost among them are Prout Catamarans, with more than 3,000 boats off their lines, by far the world's largest producer; pioneers Tony Smith and Ian Farrier, both now domiciled in the USA and producing boats

Fig 1.18 *The 18m (60ft)* Formula 1 Spirit of Apricot, *designed by Barry Noble and Martyn Smith (UK) and skippered by the indomitable Tony Bullimore. Note the clean wake as she slips effortlessly along at 15 knots in a 10 knot breeze.*

there; and a number of French firms, some of them supported by larger parent companies. Compared with the total world production of monohull sailboats, factory output of multihulls is still relatively modest, at less than 10%. But as their record of safety and racing success continues to grow each year, so do their numbers.

The features in their favour, and a few against

The ideal boat probably doesn't exist, except in dreams. Everyone is bound to be something of a compromise, either in its design, or in our own reasons for choosing it. One person's idea of a dreamboat nearly always differs from another's. So why do we go sailing, and what are our priorities?

The offshore racing sailor, with speed as his prime consideration, will usually accept spartan accommodation for the sake of performance; the day racer expects hardly any at all. Some cruising folk are content to drift along in cottage comfort, turning a blind eye to aesthetics. Others will put up with a thoroughly uncomfortable and often leaky boat for the beauty of her lines. To each his own. And then there's the matter of the budget.

Dick Newick advises his clients: 'Beware of anyone who offers you a fast, cheap, roomy boat. You can choose any two of these three: (1) high performance, (2) low cost, and (3) spacious accommodation. You cannot have all three together.' If they choose (1) and (2) they get a stripped-out racer; (1) and (3) gets them a large and expensive yacht, while (2) and (3) will be slower and heavier and probably less seaworthy than the other combinations. But if space is essential and the budget is tight, there is very little alternative.

Speed

Let us look first at performance, starting with its most obvious parameter, speed. Francis Herreshof, son of the early catamaran designer, once said that the principal function of a yacht is to give pleasure, and that the enjoyment of sailing is in direct proportion to speed. These are obvious over-simplifications, but there is more than an element of truth in them. Fast is fun. Anyone who has experienced the pure exhilaration of a 15–20 knots reach will appreciate how Art Piver felt when he went whoopin' and hollerin' across San Francisco Bay and raised a few eyebrows all those years ago. 'Since earliest times,' he wrote, 'Western man has viewed the sea as an enemy to be fought against, to be ventured upon with ships heavy and strong enough to withstand its power and perils. Eastern man, on the other hand, has looked on the sea with respect but without fear, and skimmed over her surface in light craft.' Modern yachts, both monohull and multihull, are highly developed forms of ancient concepts. One is not necessarily any better than the other; only different.

Any vessel under sail, whether it is a conventional displacement craft pushing its way through the water, or a dinghy skipping across the surface, transfers some of the wind's energy to the water supporting its hull; and a lot of this energy goes into making surface waves, which resist its forward movement. As boatspeed increases, so does the wavemaking resistance, until finally the displacement hull reaches a critical speed of around 2.4 times the

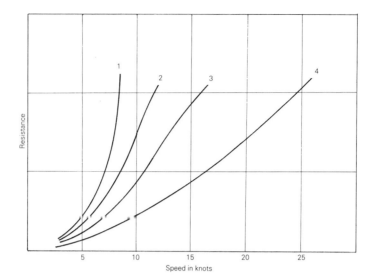

square root of its waterline length in metres (1.34 $\sqrt{WL}$ in feet). At this point, the resistance curve has climbed so steeply that the boat cannot accelerate any further. For a conventional ballasted boat with a waterline length of, say, 8m (26ft) the top speed is just under 7 knots, while a 36-footer (11m) will manage about 8½ knots. Neither can sail any faster, almost regardless of the amount of sail or engine power available – except sometimes for a few glorious seconds when surfing on a wave – because their weight prevents them from lifting clear and planing like a dinghy.

There is also the drag which – except when sailing downwind – is induced by the keel in resisting leeway; and there is a further element of resistance due to heeling. This only becomes significant when the angle of heel begins to exceed 20°, but it is increasing sharply by 30°; which is why, apart from presenting maximum sail area to the wind, a monohull should be kept on its feet – except in very light airs, when heeling to leeward will usually improve the shape of the sails – by moving the crew to the windward rail. Indeed, the majority of racing monohulls depend on

Fig 2.1 *Speed performance of four comparable hull forms.*

1. *The heavy monohull cruiser, because of its wavemaking, is unable to surmount its resistance curve.*
2. *The ultra light displacement monohull is more slippery and continues to accelerate past the resistance hump, albeit more slowly.*
3. *The high performance multihull cruiser climbs the hump even more easily, given enough sailpower.*
4. *The racing multihull makes such small waves that it experiences virtually no hump at all, and accelerates smoothly throughout its speed range.*

this, or some other form of movable ballast such as water, pumped across from one side tank to another, for stability, because without it they cannot carry the amount of sail they need if they are to win.

The remainder of the energy is dissipated in overcoming the friction of the water passing along the surface of the hull. The smaller the wetted area, the less is the friction. By far the fastest of all single-hulled sailing yachts are the new breed of ULDB (Ultra Light Displacement Boats), which combine a comparatively slim hull shape with a flat underbody to encourage early planing, and a big sailplan for plenty of power. Fast they certainly are – compared to conventionally proportioned monohulls. But their speed is still limited by the weight of their ballast keel, and is less than half that achieved by equivalent multihull racers.

Faster than the wind

The multihull, with its wide-based 'straddle stability', needs no ballast to resist the heeling force of the sails (although a racing crew will normally transfer to the windward hull) and the individual hulls are very narrow at the waterline. The result is firstly that their wavemaking resistance (discussed more fully in Chapter 3) is less than that of the broader and heavier keelboat at low speeds, and consequently they are more easily driven in light airs. Then as the wind freshens and boatspeed increases, the lightweight hulls start to rise due to dynamic lift, their wetted area and corresponding drag are reduced, and boatspeed increases still further. Under favourable conditions, high performance multihulls can sail faster than the wind itself, and often by a substantial margin. In light airs they can sometimes more than double it, but even when it's blowing hard they can still exceed the windspeed, unless the sea is very rough. For example, *Full Pelt*, a 12m (40ft) racing trimaran designed by Ed Dubois (UK), has been offi-

Fig 2.2 Racing trimarans often fly their mainhulls. This 12m (40ft) Lock Crowther design held the singlehanded Trans-Pacific, and both the single and two-handed Trans-Tasman race records. Surprisingly, she is quite comfortable for two people to live aboard while cruising (accommodation plan p. 36).

cially timed at 32 knots in 30 knots of wind.

Leeway resistance still occurs, as with a monohull, but there is of course no measurable heeling resistance, except when a catamaran flies a hull – and then it is more than offset by the dramatic reduction in overall drag as the windward hull leaves the water. Balancing on the lee hull is quite a tricky technique, requiring considerable helming skill and lightning reactions, and leaving very little room for error. It originated with the early dinghy cats and has since become standard practice in all classes of multihull racing, including the big offshore cats which are regularly flown on one hull, and even trimarans, which can often be seen flying not one, but *two* hulls, streaking along poised on a single, hardpressed float. In fact, nowadays the larger cats can only sail on equal terms with their trimaran classmates – which have the advantage of wider beam and correspondingly greater sail carrying capacity – if they are able to fly a hull in windspeeds as low as 8–10 knots. This in itself places a limitation on the maximum beam to which these cats can be designed. By comparison, the latest racing tris are designed to fly their mainhulls in 10–12 knots of wind, and are consequently provided not only with rudders in their floats, but with helming positions and all major controls too, despite the wild roller-coaster ride for the crew on the windward float in rough weather. But it is exhausting to sail on the edge of capsize, with only a knife edge dividing winning from wipe-out. It must be emphasized that hull flying is unnecessarily risky on most cruising boats, and is best avoided, even in competitive events.

Nevertheless, under the right conditions (a strong breeze and reasonably smooth water)

and with both hulls in the water, a light catamaran with a powerful sailplan can plane at sustained speeds as high as $7.5 \sqrt{WL_m}$, or three times as fast as a conventional monohull of the same size, provided of course that there is sufficient wind. It is also nearly as close-winded, tacking through 75–80°, in contrast to many of the older types of cat which had difficulty in achieving 100° – or even in going to windward at all when reefed.

Trimarans are as fast as cats, often faster, for an equivalent size, weight and sail area, and their ability to point up to windward is nowadays as good as the best of the monohulls. Generally speaking, under cruising conditions there is little to choose between the two configurations. The tri can usually sail rather faster and closer to the wind than the cat, especially in a light breeze, when the lee float is taking very little weight; and it is often quicker to tack, because as the boat's head comes through the wind, both floats are clear of the water and there is only the main hull to resist being swivelled round. Conversely the cruising cat, with a full-sized hull to resist heeling, tends to be a bit faster to windward when it is blowing hard.

Weight

We have seen the effect of light weight on boatspeed when sufficient power is available. High power-to-weight ratio also produces rapid acceleration, the ability to jump from standstill to 10 knots in just a few boat lengths as you sheet in, or as the first puff reaches you in a calm patch. Even as the heavy displacement boats heel to the breeze before they gather way, the multihull is on the move, light and eager, and unable to heel more than a few degrees, so that the wind's energy is imme-diately converted into forward motion.

The same light weight, however, can some-times result in insufficient momentum to maintain way across localized wind shadows and the dead patches in the lee of trees and buildings along a river bank. When the wind stops, the boat stops. Similarly, successive heavy wave strikes when beating to windward in a seaway may almost halt it, unless it can be kept driving fast across the smaller crests and allowed to dance away from the big ones; whereas a heavy keelboat is better able to absorb the impacts, and although slowed down, will continue to shoulder its way through the seas.

The average monohull is also able to accept a considerable load of cruising stores and equipment, provided it is distributed so as not to upset the trim of the boat, without serious loss of performance or detriment to its hand-ling, even though the extra payload may have added as much as 25% to the displacement. The slender hulls of the multi, on the other hand, are poor load carriers, and without some restrictions on the family cruising gear, it is only too easy to turn a respectably fast boat into a real clunker. A high-performance cruiser-racer, weighed down with long-distance stores and equipment, can only too easily end up slower than a lightly loaded 'country cottage' cat. The discipline is hardest to apply on the bigger boats, with voluminous locker space inviting those last minute bicycles and sailboards to be added to the holiday inventory of extra ground tackle, tools, tins and bottles. The micro necessarily offers less scope for temptation of this kind within its overall length of 8m (26ft); but essential loose gear still accounts for around 10% of its dis-

placement, so the weight of any additional items such as engine, batteries, dinghy, anchors and water storage – and where you put them – must be carefully considered if the boat is not to be overloaded at the fitting out stage, let alone later.

Windage

A yacht's performance is also affected by the aerodynamic drag caused by the wind forces acting on the hull(s) and the superstructure, including the rig. These forces are propor-tional to the square of the apparent wind-speed, so that an increase in boatspeed from, say, 5 knots to 10, will result in four times the aerodynamic drag, while at the 15 knots that can be reached by many good multihulls, the drag is nine times that of the same boat jogging along at 5 knots.

This drag is made up of three components. The first, and least important, is the skin fric-tion caused by the air flowing across the vari-ous surfaces of the boat. In contrast to the water friction on the wetted areas, it is so small that it can be virtually disregarded, most of what there is coming from the sails, which pre-sent a relatively smooth low-friction surface. Next there is the drag induced by those sails in generating their driving force. This resistance is minimized in well-designed and accurately cut sails, correctly trimmed for angle, shape and their relationship with one another. The more efficient the overall sailplan, the less is its induced drag, but some is unavoidable. Finally, and most importantly because much can be done to minimize it, there is the para-sitic drag or 'windage' of the boat, caused not only by the hulls and cabin tops, but also the mast, spars, rigging and anything else exposed

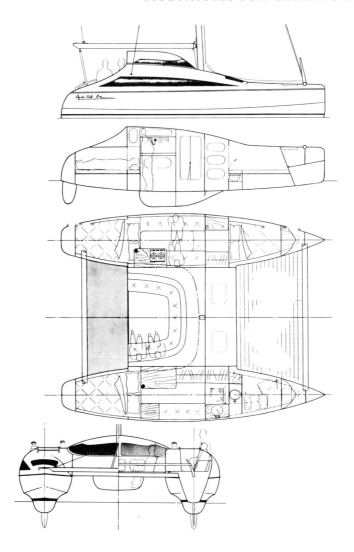

to the airstream. Remembering the 'square law' between windspeed and pressure – try putting your hand out of the window of a moving car to gauge its effect – it is easy to visualize the magnitude of the forces that a strong wind can exert on, for example, the superstructure of a big catamaran with a bluff bridgedeck saloon.

It is not only speed to windward that is affected by such drag. Pointing ability is significantly impaired, leeway is increased, and strong winds can also make the boat a handful to manoeuvre at low speed. Even with twin

Fig 2.3 *Micro with the mostest, the Clyde Cats 8m (26ft) 'Cheetah', designed by John Shuttleworth. Note the water tanks in the fixed keels, three roomy berths, and detachable bridgedeck shelter. For trailering the hulls stack on their sides, one above the other.*

engines, it is liable to skid around like a teatray unless it has deep centreboards, or a generous keel area, or unless plenty of steerage way is maintained – which can make for some hair raising exercises in close quarters handling. Careful attention to streamlining considerably reduces these effects, but they are still to be reckoned with on a large or lofty design.

The problem is less serious on a micro-cat, which besides having a more compact profile, will not aspire to much if any accommodation between the hulls, because if it is roomy enough to provide shelter for the crew, it is difficult to make it a demountable and sufficiently compact package for the road. The 8m (26ft) 'Cheetah' (fig 2.3) offers an ingenious compromise, but it needs a strong crew for assembly and dismantling, and is only intended for occasional changes of location, as distinct from weekends-away trailering. Bearing in mind that when a boat is sailing to windward, the airflow is coming from 30° or more off the bow, rather than from head on, any catamaran will present a considerable proportion of its two topsides and cabin tops obliquely to the wind when beating. The designer of a micro will therefore normally restrict freeboard to the minimum required for comfortable sitting headroom, with the side benefit of some saving in structural weight.

The trimaran scores slightly better in this respect because its floats, being smaller than the main hull, do not add much to the overall profile, except when heeled in strong winds. The monohull is still less affected by windage, not only because of its configuration, but because under most conditions it is slower than the multihull, and hence is subjected to lower windspeeds across the deck; but windage still affects the performance of even the slowest boats, and all reasonable steps should be taken to minimize it.

Passage time

The speed differential between multi- and monohull is usually reduced in bad weather, because except when racing, the prudent helmsman will deliberately slow his boat to a more comfortable pace. Not only does this subject the structure and gear to less of a hammering, but it gives a quieter ride to the crew below. Experience has shown that on any trip lasting more than a few hours, even in comparatively calm conditions, the cruising speed of a fast multihull is usually limited as much by decibels as by the motion. In fact, it can often be too noisy to sleep at any more than 9 or 10 knots, still less in rough weather, the lightweight hulls acting as sounding boards for the unending rush and rattle of the water, and amplifying the crash of the waves when the going gets rough – to a level that can make you flinch if the helmsman persists in driving hard. To be realistic, a fast 24-hour non-stop run in any but the really big multihulls is usually about as much as anyone can take, before tiredness begins to spoil the fun.

Sea-keeping, which after all is what concerns most sailors, was defined by the eminent physicist Froude as the combination of speed with habitability – which is what we really mean by cruising speed. Not everyone buys a multihull for the sheer joy of fast sailing; some people are more attracted by the roomy accommodation, shoal draught, level sailing and the feeling of security this gives. But useful cruising speed is something else. It constitutes what is arguably the single most important advantage of the high performance multihull: a comfortable cruising speed, given a moderate amount of wind, of around 1½ times and sometimes twice that of an equivalent monohull. The faster boat enables the one-day sailor to reach his favourite anchorage for lunch, and be home the same evening, instead of overnighting. It can undertake a more ambitious cruise in the allotted time, gives its crew longer ashore on visits, allows them to wait for favourable weather, or to make a dash for it and reach shelter in advance of a blow.

Average passage speeds over an entire season of sailing are difficult to assess, and they form a ready topic for discussion in the club bar. But a consensus of current opinion credits the fast multihull cruiser with around a one-third advantage over the same size of monohull, which allowing for a variety of weather conditions, translates into a net saving in passage times of three or four hours in every twenty-four. This is not to say that all multihullers have speed as their main objective. Far from it. Many of the heavier and more commodious cruising cats are only marginally faster than monohulls of the same length. But they are very seldom slower.

Shoal draught

Cruising in coastal areas and the choice of waypoints depends to a great extent on the depth of water along the route and in the anchorages and harbours to be visited. Passage planning involves charts, pilot guides, tide tables, weather forecasts, the speed of your boat – and its draught. Shallow draught is another of the multihull's happy advantages. Unlike the lifting keel monohull, most are capable of sailing to windward reasonably well with raised centreboards – if they have one at all – because of the combined keel effect of two bottoms, and the increasing lateral resistance of the lee hull or float as it is depressed.

Knowing that you need less than a metre

Fig 2.4 *Shoal draught and solitude. A Wharram 'Tiki 26', with her shallow draught rudders and no centreboards, can be sailed straight through the surf and up on to the beach.* (Photo © Hanneke Boon)

(say 3ft) of water to float in – half that if you have centreboards – allows you to save much valuable time (having regard to the weather and the state of the tide) by taking short cuts across shoals and sandbanks that would otherwise have to be given a wide berth. It opens up a range of new cruising grounds, enabling you to explore hitherto inaccessible coastlines and islands, and the upper reaches of rivers and estuaries. Shoal draught adds another dimension to the freedom of sailing.

Sneaking about in thin water, you are of course much more likely to run aground than the deep keelers. But most multihulls are so comparatively light that it is usually just a matter of jumping overboard and shoving off. Except in soft mud or strong winds, it is possible to push out through quite choppy water, provided you don't mind getting wet. On the other side of the coin, however, it has to be said that shallow draught sometimes encourages over-confidence and can lead to the taking of unnecessary risks, such as attempting to cross sandbanks or harbour bars in short, steep breaking seas. Indeed, all too often insurance companies report claims for the stranding of multihulls, although these mostly concern the larger boats that under the circumstances could not be shouldered into deeper water, or kedged off.

To the delights of sailing in the shallows can be added the joy of being able to get away from the crowd, if you feel like some peace and solitude, by creeping into some secluded spot where no keeler would dare to go. You can anchor to a short cable and dry out comfortably, or put her aground on any stretch of clean and level bottom. Or simply run up the beach, secure in the knowledge that no one can run into you in the night or drag into you

in a blow. Anyway, with your combination of light weight and draught, and a mostly rope cable instead of heavy chain, you are prone to sheer about at slack water or in a fluky breeze, so you are liable to make yourself unpopular in a crowded anchorage.

Trouble-free grounding, and being able to accept shallow moorings and mudberths, not only offers an alternative to marina berthing, for which multihulls are often surcharged on account of their wide beam; it represents a safety factor in an emergency. For if you are caught out in really severe weather near the coast, it is comforting to know that as a last resort you can take refuge by running ashore. With luck and some good judgement by the helmsman, a lightweight and strongly-built multihull will sustain little or no damage, even in surf; and it will float if holed by a rock. This is hardly a practice to be recommended, but you would probably get away with it where a monohull would surely be wrecked.

Apart from cruising performance, two other factors contribute to habitability and the quality of life aboard: accommodation and stability. It is these, as much as speed, that need to be considered while making the vital decision for or against a multihull, and in choosing between a cat and a tri. When people don't know much about either, or have no experience of them at all, their first thoughts are usually of voluminous cabin space, upright sailing and, too, a nagging question mark about the possibility of capsize. Take first the matter of space.

Accommodation

The sheer volume of living space in a medium-sized bridgedeck catamaran, let alone a large one, has to be seen to be believed. It almost takes your breath away the first time you go aboard, although in some parts of the boat the actual proportions may not be to everyone's liking. Standing down in the hulls, the width of the cabin soles is somewhat constricted by the essential narrowness of the waterline beam. But the outward flare of the topsides gives plenty of elbow room; and at eye level, with large windows along one side and the raised areas of the bridgedeck saloon – or sleeping berths – on the other, there is a pleasant air of spaciousness and luxury, enhanced by an abundance of varnished woodwork and cabinetry. On a length of around 11m (say 35ft), it is not unusual to find three or four double cabins, two heads-cum-shower compartments, a large fully equipped galley, seating for eight or more at the saloon table, with panoramic views and a doorway into a

cockpit that could easily hold another dozen guests in port without overcrowding – not to mention the vast areas of uncluttered deck for lounging on (and, inevitably, equally vast areas to be kept clean and painted). It requires a very much larger and more expensive monohull to provide such facilities. No wonder a medium-sized cat is the first choice for many live-aboards who put high initial stability, shallow draught and spacious accommodation, with protection from the elements, ahead of sailing performance; for it is generally true that the more accommodation a boat has – any boat of a given size, monohull or multi – the lower must be its level of sailing ability.

It is interesting to compare two of Richard

Fig 2.5 *Spacious bridgedeck area aboard the 13.3m (44ft) 'Casamance' offshore cruising catamaran, designed by Joubert & Nivelt and built in France by Fountaine Pajot.*

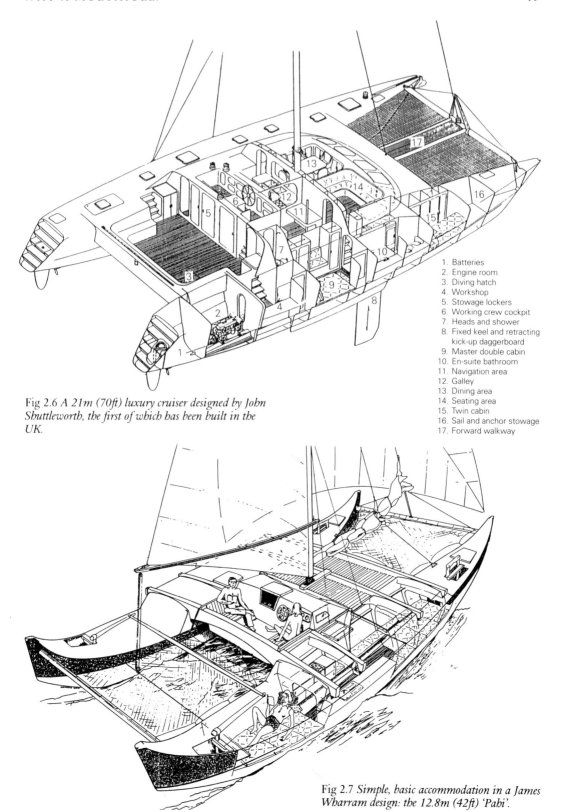

1. Batteries
2. Engine room
3. Diving hatch
4. Workshop
5. Stowage lockers
6. Working crew cockpit
7. Heads and shower
8. Fixed keel and retracting kick-up daggerboard
9. Master double cabin
10. En-suite bathroom
11. Navigation area
12. Galley
13. Dining area
14. Seating area
15. Twin cabin
16. Sail and anchor stowage
17. Forward walkway

Fig 2.6 *A 21m (70ft) luxury cruiser designed by John Shuttleworth, the first of which has been built in the UK.*

Fig 2.7 *Simple, basic accommodation in a James Wharram design: the 12.8m (42ft) 'Pahi'.*

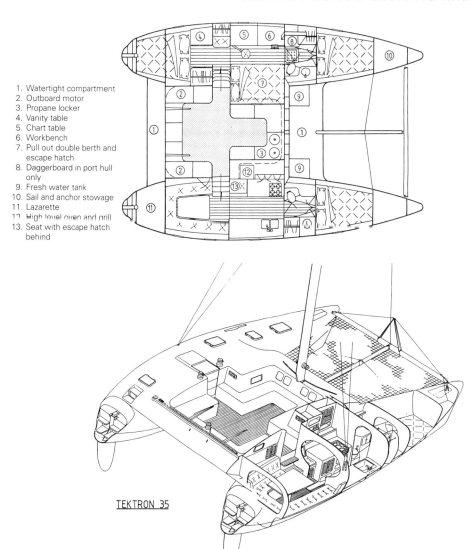

1. Watertight compartment
2. Outboard motor
3. Propane locker
4. Vanity table
5. Chart table
6. Workbench
7. Pull out double berth and escape hatch
8. Daggerboard in port hull only
9. Fresh water tank
10. Sail and anchor stowage
11. Lazarette
12. High level oven and grill
13. Seat with escape hatch behind

TEKTRON 35

Wood's 10.65m (35ft) designs, both built from the same hull moulds by Fantasy Yachts, Plymouth. One is the 'Flica', a luxuriously appointed, long-distance live-aboard boat, with full headroom throughout, fixed shallow keels, twin inboard diesels, and a conservative rig for comfortable journeying at 8–10 knots. Her sister, the 'Banshee', is a 15 knots sports cruiser with a powerful sailplan and deep daggerboards for good windward perform-ance, but with simpler and less spacious accommodation than the 'Flica', and with

Fig 2.8 *Another catamaran design by Shuttleworth, the 11m (35ft) 'Tektron' cruiser racer built in Canada. Note the spacious saloon in the stern, achieved by increasing the flare at the after end of the boat, with galley amidships.*

sitting rather than standing headroom in the bridgedeck saloon, in the interests of wind resistance, and an outboard motor.

Trimarans are different. The usable vol-ume of the main hull, even augmented by design dodges such as flared topsides and wing boxes built out below deck level, is considerably less than that of the cat's two hulls combined (though it approaches that of a monohull of similar length), it has less load-carrying capacity because of its smaller waterplane area, and it costs more to build. For these reasons, they are much less popular than cats of similar size – a recent American survey of all multihulls in the 7–12m (23–40ft) range indicated a market split in favour of cats about 40/60 (while in Europe the ratio is probably nearer to 20/80). But tris are nevertheless chosen by numbers of cruising folk in preference to cats, because of the more traditional shape and layout of their accommodation areas, and for their superior performance. Above 12m the survey found that the split actually went the other way, with the tri having sufficient accommodation for the majority of purchasers, and the cat becoming roomier than really necessary, and correspondingly bulkier to handle.

Conversely, however, as size decreases, so does the cat's space advantage; and coming down to an 8m (26ft) micro with an open area between the hulls (i.e. a trailer cat, as distinct from one with bridgedeck accommodation), it has lost out to the trimaran, which may have double the cabin width – anything up to 2.5m (8ft), the legal maximum for trailering in most countries (see p.141) – sometimes even combined with full standing headroom. Accommodation layouts are similar to those of monohulls, although not as spacious, typically comprising a double berth forward, a saloon with settee berth to one or both sides of the table, a galley and a heads compartment on opposite sides of the companionway, and an aft cockpit seating four. Except for a few 'wing-deck' designs, in which the hull and floats are

bridged by solid decking instead of nets or trampolines, the small tri lacks the cat's generous deckspace; but it does provide an attractive lounging area on the upwind trampoline, and useful storage in the floats for lightweight items such as oars, boathooks and fenders. It also offers shelter for its helmsman and crew in a secure cockpit, either conventionally located aft or in a snug central position where it provides a great sense of protection, besides concentrating the crew weight amidships – although on a small boat it undoubtedly spoils the roomy run of the accommodation by dividing it into two separate self-contained areas; and being nearer the bows, it is also inclined to require more frequent use of the sprayhood in choppy weather.

Micro-cat sailors, on the other hand, must at all times be out in the weather to work the boat, and usually have to perch on a cabin top, or spread themselves out on the trampoline or decking between the hulls – solid decking being preferable in a family cruiser because waves invariably squirt up through a trampoline. Except in a few particularly roomy designs, such as the Prout 'Scamper' and the Clyde Cats 'Cheetah' (fig 2.3), which also provide seats along the inboard sides of their coachroofs, internal accommodation in a small open bridgedeck type of cat is restricted by a cabin width of a little over one metre, and to hardly more than minimal sitting headroom – although the latter seems less of a disadvantage if you accept Nat Herreshof's philosophical view: 'the only time you need full standing headroom is if you sleep standing up.' The layout normally has a single berth at either end of each hull, making four in all, with a toilet under one of them, and one or more being used for the stowage of sails and other

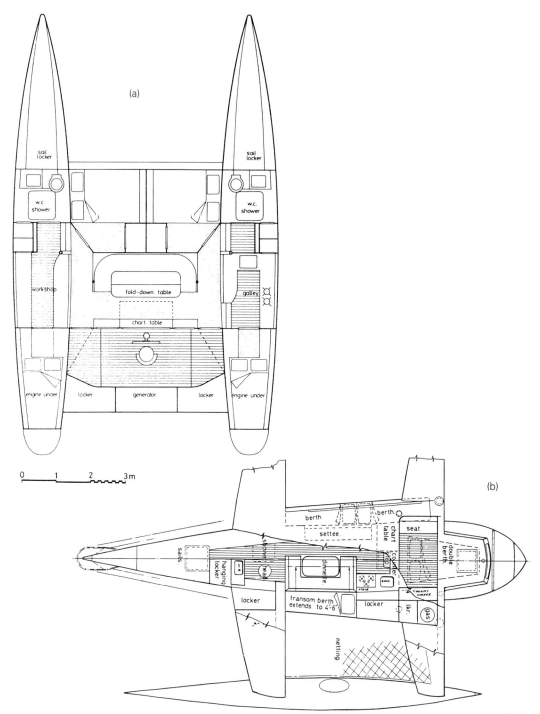

Fig 2.9 Cats and tris compared for their
accommodation.
(a) 12m (40ft) fast cruising cat by Nic Bailey and
   Jack Michel (UK). Four double cabins, two WC/
   shower compartments, galley, workshop and large
   bridgedeck saloon.

(b) 12m (40ft) cruiser/racer tri by Lock Crowther
   (Australia). One double cabin; three berths, galley
   and dinette in the saloon area; WC/shower for'd.
(c) F-27 8m (26ft) high performance folding tri by
   Ian Farrier (USA). Small aft cabin; saloon with
   standing headroom under a pop-top, cooker and

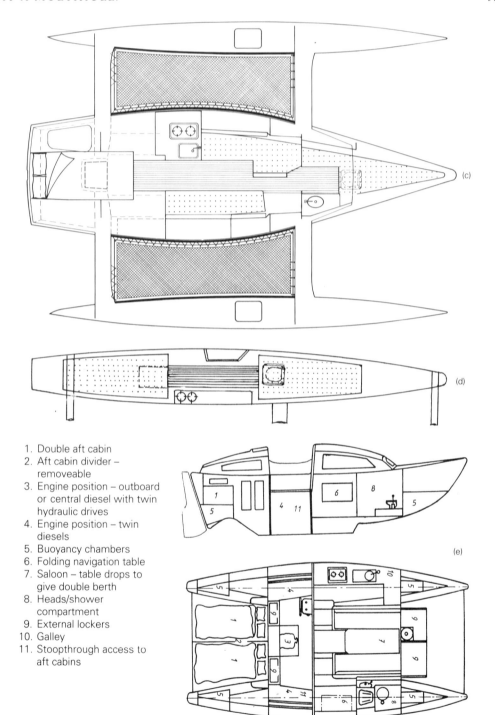

1. Double aft cabin
2. Aft cabin divider – removeable
3. Engine position – outboard or central diesel with twin hydraulic drives
4. Engine position – twin diesels
5. Buoyancy chambers
6. Folding navigation table
7. Saloon – table drops to give double berth
8. Heads/shower compartment
9. External lockers
10. Galley
11. Stoopthrough access to aft cabins

two berths; vanity unit, toilet and additional berth forward.

(d) Typical accommodation in a micro cat (both hulls are similar) totals four single berths with sitting headroom, toilet under one berth, cooker and fold-down table. OK for weekending.

(e) Still only 7.9m (26ft), but not trailerable. 'Heavenly Twins', designed by Pat Patterson (UK). Bridgedeck saloon; standing headroom in the hulls containing the galley, chart table, and toilet; two double cabins aft of the centre cockpit; and twin diesels. Comfortable cruising at modest speeds.

gear when not occupied. Off-duty crew-members sit facing one another on the ends of the bunks, with a folding table between them, and a cooking stove hinged on the cabin side or centreboard casing. It is a cosy and sociable arrangement, but decidedly cramped for pro-longed cruising; and freedom of movement becomes something of a problem in wet weather when the hatches are closed. This can be considerably alleviated, however, when the boat is berthed or beached, by means of a cock-pit tent rigged over the boom and fastened to each hull. This effectively doubles the total space and provides an agreeable socializing area, while the two separated cabins offer a big bonus in privacy – something which is other-wise very difficult to achieve in small boats.

Stability and motion

Living space is only part of habitability and comfort afloat. The ability to use that space while sailing is just as important, and under extreme weather conditions can become a critical factor. Seaworthiness can be defined as the ability of a vessel to carry her crew in safety through the most severe weather conditions, sea-kindliness the ability to do so in any sort of comfort. Both are strictly relative terms, for it's a fact that although it may be safe enough, no small boat is comfortable in a rough sea. This poses the question of just how seaworthy does the weekend cruiser, for example, need to be? Given that she is unlikely ever to be called upon to face the survival conditions that a larger boat might conceivably encounter in the course of a long ocean voyage, she should still – in the right hands – be capable of living through them; and of riding out a 'mere' coastal storm without endangering her crew.

The following graphic account of one such experience in *Summer Twins*, a 7.5m (25ft) cruising cat with full bridgedeck accommoda-tion, was written by its designer, Pat Patterson:

'Due to a very inaccurate weather forecast, Tom and I were caught off the North Cornish coast in a NNE gale. Our anemometer was showing 40 knots. We hove-to on the starboard tack with deep reef main and about 30sq ft of jib aback for 18 hours. Seas built up quickly to an estimated 12–14ft and were short. Worst of all, it was very cold – barely above freezing. We could maintain a watch from inside the saloon. We cooked adequate meals eating off plates at the table. The cabin heater kept the cold at bay, although clothes were not taken off for three days. We had to request (by VHF) one ship to keep clear. This ship confirmed our position obtained by RDF. Had we been in a 25ft monohull, to keep as good a look-out one of us would have had to keep watch in the cockpit. The chill factor was horrendous. A lot more seas would have broken over us. Cooking and eating would have been more difficult. Hypothermia and fatigue could have put us in a life-threatening situation. My conclusion is that we were, for those conditions, in a more seaworthy boat than any production monohull of a similar length.'

It is also a fact that a multihull is more affected by sea conditions than a monohull when either is driven to its limits in bad weather, as in ocean racing. At the multihull's high speeds, it's not the wind that's the worry, it's the sea-state. Yet such is the seaworthiness of the big maxis in experienced hands, that they are routinely sailed 'on the barometer', racing from one low pressure weather system to the next so as to catch the strongest winds. For them, the biggest danger is of collision with flotsam, or whales. The sea is undoubtedly more cruel to little boats than to large ones, and in a rough sea, the smaller and lighter the boat, the more exhausting is its motion. A wind-over-tide Force 7 in a micro can equate to a roaring Force 10 in a 40-footer. Nevertheless, small boats, properly equipped and expertly handled, have raced single-handed across the Atlantic, and have even circumnavigated the world. Their intrepid helmsmen must have suffered acute discomfort and hardship at times, but some boats are much less uncomfortable than others, and under cruising conditions multihulls usually come off best, provided they are sailed sensibly.

Upright sailing is another relative term, since no multihull can sail bolt upright except in flat water and light airs. In the sort of boisterous breeze that would lay most monohulls over to 30° or more, a trimaran will probably heel no more than 10° or so, depending on the design of its floats, possibly reaching 15° in a squall; and a catamaran scarcely half as much – relative to the surface of the water. It is interesting to note that the moderate heeling of a tri is preferred by some sailors as feeling more 'natural' than the cat's upright stance, and also as a more sensitive indicator of the amount of sail being carried in relation to the wind strength.

The multihull, sitting on the surface of the sea like a raft, will naturally try to conform to the slope of the particular wave she is riding, so in following the contours of a beam sea, the angle of heel will alternately increase and decrease. But profiling is not the same as rolling, which is the pendulum effect of the heavy keel that takes a monohull way past its normal heeling angle whenever the frequency of the roll happens to coincide with the period of the waves. Instead, with none of this rhythmic rolling, the motion of a multihull is relatively quick and jerky, smaller in amplitude but often unpredictable, because its light weight causes it to react accurately and almost instantaneously to the wave surfaces. A trimaran's motion is somewhat gentler and less abrupt than a cat's, because of the lesser buoyancy of its floats, compared to the cat's hulls, and the larger angles of heel they accordingly permit. Nevertheless, those who claim that no multihull will ever spill your cup of tea are guilty of wishful thinking.

Downwind, the keelboat suffers even more from cumulative rolling, due to the absence of any damping effect from the wind acting on the sails from one side. As she rolls from side to side, she becomes directionally unstable due to the off-centre drive of the heeled rig and, unless the hull is particularly well 'balanced',

Fig 2.10 *Profiling is not the same as rolling. In these diagrams, the waves are moving from right to left, and it can be seen that the multihull will try to conform to the local slope, riding it like a raft. The ballasted keelboat, however, once she has been heeled by a wave as at (a), will begin to roll on her own because of the pendulum effect of her keel. If successive waves then coincide with her natural roll frequency, their cumulative effect – despite some damping by the keel and sails – can lead to large angles of heel, as at (b).*

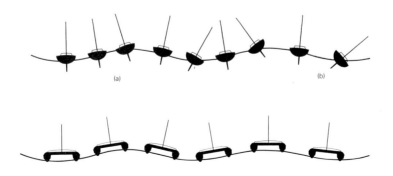

(a)   (b)

due to the dissimilar volumes being periodically immersed fore and aft of the centre of
gravity, requiring constant helm corrections to
maintain course – and in gusty conditions to
resist the tendency either to gybe, or to gripe
up into the wind and broach. The multihull on
the other hand invariably gives you a fast,
steady and relaxing ride, with comparative
freedom from roll, only small rudder movements being needed to avoid yawing and the
attendant risk of an accidental gybe. Moreover, gybing, whether accidental or deliberate,
is itself a gentler affair with less risk of damage,
because the multihull's high speed means that
downwind it is sailing closer to the true
windspeed, so that the apparent windspeed is
lower than on a monohull under the same
conditions.

Their relative behaviour in big head seas is
also different. Some types of monohull, such
as the heavy narrow-beamed boats with long
deep keels, have a slow and easy motion in
rough conditions, although they give you a
very wet ride as they slice their way through
the waves. Others, notably the modern fin keel
cruiser with broader beam and greater reserve
buoyancy, are drier but less comfortable, tend-
ing to fall out of the back of each big wave and
plunging heavily into the bottom of the next
trough.

The lighter multihull responds to the contours immediately, the motion is shorter and
sharper, and the decks stay clear of solid water.
But at a certain wave periodicity, the combination of fine bows and sterns, with the inertia of
a comparatively heavy mast and sails, sometimes leads to a violent pitching motion that
can almost bring the boat to a standstill, unless
she can be eased off the wind to pick up speed,
and then be kept driving fast through the seas.

Hobby-horsing, as it is known, can be largely
eliminated by suitable hull design (see p.64)
and lightweight spars, and by stowing most of
the heavy gear as near as possible to the middle
of the boat. Even so, it can be a nuisance on
occasions.

One aspect of rolling and heeling that is
not often recognized is that at an angle of, say,
30°, there is insufficient space in a small boat
for a person to maintain himself in a vertical
position when moving about in the accommodation, or trying to cook, or using the heads;
even the sleeping berths become untenable
without the restraint of leecloths. One's body
must adapt continuously in order to maintain
its position, needing the constant use of hands
and feet to preserve balance as the boat rolls
from side to side, pitches or corkscrews. All
this is very tiring after a time, and the motion
itself encourages the onset of seasickness.
Tiredness leads to mistakes and wrong – sometimes dangerously wrong – decisions; seasickness to an awful inability to make any
decisions at all.

With less heeling to displace the body from
the vertical, and no pendulum rolling, the
multihull's quick and often erratic motion is
much less tiring, and at the same time less sick-
making. It provides a comparatively stable
working platform on which the crew are able
to rest, cook and enjoy their food for longer
into any oncoming spells of foul weather, and
the boat can remain both fast and safe in conditions that would exhaust the same crew in a
monohull, to the point of turning a first class
boat into an unseaworthy one. This is just as
well, for there is no doubt that the multihull
needs to be sailed attentively and nursed
through the worst patches, whereas a good
monohull can be left to look after itself, pro-

vided a regular lookout is maintained, while the crew try to get some rest.

Which brings us to the crunch question of capsize.

Causes of capsize

More people have been dissuaded from buying a multihull by the fear of turning it over than for any other reason. And no wonder, in view of the sensational nature of the capsize reports that have appeared in the press over the years, and which continue to attract the occasional tragic headline. As experience in the design and handling of multihulls has accumulated during their short history, however, so these accidents have become much less frequent, confined largely to the big time ocean and circuit racers; but when they do occur, they are sensational, like the boats themselves.

Unfortunately, however, while the technological spin-off certainly benefits cruising boat design, such incidents tend to tarnish the multihull image – unlike motor racing, where grand prix accidents are never even remotely associated with the family car. Driving a big multihull on the brink of boatcrash is a very dangerous game indeed – much more dangerous than racing a monohull, because of the enormous power and speed of these machines, many of them (to paraphrase Dick Newick again) 'built so light and sailed so hard that they are sure as hell going to win something . . . if they ever get there'. Similarly, there is a much greater difference between big boat racing and cruising in multihulls than there is in monohulls.

The primary cause of capsize is sailing with too much sail up in rough or confused seas, notably on a close reach with centreboards lowered, when a sudden squall or wind shift can turn the boat over before the sheets can be released. You can nearly always get away with it on a monohull – at the cost of some excessive heeling which slows the boat – because it is self-righting. A multihull is not, and because it has such great initial stability, the crew can be lulled into a false sense of security, particularly on a catamaran which heels so little. But an alert skipper will be able to judge when his boat is becoming overpressed long before the weather hull begins to lift out. On a tri, it is easier to judge when to shorten sail, because it heels more than a cat; and anyway, you can keep an eye on the lee float and take action if it starts getting buried. Under 'survival' conditions, with all sails down and centreboards up, a broad-beamed cat or a tri with high buoyancy floats will surf sideways in breaking seas.

The length of a cat's connecting structure is limited for reasons of stressing, so the tri invariably has a wider overall beam, which gives it greater ultimate stability. Consequently it can be sailed harder than a cat, assuming that its floats are of the high-buoyancy type, each capable on its own of supporting the total weight of the boat plus a large reserve. It is sometimes argued that if you have floats that big, why not take away the centre hull and have a catamaran? This makes a lot of sense if you are looking for a mid-sized cruising boat, but it doesn't give the small trimaran credit for its roomy accommodation. And it must be remembered that a tri in light winds sails primarily on its main hull, with consequently less wetted surface and hence less resistance and usually better performance than an equivalent cat.

The one big disadvantage of a trimaran's

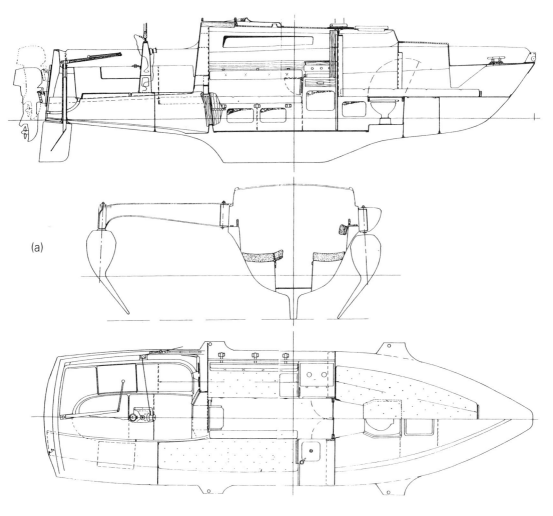

(a)

(b)

broader beam is that it is harder to find dock-ing space, although some designs incorporate floats that can be folded when the boat is still on the water, while retaining sufficient stabil-ity for motoring or gentle sailing. Current examples are the F-27 and the Ocqueteau 'Speed 944' 31-footer, in both of which the inboard ends of the crossbeams lift up on link-ages that bring the floats in alongside the main hull; and the 'Argonauta', where instead they swing back in parallelogram fashion, as in the late John Westell's original 'Ocean Bird' and subsequent designs, some of them as large as 12m (40ft). Apart from ease of berthing the larger boats, this greatly reduces the time normally required for demounting a micro on to its trailer and for reassembly prior to launching.

A few trimaran designs still feature low buoyancy floats, which offer considerable savings in weight and windage. But these are too easily driven under when sailing hard in strong wind conditions, or if the boat is thrown over by an extra large wave while lying a-hull in heavy weather; and this can put the boat at risk of pitchpoling over the lee bow. Under normal circumstances nothing so spec-tacular occurs, because the main hull lifts to the approaching wave sufficiently to take the weather float out of its reach; and before the lee one has dropped enough to induce any tripping force, the wave passes under it and lifts it back. With high buoyancy floats (more about these on p. 72) – and similarly with cats

Fig 2.11 (a) Spacious for only 6.8m (22ft). A swing-wing trimaran by the late John Westell (UK). Beam for sailing is 6.8m (19ft), folding to 2.4m (8ft) for trailering. (b) Application of the same principle on the 7.9m (26ft) 'Argonauta', designed by Dick Newick and built by Tremolino in the USA. The Quorning 'Dragonfly' 800 and 31 are the latest trimarans to adopt this principle.

provided that their leeward centreboard has been raised – whenever the boat is thrown sideways after being hit by a beam sea, it will skid down the face of the wave until the crest picks up the lee hull and equilibrium is restored. In sailing any multihull, the golden rule is to recognize and respect its operating limits, and not to approach them too closely.

The same reasoning has always applied to unballasted, flat-bottomed monohulls, such as the traditional Thames barge, and the many types of Dutch barge and barge yacht, none of which has any notable history of capsizing, because they are sailed sensibly. Most multi-hulls are potentially high performance craft. And just as a powerful, thoroughbred sports car doesn't have to be driven flat out – at half-throttle it is much safer than a slow vehicle pushed to its limits – so the multihull, sailed with reserve, can still keep pace with the hard-driven monohull. This doesn't necessarily mean sailing slowly; merely less fast. The fast boat which is deliberately slowed down in heavy weather is much less uncomfortable than a slow one pushed to its limits. When it begins to blow a honker, the motto should be 'Ease back and enjoy the ride'.

Nevertheless a multihull *can* capsize, although it has to be sailed without much regard for good seamanship – or in other words, very rashly – for this to happen, except when racing. Racers in major international events take calculated risks in driving their boats close to the ragged edge of safety; but when occasionally lives are lost, it is usually from failing to clip on to a lifeline, and falling overboard in heavy seas. Capsized and dam-aged multihulls are almost invariably recov-ered – sometimes many months later – and repaired, to sail another day. So in the last

(c)

(a)

Fig 2.12 *Ingenious float folding geometry devised by Ian Farrier (Australia and the USA). (a) and (b) Farrier's 'Command 10' design for a 10m (33ft)*   *cruiser-racer for home building in sheet plywood. (c) the 9.5m (31ft) 'Speed 944', produced in France by Bateaux Ocqueteau, uses the Farrier folding system.*

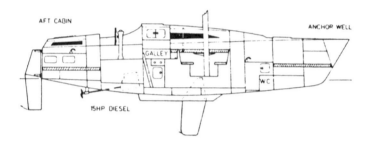

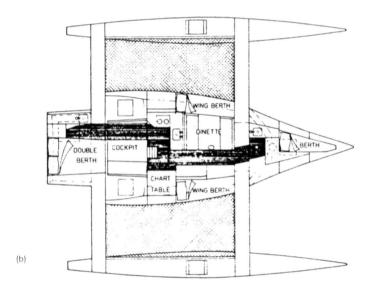

(b)

resort, if you should find yourself in the water with an upside-down boat, it's comforting to know that your life support system can't sink, provided that it has built-in buoyancy, which virtually all multihulls do – whereas a monohull can be overwhelmed and dragged under by its heavy keel. Neither is at all likely, but nor can either risk be entirely eliminated. They just have to be accepted if we want to go sailing for pleasure.

Cost

The final parameter to be considered in choosing the right kind of boat is the budget from which it will be funded, starting with the purchase price. Partly because of the relatively small numbers of any one type of multihull to be built commercially, compared to the flow-line production of most small monohulls, and partly because you are to some extent buying two boats at once, cost being related to surface area, the price of a professionally-built cat is in the region of 20%–30% higher than that of an equivalent monohull of the same *length*, with the tri rather more expensive still. There are as yet comparatively few commercially produced multihulls to choose from – except in France, where several major yachtbuilders are running a multihull line, mostly of big boats, alongside their normal production; and a number of smaller companies are offering micro-multi-hulls off the shelf. Among amateur-built designs, the choice is much wider, and many of

Fig 2.13 *The 'F27' in action: sailing, folding and trailering.*

these boats are soundly constructed and fin-ished to standards that would be uneconomic in a professional product. Some, on the other hand, are so poorly put together that they do nothing but make the owner's life a misery and damage the reputation of home-builts as a whole. This is reflected in their second-hand values, which are considerably lower than those of the factory product. But if you find what you think is a good one, and your sur-veyor agrees with you, you have probably got yourself a bargain.

Running costs are also inclined to be higher than those of a monohull. Apart from the berthing surcharges on beam, imposed by some marinas, there is more boat to clean and paint – although the increased cost of main-tenance will not be significant if the owner does most of the work himself. On insurance, unfortunately, it will. The premium for a 'series' multihull – one that is produced on a fairly large scale, such as the Prout catamarans – is currently around 1.2% of its insured value, compared with 1.0% for an equivalent mono-

hull. Those figures exclude the overseas exten-sion you would need if you were to take the boat abroad on a holiday trip. But for a cat or tri built professionally but in small numbers, or a home-built one-off, the rate is nearer to 2%. Three hundred pounds per annum on even a £15,000 boat is enough to make one think twice, let alone the premium on a big cruiser. Some don't insure; but suppose your boat were to break loose in a storm and damage someone else's, or you collided with a boardsailor, or inadvertently caused an acci-dent to another boat. A third party claim could cost hundreds of thousands. Fortunately a few enterprising insurers now offer third party cover at comparatively modest rates. Virtually all countries recommend that visiting yachts-men should carry third party insurance; in a few it is compulsory.

We are faced with these punitive pre-miums because the marine insurance under-writers are obliged to base their rates on the frequency and size of the claims for total loss. And it is an unfortunate fact that the pattern

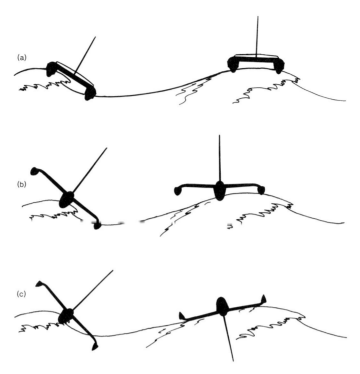

Fig 2.14 *Heavy weather behaviour of catamarans and trimarans in a beam sea. (a) The cat readily surfs sideways, until the wave crest picks up the lee hull and the boat comes upright. (b) A trimaran with high buoyancy floats behaves in similar manner, although the angle of heel may be greater (depending on how the tri's half-beam compares with the overall beam of the cat) while the lee float is deeply immersed in supporting much (occasionally all) of the total displacement – until the crest runs under it and rights the boat. (c) A low buoyancy float may dig in sufficiently to trip the boat, leading to capsize.*

has been set, and is currently being maintained, by the accidents to a comparatively few big, fragile and enormously expensive racers, which are effectively spoiling the market for the cruising sailors, who can only console themselves with their no-claims bonuses.

Although it is impossible to generalize in the matter of cost, it is probably fair to say that overall, the multihull is at the most about one-third more expensive to buy and operate than the monohull; and in the opinion of nearly everyone who has tried both, it is well worth it.

Last but by no means least, there is the important matter of emotional appeal to be considered. Can a multihull ever touch the yachtsman's heart in quite the same way as a traditional sailing boat? The answer is prob-

ably no – except perhaps in the case of the picturesque Wharram cats. But then there are some who say there's little to really stir the senses in today's mostly bland and look-alike monohulls. They have lost so much of the individual identity and character of their hand-crafted predecessors – though again there are exceptions. In comparing fast modern cruising boats, any disadvantage the multi-hulls may have in their visual attraction is, for most of us, outweighed by their superiority in other respects. Traditional beauty, seakindli-ness and habitability, combined with very high performance, and all at an affordable price? Alas, this is the stuff that only dreams are made of.

The choice is yours.

Multihulls and monohulls compared

MULTIHULLS

For

Most designs cannot sink

Lavish accommodation for live-aboards

Usually faster, with reduced passage time

Exciting acceleration

Shallow draught and ease of drying out opens up new cruising grounds

Don't heel or roll much

Motion is less tiring

All-round view from spacious bridgedeck saloon

Easier downwind helming

Mostly suitable for amateur building

Lightweight, and easy to trail (micros)

More deck space for working and sail handling

Against

Can capsize, not self-righting

Shape of accommodation (except on big trimarans) offends some traditionalists

Fewer opportunities for racing

Stop when the wind stops

Sometimes difficult to find space in yards and marinas

Poor weight carrier

Need attentive handling in bad weather

Much less choice of production designs

More difficult to sell if home-built

Usually take longer to dismantle and re-assemble than monohull trailer sailers

More expensive to insure

BALLASTED MONOHULLS

For

Usually self-righting after a knockdown and can survive a 360° roll

Look after their crew in bad weather

Good accommodation, even in small boats

Easy to find berthing space

Wide choice of types

Good resale value

Against

Can sink if overwhelmed by the sea or following a collision (except for a few monohulls that have built-in buoyancy)

Heeling and rolling is tiring and can lead to seasickness

Helming is more difficult off the wind

Deeper draught of fixed keel boats restricts cruising grounds

Slower speed means longer passages

CAT v. TRI

Cat

Heels less

Cheaper to buy or build

More accommodation on mid-sized boats

Better load carrier

More deck area for anchor handling and lounging on

Two separate hulls give more privacy

Less overall beam causes fewer problems on narrow waterways

One less hull to scrub and paint

Tri

No bridgedeck pounding

Motion less abrupt than a cat's

Safety of three hulls in the event of holing

Better living space on micro-tris

Faster in light winds, handles better, and tacks more quickly

Wider platform for shrouds; better support for fore and aft stays gives superior pointing

Greater ultimate stability

Some designs have folding floats for ease of berthing and trailering

Handicapping, hull shapes and computer-aided design

It is important, as well as interesting, for a sailor to have some understanding of the way in which the various aspects of design affect the character and behaviour of his boat, or of the one he is thinking of buying. The old adage, 'if it looks right, it *is* right', has traditionally enabled those with an experienced eye for a sweet-handling and seaworthy hull shape to recognize one at a glance. Nowadays it is not so simple. First appearances have become deceptive as new technology, developed in the design of high performance keelboats – and the majority of multihulls – has changed the delicate balance in the relative importance of the various design parameters, and our understanding of the ways in which they interact on one another. As a result one sees some aesthetically strange, and occasionally even ugly, monohulls that are in fact miracles of computer-predicted performance, though sometimes at the expense of habitability, and possibly ease of handling too. The underwater shapes of most multihulls, on the other hand, have always looked sleek and graceful, and still do; but in the last forty years, their designs have become a much more complex blend of the qualities shown by seagoing experience to be needed in a successful boat.

Some of these qualities are, of course, sacrificed in the design of a dedicated racing boat; but for a cruising multihull they can be defined as:

1. Safety and seaworthiness. A cruising boat must be designed for heavy weather, with sufficient reserves of strength and stiffness for it to be driven hard when necessary, and with watertight compartments large enough for it to continue sailing if partially flooded, and to float high in the water if inverted.
2. Good performance, especially to windward, with high pointing ability.
3. Comfortable crewing stations and spacious accommodation, especially in harbour. If a cruising boat isn't roomy (at least for its size), practical and comfortable, it won't sell – or resell – no matter how fast it is.
4. Handling characteristics should be docile, with a light helm, and the boat must tack easily.
5. In the case of a micro, which has to be trailerable, it should also be as light as possible, both for performance and for towing, and be easily assembled and dismantled.

Let us look first at the matter of speed, not that it is necessarily the most important but because it is the one parameter that links cruising with racing.

Speed

We have seen how fast multihulls can sail, because of their relatively high power-to-weight ratio and low drag. But by no means all owners or would-be purchasers of multihulls are interested in racing their boats, nor are they particularly concerned with racing performance. When choosing a boat large enough for extended cruising, most multihull owners put comfort and safety a long way ahead of speed – provided it is at least as fast as any comparable monohull. But speed is a very

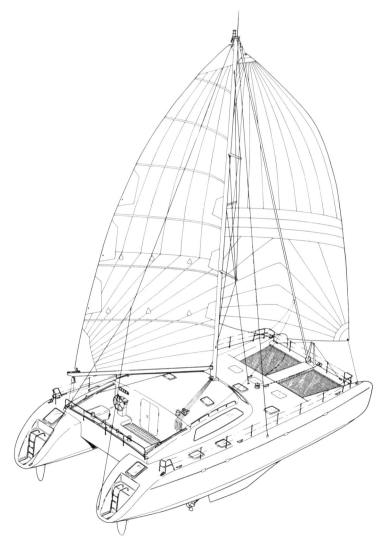

Fig 3.1 *Sleek and graceful, the 'Freebird 50' 15.2m (50ft) fast cruising cat was developed from the classic 'Firebird' micro. Built in Cornwall by Modular Mouldings.*

important design consideration; and even the most pottering-orientated sailor likes to know what his boat would do if he ever needed to 'push it'. Looking at it another way, a boat that can be safely sailed at high speed and raced through a gale is going to feel more secure for cruising in bad weather than might a more pedestrian design.

There are several methods of comparing the speeds of different boats. The most elementary and now somewhat outdated basis is the Bruce Number. It is mentioned here because it is still often referred to, and it gives a

clear indication of whether one boat is likely to be faster than another. The Bruce Number is simply the square root of the sail area (in sq ft) divided by the cube root of the displacement (in pounds); the larger the number, the greater the power-to-weight ratio and the faster the boat should be in a breeze. Taking two widely differing examples, a 'Dragon', which is a traditional racing keelboat, has a BN of 1.06, compared to 1.72 for a 'Tornado' two-man Olympic catamaran. The 'Tornado' is certainly the faster boat, and by very much more than the 60% difference in the Bruce Numbers, for reasons that will be explained later. A BN of 1.00 is generally accepted as the approximate dividing line between so-called fast and slow boats.

Various other methods have been devised to present a fair comparison of multihull performances, based like the Bruce Number on power-to-weight ratio, but introducing the important variable of length, as this affects drag, in the form of sail area multiplied by length and divided by displacement. On this basis, an easy way of calculating the relative top speeds of different boats, or to assess the effect of changes that you might make to your own boat's sail area or weight, is to work out its Measured Rating using the formula

$$MR = 2\sqrt{\frac{SA \times WL}{\Delta}}$$ where:

SA = Mainsail area + 100% foretriangle (m²). The foretriangle, as its name implies, is the area formed by the forestay, mast and deck.

WL = Waterline length (m)

Δ = Displacement (kg)

If you prefer to work in feet and pounds, use

$$0.5\sqrt{\frac{SA \times WL}{\Delta}}$$

Suppose that your top speed is around 12 knots, and that your SA = 30m², WL = 7.5m and Δ = 850kg. Your MR works out at 1.03. Now you take on extra stores and a couple of extra crew for a holiday cruise, adding 200kg to your payload. Your MR falls to 0.93, and since this is directly proportional to speed, this drops to 10.8 knots.

In practice, it has been found that this simple formula tends to exaggerate the effect of changes, particularly in displacement, and the problem has been to find the correct emphasis to place on each of the three primary criteria affecting 'base speed' – typically, average speed round a triangular course, or over a day's run – bearing in mind that yachts spend nearly half their time close-hauled, and hence at much less than their top speed.

Handicapping

In awarding racing handicaps, with the object of allowing widely differing types of boat to compete on as near equal terms as possible, there are two fundamentally different methods of assessing relative performance. One is theoretical, using one of several highly refined and somewhat complex derivations of the basic MR formula in which powers varying between 0.25 and 0.50 are applied, instead of an overall square root, each boat (or type) being weighed and measured – which is time-consuming and sometimes expensive – to produce a rating figure. The other is purely statistical, based on race results instead of measurements, and is known as a yardstick number.

PERFORMANCE YARDSTICKS

The most widely used formula in both the UK and the USA is the RYA (Royal Yachting Association) Portsmouth Yardstick. As distinct from a calculated performance rating, this is a form of all-round racing handicap derived from the time taken by different types of boat to cover the same distance in races. Hence during one typical racing season, again instancing the 'Dragon' and the 'Tornado' (not that such boats would be likely to race against one another), the 'Dragon' had a PY of 103 and the 'Tornado' 75, because it had been established by the RYA from seasonal returns from the sailing clubs with either class in their fleets, that on average Dragons took 103 minutes to sail the same type of course that was covered by Tornados in 75 minutes. The handicaps, which are revised from time to time in line with reported race results, are applied by multiplying the elapsed time of each competing boat by 100 and dividing by its PN. Putting it on a simple percentage basis, a fast boat with a PY of 75 is expected to finish in 75% of the time taken by a boat with a yardstick of 100; whereas a slow boat with a PY of 120 can take 20% longer and still finish level on handicap.

The system works reasonably well in cruiser racing among monohulls, but not in mixed mono- and multihull fleets, partly due to lack of club racing experience with most multihulls other than the dinghy types, but mainly because of the wide variation in their performance from light to strong wind conditions. Accordingly MOCRA (the Multihull Offshore Cruising & Racing Association) awards its own Performance Yardstick to members' boats, again based on race results, but using a slightly simpler system of handicap adjustment to suit its smaller fleets.

The disadvantage of yardsticks is that because they are derived from race results, good design and efficient crewing tend to be penalized, while a badly prepared boat or sloppy helmsmanship is rewarded – except, of course, when any one type of boat is raced in sufficiently large numbers to average out the anomalies between individual entrants. A brilliant crew may be 10% better, a poor crew 15% worse than average, but the differences can to some extent be ironed out by introducing a Crew Skill Factor, which clubs are asked to apply before making their national returns. This is supposed to take into account preparation, sailing and technical skills, and can also be allocated on an individual crew-and-boat basis in local racing. The object of any handicapping system is to even out the fleet so as to ensure that not only the fastest boats have a chance of winning. Nevertheless, in practice, the slowest ones seldom seem to, unless the averaging process is overdone, and the fast ones quite often do, despite the fact that they require more skill to win on handicap, because mistakes cost more effective time. There will always be some competitors who feel they are unfairly treated. No system has yet been devised that is fair to everyone; this goes for ratings too.

RATINGS

The alternative to yardsticks are the various rating systems that are in current use. These take the form of a Time Correction Factor (TCF) which is multiplied by the boat's elapsed (stopwatch) time over the course to give a corrected time on which the race results are based. Among the best known is Holland's Texel Yardstick – something of a misnomer, for it is in fact a measured rating, although it is calculated from a statistically based MR formula – which is widely used for handicapping dinghy cats and other beach boats, although it also works quite well for larger multihulls. Then there's the IMMCA (International Micro-Multihull Class Association) TCF, which is similar to the Texel system, but was expressly devised for micro racing. And most wide ranging of all, the IOMR (International Offshore Multihull Rule) which is applicable to all cruising and racing multihulls, regardless of size, and is administered on a worldwide basis by the International Yacht Racing Union. It is established in the United States, notably on the West Coast under the auspices of the Pacific Multihull Association (PMA), and in Australia, Scandinavia and most of continental Europe, including France, where it is also referred to as PMA rating.

Each rating is computer calculated from a comprehensive set of hull and sail measurements and weighing routines, differing mainly in the complexity of the procedures adopted and the way in which the respective formulae take account of the area of individual sails (and of the wingmast, if fitted). The IMMCA and Texel ratings are generally much simpler to apply, because not only are their formulae far less complex than the IOMR's, but under their rules a single handicap holds good for all boats of a particular design, with allowances for certain variations in equipment, whereas under the IOMR every boat must be individually weighed and measured, and the subsequent calculations run to several pages.

There is a certain amount of controversy as to which is the best system, with designers pressing for various sections of the rules to be amended in the light of the latest technology. But unless or until they are replaced by a single acceptable method of rating, you will need both if you are going to race against rated boats in continental Europe and Scandinavia. A performance yardstick is undoubtedly a simpler method of handicapping, involving as it does no weighing or measuring. But it can be no more than an overall and necessarily approximate measure of the capability of a boat with a particular crew, and it is subject to the uncer-

tainty of arbitrary revision by a local club (or nationally in Britain by the RYA or MOCRA). A rating, on the other hand, is supposed to represent the potential performance of the boat itself. It remains constant until any modification, such as the size of a sail or a change in equipment, is made to the boat, which must then be re-rated.

Virtually all new micros are optimized for one or other system of TCF calculation at the design stage, and existing boats are often modified so as to sail to a more beneficial rating. A reduction in sail area, for example, would achieve this: speed on the water would of course be reduced, but the chances of winning on corrected time would be improved. Hitting the rating just right – the object of every racing boat designer – would result in a boat capable of winning on handicap as well as being first over the finishing line.

The very fact that multihulls are so fast only serves to accentuate any disparity between the performance of similar boats, when a single small error of judgement can result in a major loss of distance, compounded by the big changes in speed with varying wind strength. Quite apart from the crew factor, there are often performance differences between boats of the same class – even among strict one-designs. Some designs, moreover, have a range of windspeeds, seastates or wave patterns in which they perform best, so there will be differences in results between sea areas with strong prevailing winds and those with more sheltered water. This too can make a nonsense of yardsticks as much as ratings.

Class Racing

It has to be accepted that no handicap, on whatever basis, can be relied on to be completely fair to all competitors in every race. Furthermore, many people feel that there is limited fun in winning on handicap when other boats are actually faster on the water. This has led to the popularity of what has become known as 'Formula 26', under which any micro racing in UK National or European championship events can also win points on a 'level rating' basis – i.e. regardless of handicap, the first boat across the line wins. These are essentially cruising designs. With the increasing number of 'built-to-rule' racers on the water, flat out boat-for-boat competition is becoming more widespread than handicap events, and the fastest growing class is currently Formula 28. Originally conceived in France in 1986 as a low-cost alternative to Formula 40, when these 40-footers became too exotic and expensive for unsponsored amateurs, Formula 28 boats have the added advantages over their big sisters of being built without any limitations on minimum weight or maximum sail area – typically around 650kg (1430lb) and 45m² (480ft²), a scintillating power-to-weight ratio which is reflected in their performance; and they can be trailered from one race to the next. About the only class rules are an overall length of 8.5m (28ft), an overall width on their trailers of 2.5m (8ft), and a maximum mast height of 14.5m (48ft).

Among several more recently introduced classes are the French Multi 30, which has no design restrictions at all, other than a length of 9m (30ft); in America, Formula 500 – 500kg (1100lb), 46m² (500ft²), 9–10.5m (30–35ft) LOA, another cheaper alternative to Formula 40; and half a dozen others. One wonders how many will be around in a few years time. Such formulae are apt to produce some extremely fast but questionably frail boats, thrilling to sail but only able to retain their places in the top echelon of racing for a season or two, such is the pace of technology. By comparison, the majority of micros are designed primarily as fast cruisers with racing potential, costing less than a dedicated racer, and with a much longer 'shelf life'.

The history of Grand Prix multihulls has its parallel in motor racing, each successive class being introduced with the object of reducing the price of participation in the sport, only to develop into such a sophisticated and costly collection of machines that a further stepdown became necessary after only a few seasons. The enormous cost of building and campaigning the 75ft (now 60ft) Formula One maxi-multihulls, and the expense of moving these monsters from one race venue to the next, led in 1985 to Formula 40, the size being chosen as the largest that would fit into a standard 40ft shipping container. But as rising prices have in turn lifted F40 beyond the reach of those it was supposed to attract, many of its sailors are moving down to F28. These boats are now being built – some on a series production basis – in various parts of the world, notably France and Italy. The European fleet alone totals nearly 100, and attracts sufficient advertising support to pay the competitors' travel expenses, which are considerable as the 'circus' tours from one country to the next. At the same time, other major sponsors of professional open racing are abandoning F40 in favour of Formula One, having found that despite the very high cost, the adventurous nature and undoubtedly dangerous aspects of long-distance racing in these maxis attract more publicity and a better return on investment than the inshore regattas with their one and a half hour races, spectacular though these are. Indeed, at the time of writing, the future of F40 looked uncertain, with few new boats being built. Not that the future of Formula One looks all that rosy. With the price of a new boat having risen from around £250,000 only a few years ago to approaching £1 million today, the overall cost of campaigning it is beginning to overtake the returns, and there is a disquieting trend towards updating last year's boats instead of designing new ones. Nevertheless even the pessimists concede that big boat racing, in one form or another, is here to stay.

Racing apart, size and speed largely define the character of a cruising boat. We already know that, generally speaking, the longer the boat (for a given weight) the faster it can go. Not surprisingly, size also brings with it a marked superiority in sea-keeping ability. When the size of a yacht of similar form to another is – for example – doubled, Froude's Law of Comparisons tells us that its sail area will be about four times greater, displacement eight times, and stability sixteen times greater; that is to say, it will be sixteen times more resistant to capsize in the same wind strength and sea state. What is more, it will be able to power through waves that would slow or even stop the smaller boat. Clearly, a big boat is preferable to a small boat, but for its costs and crewing requirements – two big 'buts' which usually dictate the size of boat we can afford. A third consideration is trailerability; for if a boat is substantially longer than 8m (26ft) overall, which is the limit for a micro-multihull, it becomes too large and heavy for an amateur to tow around on a trailer.

Wavemaking resistance

As a hull moves through the water, it generates two separate and easily discernible wave systems, one divergent and the other transverse, near the bow and stern and travelling forward with the boat. You have probably seen them, from an aircraft or distant hillside, as a geometric pattern of ripples fanning out in the wake of a ship. The divergent waves remain separate, never interfere with one another, and have no more than a marginal effect on hull drag. But the transverse waves certainly do. The distance between their crests – the wavelength – is a function of boatspeed (v) and the force of gravity (g), and increases with the square of the speed. It is expressed as $2\pi v^2/g$. Taking the case of an 8m (26ft) ballasted keelboat: sailing at 2 knots, it will have eight

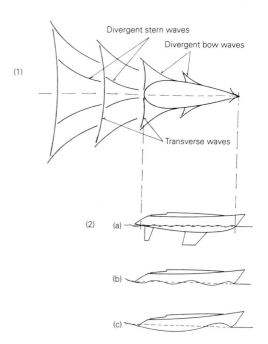

Fig 3.2 *(1) The pattern of divergent and transverse waves, seen from above. (2) Variation of transverse wavelength with boatspeed for an 8m (26ft) keelboat. (a) at 2 knots (b) at 4 knots (c) at 6 knots.*

waves along its waterline. At 4 knots there are only three waves, spread out between bow and stern; and at 6 knots little more than a single one, with the old bow wave beginning to mount the stern wave, and the stern itself starting to squat in the deepening trough as the bow clambers up its new wave. Eventually, when boatspeed reaches the critical value of $2.43\sqrt{WL_m}$ ($1.34\sqrt{WL}$ in feet), the wavelength equals the waterline length, and the stern is finally dragged down by hydrodynamic suction into its own trough. Our conventional 8m monohull is making 6.9 knots, and can sail no faster. Even the brute force of a powerful engine would have little effect, beyond increasing the downforce still further; boats have sunk when towed too fast.

To be driven through this barrier and up the slope of its bow waves – which is what happens with fast 'semi-displacement' power boats, and in the manner of the ultra light displacement sailboats and dinghies, a hull requires not only a high power-to-weight ratio, but an essentially flat afterbody that develops little or no downforce. Once past the critical speed, the resistance curve continues to rise steeply until speed approaches $3.0\sqrt{WL_m}$, when increasing dynamic pressure under the hull begins to lift it, wave drag starts to relinquish its grip, wetted surface area decreases, and the gradient of the resistance curve eases off; the boat is now said to be semi-planing. Given enough power, speed goes on increasing until somewhere in the region of $5.5\sqrt{WL_m}$ – call it 15 knots for an 8m (26ft) boat or 18 knots for an 11m (37 footer) – the hull has emerged almost completely from the water and is truly planing. It is now skimming across the surface of the water, supported entirely by dynamic lift and making virtually no waves at all, its only resistance being that of friction on the remaining wetted surface.

Displacement, length and beam

The structural stresses imposed on a fast multihull require a stronger and correspondingly heavier form of construction than is necessary on a monohull, to achieve an equivalent safety factor – or alternatively, a more sophisticated and hence more costly one. The actual magnitude of the transverse waves depends on a hull's fineness and its displacement-to-length ratio, which is a useful measure when comparing similar boats to judge whether one or another may be rather heavy for its length. For any given displacement, the narrower the beam at the waterline, the smaller the waves the hull will generate, and the less drag they will cause. The slender underbodies of a well-designed multihull, unless it is overloaded with cruising stores, slip easily through the water, creating a minimum of disturbance, and with only a small – if any – transverse wave formation. This only starts to become significant, and then to increase rapidly, as the boatspeed approaches the critical 'hump', when the length-to-beam ratio falls below approximately 8:1. Such a figure is bettered – or at least equalled – by the majority of multihulls, including even the big cruising cats. These are usually given a fairly generous beam – hull beam on the waterline, that is, not the overall width of the boat – so as to improve their load carrying capability at the sacrifice of some speed, in contrast to the slim but easily overloaded hulls of high performance boats. By comparison, most monohulls fall in the range 2:1 to 3:1, though this is inevitably complicated by having to take into account the angle of heel, which affects both measurements.

It is particularly important for a multihull to avoid transverse wavemaking, because in addition to creating drag in the way we have seen, there is the likelihood of wave interaction between the hulls of a catamaran, leading to additional resistance, and in choppy weather to the formation of wave crests which pound heavily under the bridgedeck. This was an unfortunate feature of most of the early cats with narrow hull spacing.

Most trimaran hulls are slimmer than 8:1, usually exceeding 10:1 with racing boats, and their floats are so narrow that they can be disregarded in this context. Catamarans also start at around 8:1, with one or two fat exceptions; but because their total static displacement is divided between two hulls, fineness is easier to attain, and all but a few heavy cruising designs

nowadays achieve a ratio of between 10:1 and 13:1, with some of the racing boats – and, incidentally, the Wharram designs – exceeding 16:1, although such extreme slenderness can sometimes attract other problems, as we shall see later.

Another very important consideration is the centreline spacing between the hulls of a catamaran or a trimaran's floats, for this governs not only the stability of the boat and the amount of sail it can carry, and hence its performance; it also dictates the size of the accommodation that can be built across the

Fig 3.3 (a) Central nacelle underbody (1) on the 11.3m (37ft) Prout 'Snowgoose'. (2) Water tanks in keels (3) saloon seating (4) steps (5) galley area both sides (6) cooker (7) slide-out chart table (8) lockers. (b) Design for a 13.7m (45ft) fast cruising cat by Robert B. Harris (Canada). All accommodation is in the nacelle, which can be detached from the crossbeams to act as a motorboat or survival capsule.

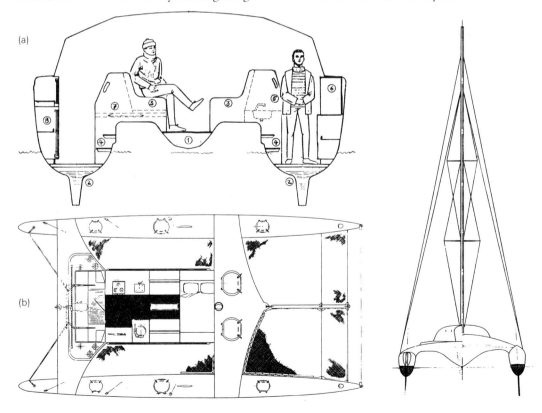

bridgedeck of a cat. Both increase significantly with overall width, but so too does the stuctural weight. This, as much as social acceptability in marinas, and the width restrictions on inland waterways – for example, 5m (16ft 5in) throughout most of the French canal system – limits the design of many cruising cats, even those of contemporary lightweight construction, to an overall beam-to-length ratio of around 60%; and the more heavily built boats that are still favoured by many offshore voyagers and live-aboards, to whom performance is less important, to 50% or under, with correspondingly modest sail areas.

In order to preserve adequate headroom in the bridgedeck accommodation without resorting to an excessively high superstructure, wave clearance under it has also to be somewhat restricted. Consequently a certain amount of slamming is almost inevitable with these boats, and most of them feature a streamlined pod or nacelle between the hulls, which effectively softens the wave impact and at the same time increases the headroom in the centre of the main saloon and stiffens the entire bridgedeck structure – at the cost, it must be said, of some small additional drag in rough

Fig 3.4 *The 9.7m (32ft) 'Podcat' by Kirk Fuller (USA), made entirely of reinforced plastics including the rotating unstayed mast. All accommodation is in the pod, with stowage for cruising clutter such as bicycles and windsurfers in the self-bailing floats. As with the big Harris cat, the pod, which has a stable hull shape, can be separated from the floats to act as a survival capsule.*

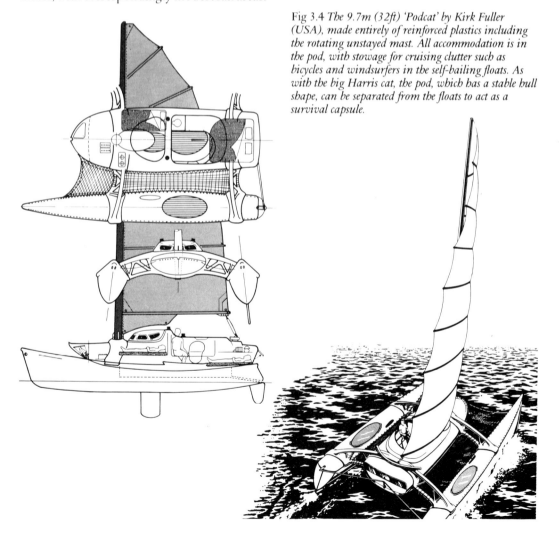

weather and in some designs a rather awkward series of changes in the level of the cabin sole that have to be negotiated when crossing from one side to the other, although owners soon get used to it. Neither problem occurs on the larger boats, where the after end of the pod can also serve as a convenient garage for the dinghy.

The weight-for-width penalty is far less significant in the case of high performance cats with open bridgedecks, for which beam-to-length ratios of 75–80% are not uncommon, being limited only by the rigidity and ultimate integrity of the structure, and wave clearances can be more generous. Trimarans on the other hand, needing relatively short crossbeams, can be built virtually square (see Chapter 4) and can safely carry a much more powerful rig. However, the exceptional width of most big tris can often be an embarrassment, posing considerable docking problems, and certainly ruling out the passage of canals and narrow rivers.

Frictional resistance

Apart from some residual drag due to heeling, resistance to leeway, rudder action (p. 84), divergent wavemaking and general turbulence, all of which consume a certain amount of energy, the remaining hydrodynamic drag is all caused by skin friction. This in turn is proportional to the square of the boatspeed, the wetted surface area, and the coefficient of skin friction which depends on the smoothness of the hull surfaces. Weed and other marine growths can actually double this coefficient, and with it the frictional resistance which is directly proportional to it, so it is important to keep the bottom clean and smooth.

Hull cross-sections

For any given waterline length, the wetted surface area of a hull is determined by its cross-sectional profile, and by the way in which its volume is distributed along the boat's length. In terms of construction, the simplest shapes are the straight vee from keel to deck and its

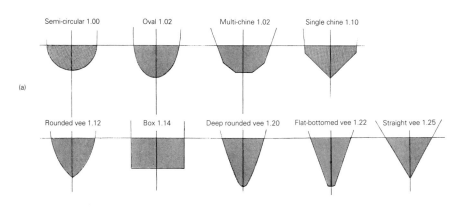

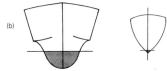

Fig 3.5 (above) These hull shapes all have the same cross sectional areas. The figures denote their comparative wetted surface areas. (below) Typical midships hull section for a cruising catamaran (left) and a trimaran float (right).

derivative, the flat-bottomed vee. They are both well suited to home-building in sheet plywood, the first forming the basis of all of Jim Wharram's many designs in the well-known Polynesian style he adopted more than thirty years ago, and the other favoured by Janbart de Jong in the Netherlands for his shoal draught cats. Both offer strength and structural integrity, comparative freedom from pounding or slamming in a head sea, reasonable load carrying capability, and enough leeway resistance to sail reasonably well to windward without the complication of any additional keel surface – although they cannot, of course, point up as close to the wind as a keel-equipped boat. Nor can they be potentially as fast as other hull shapes, because for the same cross-sectional area, which is proportional to displacement, they have a comparatively large wetted surface area, and hence a higher induced drag.

At the other end of the speed range, the semicircular or canoe-shaped hull has the least possible wetted surface for a given displacement, and uses the minimum quantity and weight of materials; but it requires additional lateral plane in the form of a keel or centreboard in order to sail to windward, and it is more difficult for the amateur to build.

Between these two extremes lie a variety of derivatives, and fig 3.5 illustrates a selection of them, with the relative surface areas that would be arrived at if you were to measure the girth of each by stretching a tape under it from one waterline to the other.

Comparing a canoe-hulled cat in light airs with a tri of the same shape, length and displacement, the combined surface area of its two hulls will be some 40% greater than that of the tri's main hull, which will be supporting the whole weight of the boat, with the floats only just touching the water; hence the tri will have less drag and better performance. However, as the wind increases, the tri begins to heel more than the cat, until its lee float is sharing the downforce equally with the main hull, while the cat's windward hull is left with only about a quarter of the total displacement, so that in medium airs the immersed areas and resulting drag of the two boats becomes roughly equal. Finally, in strong winds, both are virtually sailing on their lee hull or float, but the cat's is depressed less. It is better shaped to support any additional displacement and consequently has the lower drag of the two configurations under these conditions. It would always perform better, were it not for the relative flexibility of its structure compared to the tri's (discussed later), and for the same reason, the cat is a much better load carrier than the tri when it comes to cruising stores or extra heavy gear.

Accommodation volume

The cross-section chosen for the majority of multihulls is based on a rounded bottom with the sides flaring outwards instead of rising vertically, starting just below the waterline so as to sink less, and pick up buoyancy more readily, whenever the loading on the hull is increased by sail forces or payload; and conversely, to lose waterline beam more quickly as the hull lifts with increasing speed. It is important, however, to avoid excessive flare in the region of the waterline, because of course this moves up and down in a seaway, and the more the hull sides slope outwards, the more disturbance they cause. For this reason, flare or reverse curvature is usually kept slight until it reaches a point well above the waterline, where it helps to keep the boat dry by turning over the hull-generated waves and spray – an effect which can conveniently be increased by means of a pronounced chine or 'spray knuckle'. Above this, the topsides continue outwards to near deck level so as to provide as much accommodation volume as possible, and a reserve of buoyancy at extreme angles of heel.

To conform to the micro rules, there must be at least three berths, two of which are suitable for use at sea. There must also be a minimum of 1.22m (4ft) headroom over a length of 1.35m (4ft 5in) cabin sole. In a trailer cat, maximum cabin width is usually restricted to approximately 1.2m (3ft 9in), in order that the two hulls may lie side by side on the trailer without exceeding the maximum width of 2.5m (8ft) permitted by the regulations in most countries. As we saw previously, small trimarans show to considerable advantage in this respect, with no such limit on the amount of flare that can be built into their topsides, and their internal space is usually augmented by projecting wing boxes that can house additional lockers or sleeping berths.

Among home builders of boats in the 10–15m range (33–50ft), straight vee hulls remain deservedly popular for their ease of construction and low cost. In the smaller sizes, however, they are without doubt cramped from the cabin sole up to about knee height, owing to their geometry, and until you get used to them they feel decidedly coffin-like in the lower regions of their cabins. This is avoided in hulls built by the kit panel method (see Chapter 7), which combines the vee and box shapes, by joining up a series of flat sections with rounded corner mouldings, to produce a com-

paratively roomy hull with a broad cabin sole. It is nowhere near as simple to build as the straight vee, but easier than the fully rounded bilge form, and has proved an effective compromise between speed and space.

Prismatic coefficient

The next most important criteria affecting the shape of the waterline and the hull's behaviour at sea are, firstly, the location of the centre of buoyancy at the desired trim – which coincides, when the boat is stationary, with its centre of gravity; the designer works this out from a series of weight calculations, or by using computer graphics. Secondly, there is the way in which the volume is distributed along the length of the waterline – in other words, how 'full' the ends of the hull are, compared to its fattest cross-section. A fine, sharp entrance is needed to slice through the water with the minimum of resistance and for good windward pointing; but not so fine that the bows will be driven under when sailing fast off the wind. For these conditions a fuller, more rounded shape under the forward areas of the waterline helps to lift them; but if the underbody is too flat in this region, it will slam badly in a head sea. A flattish run aft, on the other hand, produces additional buoyancy near the stern, which lessens the tendency to squat at high speed, and encourages early planing. But here again, it is important not to overdo the buoyancy (explained later under 'Pitching').

The figure which gives us an impression of how full or fine the ends are is known as the prismatic coefficient (C_p). It is arrived at by multiplying the area of the maximum underwater section, which usually occurs around mid-length, by the waterline, giving us the volume of a shaped but parallel-sided block; the ratio of this to the actual displacement volume – easily calculated from the weight of the boat – is the prismatic coefficient. When the C_p is low – a typical figure would be 0.55 – the ends of the boat will be very fine, she will be easily driven at low speeds, the performance in light airs will be good, but she may be given to pitching. In stronger winds and at higher speeds, experience has shown that while a low C_p suits some of the very lightweight designs, and the dinghy cats which sail mostly on one hull and are trimmed by their movable crew weight, most boats of micro size and upwards need a higher C_p – in the range 0.6 to 0.7 – to encourage the bows to lift, and to reduce wave-making resistance by making the boat appear slightly longer than it really is. Choice of C_p has to be a careful compromise.

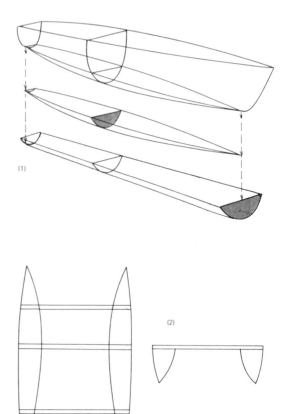

Asymmetry

The waterlines we have been discussing do not necessarily have to be symmetrical in relation to the fore-and-aft centreline. There used to be a school of thought that favoured asymmetric hulls for cats, with the inner waterline being more generously curved than the outer one, resulting in lopsided profiles after the manner of some of the Hawaiian canoes.

The idea, which has been tried over the years with varying degrees of success, is that as the windward hull rises, the aerofoil shape of the leeward hull develops some sideways lift and the boat claws up to windward. However, the actual lifting force can only be relatively small for the amount of drag it induces, due to the extremely low aspect ratio presented to the

Fig 3.6 *(1) Prismatic coefficient is the volume of the hull below the waterline – the displacement volume (centre) – in relation to that of its largest cross-section (below). It has a major effect on wavemaking resistance and hence on the performance of the boat.*

(2) Asymmetric hulls on a catamaran. The inner sides develop lift towards one another, so one must be kept at least partially clear of the water (by heeling the boat) for the other to be effective.

(3) Rocker is the longitudinal curvature of the hull's bottom profile. Both these hulls have the same draught, but the lower one has more rocker than the other. Too much rocker encourages hobby-horsing, too little can make the boat difficult to turn.

water flow and hence its relative inefficiency as a lifting foil. Although in theory a pair of asymmetric hulls begin to generate lift to windward as soon as the boat is heeled, the principle can really only become effective on catamarans at high speeds when flying a hull; but since (with the exception of dinghies and racing boats) catamarans are designed to sail with both bottoms in the water, each asymmetric hull cancels out the other's lift under normal conditions, while at the same time generating unnecessary induced drag, and probably causing wave interference between the hulls unless they are exceptionally widely spaced.

On the other hand, when the asymmetric principle is used in the design of trimaran floats, only one of which is immersed when sailing, it would seem reasonable to expect some benefit in pointing ability.

Rocker

The other variable in the shaping of a hull is the longitudinal curvature of its bottom, known as rocker. Viewed from the side, the deepest point of the profile in modern designs is usually around the midships section, sweeping down from the base of the stem – which must be sufficiently immersed to prevent the bows from 'blowing off' in a crosswind – and then starting to rise in a gentle curve to carry the stern just clear of the water. The amount of this clearance is also important, because it determines how much load can be carried without actually immersing the transom and causing extra drag, while the length of the overhang and its volume govern the rate at which the stern will pick up buoyancy as it is forced down. The Polynesian hull form, with its steeply raked bows and sterns, combined with heavily rockered hulls, scores well in this respect. Too little rocker, with a long straight keel line, will result in a high resistance to turning and difficulty in tacking; too much, and the deep-chested hull will develop excessive drag at speed.

Pitching

A major problem arising from too much rocker, when this is combined with a fine stern whose buoyancy happens to match that of the bow (low C_p), is an increased tendency to pitch. In still water, if a bow is depressed, the stern will rise at the same rate; and as the stern drops back, up go the bows like a seesaw. Should the boat be sailing in a head sea and encounter waves at the same frequency as its own period of pitch, a pendulum effect – made worse by a tall, heavy rig and any weighty objects that instead of being located fairly centrally, as they should be, may be positioned near the two ends of the boat, so as to form a 'dumb-bell' – builds up into a sometimes quite violent hobby-horsing that shakes the wind out of the sails and, combined with the extra frictional resistance caused by the vertical movement of the hull in the water, can slow the boat to a virtual stop. It can be further aggravated by the aerodynamics of the sails themselves. When sailing off the wind with sheets eased, the tops of the sails can stall and unstall as the boat pitches, driving and forcing the bows down as the masthead swings forward, and stalling as it swings back, encouraging the bows to rise.

To guard against this at the design stage, the first step is to draw the bow with a reasonably fine entry, but with sufficient rake and flare above the waterline to provide a good reserve of buoyancy with the CB well forward of the rig's CE, so as to resist any tendency to pitchpole; and to match this with a somewhat broader stern with a fairly flat run aft to it. As well as helping to minimize squatting at speed, and the danger of tripping if the boat should fall back off a wave, this ensures that the two ends of the boat have widely differing pitch frequencies which tend to cancel each other out. Too broad and buoyant a stern, however, can not only aggravate any pitching problem, but will result in a bow-down attitude on a reach, when it is least welcome; and it can allow a following sea to pick up the stern too rapidly and drive the bow down before the boat has time to accelerate and ride the wave. Moderately tapered, low-buoyancy sterns, despite any restrictions they may impose on performance and on the after accommodation spaces, remain a feature of many safe and successful offshore cruisers, including all of the Prout and Wharram designs for the past 35 years.

In any cruising boat the designer will, in the interests of comfort, try to make the best possible use of the living space close to the centre of pitch rotation – usually just aft of amidships – since this is the area least affected by the motion of the boat in a head sea and also where heavy weights such as tanks and batteries should be located.

In the case of a trimaran, pitch damping can be further improved by ensuring that the centre of buoyancy of each float is well ahead of the centre of gravity of the whole boat, and that flare at the bow of the float will cause the CB to move forward with increasing immersion. What happens then is that as the boat meets a wave, a diagonal twisting moment is created to resist the natural inclination to pitch about a transverse pivot line; and as the wave reaches the stern and tries to lift it, the tendency to drive the bow down is again resisted by the forward buoyancy of the floats. Another remedy for bow burying that has proved effective on some high performance craft is the fitting of anti-dive plates, to give additional lift when the boat is hard pressed.

A similar effect can be provided for a catamaran by giving the forward sections rather more flare above the waterline than the aft sections, causing the centre of buoyancy to move forward in the leeward hull and back in the weather hull as the boat heels. Raked bows add to the reserve buoyancy and give a drier boat, but because class rules stipulate a maximum length, the current trend for racing boats is towards vertical stems, which draw the waterline out to almost the overall length of the boat in the interests of speed. This has the effect of increasing the initial buoyancy while losing the reserve contained in the overhang. The designer has to be careful, however, not to overdo the forward buoyancy, because experience has shown that excessive lift from the downwind bow will force down the stern into a squatting attitude, with a resultant loss of boatspeed.

Computer techniques developed in recent years have made it possible to predict and correct behavioural patterns such as this on the drawing board – or rather, on its electronic equivalent, the visual display monitor; and to manipulate and modify the shape, structure, layout, and even the performance, of a new boat before ever its plans are passed to the builder. The techniques are complex compared to the design of cars and aircraft, because whereas these travel in only one element, parts of a sailing craft are moving through water, parts of it in the air, and the interfacing areas at times in either or both. With such seemingly imponderable parameters and random dynamics, only a computer could make the necessary design calculations with any degree of accuracy. Small wonder that CAD has revolutionized the high-tech sailboat industry.

Computer-aided design

Instead of sharpening his pencil, today's designer switches on his machine, inserts a program disk, reaches for the 'mouse' switch that moves the screen cursor, and starts to draw. A new design begins with two control points placed on the screen, or keyed in numerically, to define the length of the boat, and another pair for its maximum beam. A click of the mouse and the hull appears in plan view as a simple kayak canoe, symmetrically curved and pointed at both ends. Two more

Fig 3.7 *Stages in a computer-aided design for an 8m (26ft) micro by John Shuttleworth. (1) Simple canoe (2) Shape at deck level (3) Profile (4) Cross sections (5) Perspective net of control points (6) Resulting 3D surface model.*

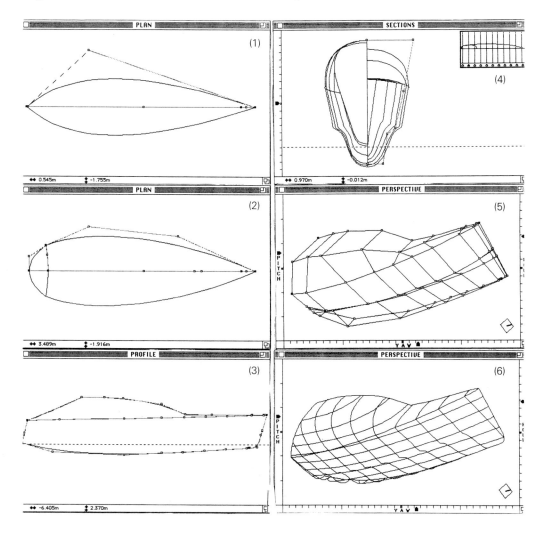

clicks give it a transom stern, a few more here and there along its sides alter the curvature of the shape required at deck level. So far, the process has taken less than half a minute.

A draughtsman traditionally uses flexible splines of various stiffnesses, held down to his board by a set of weights, as guides along which to draw smooth curves. The positioning of these weights, which defines the amount of the curvature, is simulated by the location of the computer control points; and the stiffness of the imaginary splines, which can be chosen on the screen menu, influences how literally the computer links the points or interprets a fair curve through or close to them. In order to avoid initial errors of alignment in the positioning of the points, which would result in unintended kinks or hollows in the curves, the points can be displayed as a network of straight lines linking the points in each plane. Using this control net, it is much easier to recognize any anomalies and to correct them before the lines are faired into curves.

Thus the degree of curvature can be varied for different parts of the surface, the closeness of the control points accentuating or subduing the modelling in their immediate vicinity, allowing local bumps and creases to be created without affecting the rest of the hull surfaces. The boat is progressively sculpted on the screen as each line is dragged out or dented, and the designer can watch the effect on the overall shape each time he manipulates a part of the curve by moving a control point, or by clicking in some more where he wants to improve local definition.

The process is repeated for the side view, in which the designer defines the draught of the boat, the shape of its stem and stern, the curvature of its bottom profile and the position of the waterline.

Next on to the screen is an elevation of the hull as seen from ahead and astern, starting with a mid-body cross section and followed by a series, like slices through a cake, at specified distances from a convenient zero point such as the bow. A complete set of sections is then drawn, almost instantaneously, from what the computer knows at this stage about the plan and profile. As the designer manipulates each particular section into the shape he wants, its neighbours are simultaneously aligned and smoothed, to produce faired lines which will automatically appear on the other two orientations, the degree of fairing varying from a local bump with sharp changes in curvature – such as a sharp spray rail – to a gentle swelling without local discontinuities, depending on the spline stiffness selected. As each curve is modified by dragging a control point into a new position, the complete hull is redrawn in all three dimensions – in about three seconds.

Switching between plan, profile and sections, the designer can continually examine the effects of his modelling from any direction and at any scale, shrinking the picture so as to stand back from it, or panning and zooming in for a closer look at a small area, or at a single item such as a rudder, in magnified detail. Most eye-catching and creative of all, he can call up an animated perspective, a 3D surface modelling generated by the computer in the form of a geometrical mesh of all the lines appearing on the three basic orientations. The picture can then be rotated one step at a time, as if the designer were holding a solid model in his hands, or continuously like a chicken on a spit, and the axis can be additionally tilted to vary the viewpoint as the work proceeds.

To the hull may be added the floats, cross-

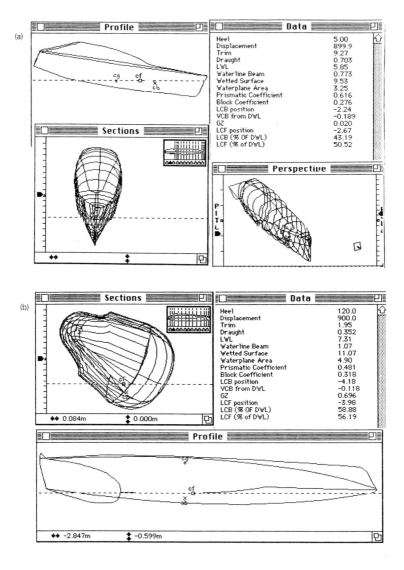

Fig 3.8 *The same micro-cat is 'free floated', using a hydrostatic programme in the computer.*
(a) Trimmed bow down and 5° roll, with the hull bearing the total displacement. (b) Heeled to 120° to test the flotation position for self righting.

beams, centreboard, the rigging, with its complex and varying load patterns, and the wingmast – which can sometimes require almost as much design effort as the rest of the boat – together with the cockpit and cabin superstructures, for an assessment of windage, overall appearance and how they blend with one another and the rest of the boat; and what the accommodation will look like from the inside, its headroom and seating layout, the location of companionways, furniture, fittings and locker spaces, and in the case of larger and more complex designs, details of the machinery, tanks, pipe runs and electrical circuits.

The computer also keeps track of all the changing dimensions, areas, volumes and weights as the designer works through his complex programme of structural calculations, analysing the stress forces, pinpointing areas where thinner or lighter materials can be used without compromising strength, optimizing such factors as the strength, stiffness and weight of every component, and selecting the materials, laminates, bondings and fastenings for each. He has only to call up a 'spreadsheet' on to the screen and point to any of the tables of optional formulae to see the effect of every addition or alteration on total displacement, sinkage per kg of increased weight, girth, immersed surface area, maximum and waterline beams, prismatic coefficient, costings, wastage factors and building times. By specifying the location and weight of each fitting or inventory item, he can also keep an eye on the resuting alterations to the centre of gravity, centre of buoyancy and draught.

Next, by using a special hydrostatic pro-

gram, the designer can 'free-float' the design while he studies the effects of moving the waterline to alternative positions, changing the fore-and-aft trim or the angle of heel, and the amount of hull sinkage. In the case of a multihull, the computer is performing an enormously complex series of calculations, because the hydrostatics of each hull change as one is lifted and another is increasingly immersed. Simulating sailing conditions in a

Fig 3.9 *(a) Integrated structural stress analysis diagram by John Shuttleworth, using the computer to determine the loads at key points throughout the boat. By this means, the appropriate quantities of fibres to be used in the building process can be aligned in the direction of stress, in order to optimize the strength-to-weight ratio and to avoid local stress concentrations anywhere in the boat. (b) 3D computer model of the race-winning 10.7m (35ft) cat 'Alien', designed by David Alan-Williams.*

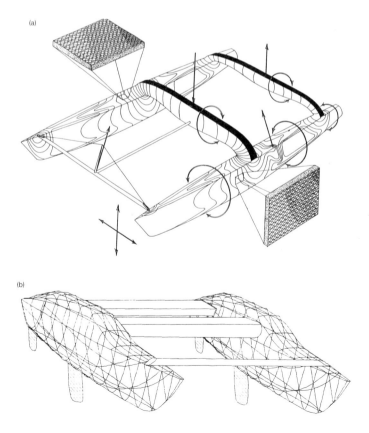

wide range of wind strengths, the designer can superimpose lateral and longitudinal down-forces, and measure the movements of the CG and CB in relation to one another, analyse the boat's behaviour as it pitches, rolls and yaws, and calculate its reserves of stability in all sailing attitudes, including flying one or more hulls. He can even check the trim of the boat floating upside down after capsize, in order to position the escape hatches.

In addition to original design work, the same techniques can be applied to re-proportioning existing craft, adding a feature such as a bridgedeck pod, or altering the rig. It might, for example, be a modified version of some boat that a client particularly admires, or one of the hull shapes that the designer would have 'saved on to disk' to form part of a database for future projects.

The lines can be plotted or printed out on paper or film at any stage to verify the shape generated on the screen, and at any scale. This makes it possible to supply the builder with full-size computer-generated drawings of the frames and building templates, saving him the laborious and time-consuming process of lofting the hull from a numerical table of offsets; and when the mould is built, or the frames are skinned or planked, he can be sure that the hull will be perfectly fair and free from ripples.

In the same way, the entire sail wardrobe can be designed on the screen, the measurements and data being integrated as necessary with those of the spars and hull. Next, detailed shaping and construction details are planned out by the sailmaker, who uses a computer-driven plotter to draw the outlines of each sail panel direct on to the cloth, ready for the scissors; or in the more elaborate installations, to actually cut them out, with great speed and precision, by means of a computer-controlled laser working inside an envelope of inert gas (helium) to prevent the surrounding fabric from scorching.

About the only thing the computer can't do is design the boat. Not yet.

Stability and the dynamics of capsize; floats, keels,
centreboards and rudders

Trimaran floats

The choice of hull form for a trimaran float is
subject to the same considerations that apply
to the main hull, except for accommodation
space – which is not required of it – and one
other critical factor: the amount of buoyancy it
is to provide.

If heeled under static conditions so as to
completely immerse one float, and its total
displacement was then the same as that of the
whole boat at rest, that float would be said to
have 100% buoyancy. The case in favour of
low buoyancy floats – those with less than
100% – is that they save weight, offer less
windage, and by permitting larger angles of
heel, give a more gradual warning of when it is
time to reduce sail. It also happens that if the
float is driven under by the downforce of the
sails in a gust, or by wave action under the
main hull, the angle of heel becomes sufficient
to spill wind from the sails and usually allows
the boat to recover, in the manner of a
monohull. At the same time, it will tend to be
swung round by the drag of the submerged
float and to run off downwind.

CAPSIZE RISK

On the other hand, the extra heeling reduces
the effectiveness and maximum power of the
rig under less extreme conditions, besides
making life less comfortable for the crew; and
it also causes rather more drag, as the waves
break along the part-submerged float deck and
wash over the lower ends of the crossbeams.
But more serious for a trimaran is the
increased possibility of capsize. It must be
recognized that the less the buoyancy of the
float, the more likely it is to 'stub a toe' into an
approaching wave and capsize the boat diagonally over the downwind bow; or even to bury
both floats when surfing down a steep wave
with the wind astern. When this happens,
helped by the downforce of the sails – and particularly the enormous leverage and momentum of a full spinnaker as the boat suddenly
slows – it can pitchpole bodily forwards. Similarly, if the boat should fail to surmount a large
wave when beating to windward in rough conditions, and fall back on her lee quarter, the
small float might allow her to capsize diagonally across its stern; or to trip sideways over
its submerged length if the boat were to be
thrown sideways by a wave while lying a-hull
with sails down. A number of such accidents
have been recorded over the years, yet there
are still some trimarans being built, happily
sailed and successfully raced with float
buoyancies as low as 70%, as compared with
the accepted lower limit of 85–90%. Admittedly they are mostly small, inshore boats
which would seldom if ever be exposed to
extreme wave action. But without doubt they
are, with a few exceptions, potentially unsafe
in any but the most expert hands – and sometimes even then.

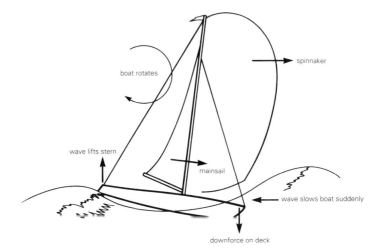

Fig 4.1 *Surfing at high speed down a steep wave with the wind astern and too much sail up, it is possible to bury the bows into the next wave. When this happens, helped by the enormous leverage and momentum of a full spinnaker as the boat suddenly slows, it can pitchpole bodily forwards.*

One such exception is one of John Westell's last designs (fig 2.11) which features a shallow keel under each float, in the form of a fin which is canted inwards so that it will produce lift as well as some resistance to leeway when it is pushed sideways. A few other designs, notably among Class 1 and Formula 40 racers, rely on a hydrofoil under each float for additional support, its lift increasing as the boat accelerates, until at high speed the float is carried clear of the surface. But it is essential to keep these boats sailing, because of course foils are ineffective when the boat is lying stopped and vulnerable to beam waves.

HIGH BUOYANCY FLOATS

The majority of today's trimarans incorporate floats of at least 150% buoyancy – more often exceeding 200% – with an overall length approaching that of the main hull itself, in order that potential boatspeed is not reduced by a shortened waterline length when the main hull starts to lift out. This ensures good diagonal stability; and by keeping their maximum buoyancy well forward, with the sterns swept up clear of the water and tapered off to reasonably fine ends, so that they do not try to

drive the bows down as the crest of each wave passes under them, they help to avoid pitching. Conversely, too much forward buoyancy will spoil the pointing ability, and a certain amount of reserve buoyancy must be retained in the stern sections in order to help control the attitude of the boat at high speed when the bows meet a wave.

The location of the floats in relation to the main hull also has a bearing on the boat's behaviour. In addition to being canted outwards – typically by about 8° – so that they meet the water squarely when the boat is heeled, for best performance they should both just miss or kiss the surface when at rest, taking at most about 10% of the total displacement. Any more static immersion causes unnecessary drag at low speeds; while conversely the higher-level floats favoured in some racing designs, to allow the boat to ghost along in light airs, balanced on its main hull with both floats well clear of the water, result in much

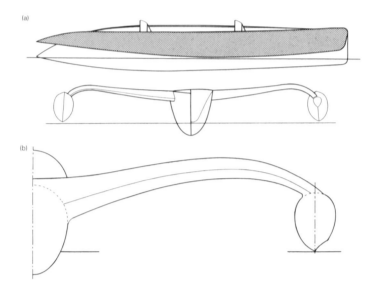

larger angles of heel, with the consequent disadvantages under most other sailing conditions.

Opinions differ as to the optimum underwater section for a float, the choice lying between the semicircular and the vee bottom. The former shape has less drag and can slide sideways with very little overturning force, but it is liable to pound in a head sea and can sometimes produce a snap roll when sailing off the wind, the boat flopping from one float to the other with a quick, jerky motion. The vee shape, with more deadrise angle on its bottom section, gives a much softer ride and some keel effect, which helps the boat to go to windward; but with more wetted surface it has correspondingly greater resistance. A combination of a vee-shaped forward part of the float with rounded aft sections has proved an effective compromise. An interesting derivative is the 'new-moon' asymmetrically profiled float devised by Dick Newick and used in several of his recent boats, but experience with them is limited at the time of writing, and at present most designers still opt for the rounded vee

Fig 4.2 (a) Example of high buoyancy floats on 12.2m (40ft) transatlantic racer by Nic Bailey (UK). Note their size in relation to the main hull, and the way in which they are canted outwards and are carried just clear of the water at rest. A cruising design would immerse them by up to 10% when the boat was fully loaded. (b) Dick Newick's 'new-moon' asymmetric float. Unusually, it is not canted, being designed to develop dynamic lift as it becomes immersed at speed, as well as resisting leeway.

compromises that are to be seen on most contemporary trimarans.

Effects of heeling

Bearing in mind the relationship between wetted area and skin friction, it is worth noting the different ways in which these are affected by the angle of heel on cats and tris.

When stationary, nearly all the weight of a tri is supported by one main hull, whereas the cat's is shared between two. However, these have a combined wetted area some 40% greater than that of a tri of the same displacement, which is why the tri is usually faster in light airs.

As the windspeed increases and the boats

begin to heel, the tri's advantage starts to diminish, and by the time the windspeed has reached 15–20 knots, or around Force 5, some three-quarters of the cat's displacement is being supported by the lee hull, whereas the tri's leeward float is sharing the load equally with the main hull. With the arrival of still stronger winds, the cat has developed a drag advantage, because although its lee hull is by now bearing virtually the whole weight of the boat, it is well shaped to so so, while the tri's slender float – even a high buoyancy one – has become quite deeply immersed under the same load, with a wetted area greater than the cat's.

In practice, the total loading on the lee hulls of the two boats is not quite the same under these conditions, because as the tri heels more than the cat, it spills wind more readily from its sails, reducing their downforce at the more extreme angles of heel. Despite this, the cat usually remains the more easily driven when beating in strong winds. But heavy weather racing experience between comparable boats has shown that the two configurations are surprisingly evenly matched, and the reason for this seems to be that the tri is better able to maintain its rig tension when the going gets rough.

Crossbeams and rig tension

The force in the sails, and hence their power, increases as the square of the windspeed: four times the windspeed – for example, from 5 knots to 20 – means sixteen times the sail force, and sixteen times the load on the rigging and on the structure to which it is connected. If the boat is not stiff enough, it will flex and release some of the tension in the rig, with the result

that power will be lost as the mainsail leach opens up and the jib luff sags away to leeward.

A trimaran's crossbeams are relatively short in their unsupported span, and have only to resist the lift and dynamic loads from the floats, the mainhull monocoque forming a rigid longitudinal girder which carries the mast and most if not all the rigging. The beams should be carried as high as possible above the water, so as to minimize wave strikes when the boat is hard pressed; and on some designs they are splayed out towards the ends of the floats, instead of running athwartships, in order to minimize the unsupported length of each float, particularly at the bows where they are subject to the greatest loading. The beams can also be triangulated by lower struts for even greater rigidity; alternatively, they can be tensioned by waterstays running in from each float to the mainhull bottom – although their vulnerability to flotsam, and the fact that their end fittings are more prone to shock loading and fatigue failure than those above water, has to be recognized.

By comparison, the beams of a high performance cat are not only much longer, but at mid-length they normally have to resist the downforce of the mast. A solution adopted by some designers, such as New Zealand's Malcolm Tennant, is to relieve the mainbeam of this load by allowing the mast to move freely through the beam, and to carry its heel on a dolphin striker with wires tensioned out to the hulls. On a small boat, these can throw up a considerable amount of spray through the trampoline, and the helmsman must beware of sailing over a mooring buoy. Apart from mast loads, the beams also have to keep the forestay tight (using another dolphin striker, but triangulated upwards in this instance to brace the beam, and more correctly called a seagull striker), hold the hulls together, and above all prevent the two from twisting. (We are not talking here of cruising cats with bridgedeck accommodation acting as a girder, and usually with less widely spaced hulls and correspondingly less powerful rigs.)

As in motor racing, it has been said of multihull construction 'If it bends or breaks, it wasn't strong enough. If it doesn't, it's too heavy.' Weight is always a deciding factor in the design of high performance boats. For a very fat cat to be rigid enough to hold its rig in tune, its beams and their supports have either to be massively engineered and heavy, or expensively built from exotic materials. Because of this constraint on hull spacing, a cat as wide as a comparable tri would almost certainly be too heavy – and incidentally, very difficult to tack.

An alternative philosophy applied by Jim Wharram, whose cats are designed throughout on the basis of what he terms 'adequate technology', is simply to allow the hulls to twist, by using flexible beam mountings of

Fig 4.3 *Articulated floats on Meade Gougeon's Formula 40* Adrenalin *(USA).*

rubber, or even rope lashings, and to accept any adverse effect on sail efficiency. This doesn't win them races, but it allows the boat to 'give' to the waves, and the hulls to twist out of line without strain when sitting on uneven ground. Interestingly enough, the same principle has been applied on a number of high performance trimarans whose structures allow the floats some degree of flexibility, the shrouds being carried to neutral points on the crossbeams so as to maintain constant tension in the rig; and on Meade Gougeon's race-winning Formula 40 trimaran *Adrenalin*, whose floats are actually hinged to articulate, within limits, in the vertical fore-and-aft plane.

Stability

It will be recalled that Froude's Law of Comparisons tells us that stability, which is directly related to sail carrying ability, grows more quickly than heeling moment as boat size increases. The reverse of this scale effect emphasizes the importance of giving a small multihull as much overall beam as possible, within the limits of structural constraint.

Whereas the older types of multihull were often built with length-to-overall beam ratios of around 2:1, and a few were even narrower, the modern wide beam, high stability cats are down to 1.5:1, and some racing tris are nearly square, at 1.1:1.

The formula for static stability in smooth water, indicating the theoretical windspeed at which a boat will become unstable, is written as:

$$W_s = 4.475 \sqrt{\frac{\Delta \times B_{max}}{SA \times b}}$$

Where W_s = Windspeed (knots)
Δ = Displacement (kg)
B_{max} = Distance (m) between centrelines of hulls or floats
SA = Sail area (m²)
b = Height of rig's centre of effort (CE) above waterline (m)

To be precise, CE should be measured from the hull's centre of lateral resistance (CLR), which lies somewhere below the waterline, depending on the shape of the hull and the depth of the keel or centreboard. But the approximation of height above WL is sufficient for this calculation.

What is often referred to as the CE is in reality only the geometric centre of area (CA). This is easily found, as indicated in fig 4.4, and the height of both centres is near enough the same for the purpose of calculating stability. It should be appreciated, however, that CA only coincides with CE when the wind direction is at right angles to the rig, which is then completely stalled and acting as a flat plate. As soon as the wind starts to blow at an angle, allowing the sail to act as an aerofoil, CE moves a little forward of CA by an amount depending on the cut (fullness) of the sail and the way it is trimmed. This shift can only be estimated by experience, and affects the longitudinal positioning of the keel or centreboard; but it has no significant effect on static stability.

Taking as an example a micro-cat displacing 900kg (1980lb), with a centreline breadth of 4.4m (19ft), and a powerful sailplan totalling 30m², whose CE is located 4.0m above the waterline, the formula indicates that it would be likely to capsize when the windspeed reached 26 knots, unless sail was

Fig 4.4 *A simple way of finding the centre of area of a rig is firstly to determine the individual geometric centres of the mainsail and headsail, by joining the halfway point along any two sail edges to its opposite corner (taking the leech as a straight line by cutting off any roach). A further line is then drawn between these centres. The common CA lies along this line, at a distance from either end proportional to the area of each sail, and nearer to the larger one. Its height (h) above the waterline is the figure to use in the stability formula.*

reduced. This assumes that the boat is on a close reach, the fastest point of sailing, with the sails trimmed so that they are developing their maximum power – and hence their maximum downforce (fig 5.3). But the limit may be reached at a much lower windspeed, depending partly on the boat's angle of heel when it reaches the point of maximum stability, and partly on the weather conditions. It is possible for a gust to exceed the steady windspeed by as much as 40%, which doubles the downforce of the rig, so it is realistic to reduce the theoretical

stability limit by some 25% to allow for this, bringing our example down to 19 knots, which is the design figure for most micros.

However, this still ignores the random dynamic action of large waves on a boat already heeled on their steep slopes, and the boat's own rotational momentum. There is also the outside chance of a boat, with full sail up, beating to windward and already close to its stability limit, bearing away on to a reach and capsizing as the sails develop more power and downforce; or of running full tilt into the back of a big wave, stopping abruptly, and pitchpoling or capsizing diagonally as the apparent windspeed suddenly exceeds the limit. So in really rough seas, the stability limit may be as little as half the formula figure – say 13 knots for our hypothetical micro. Compared to the nominal stability figure of 19 knots, the equivalent for a 35ft (11m) cruiser–racer is around 25 knots, and for a pure cruising boat as high as 35 knots. Even these figures start to look alarmingly low when you apply the rough seas factor – 17 and 24 knots respectively – but it usually takes time for an unstable state to build up, and it becomes obvious when a boat is becoming overpressed. The prudent skipper will reduce sail long before the limit is approached.

The stability formula also approximates the effects of displacement, because in practice stability is additionally affected by the way in which the weight is distributed throughout the boat. Nothing much can be done about the rig aloft, except to keep it light without compromising on strength, and as low as possible without sacrificing too much sail efficiency. But by placing any other heavy items as near to the bottom of the boat as possible, the centre of gravity (CG) can be lowered to good effect.

The stability of a yacht is determined by the relative positioning of the CG and the centre of buoyancy CB. At rest, these of course coincide; but as soon as the boat starts to heel, a distance GZ is established, the point Z occurring at the intersection of a horizontal line through the CG with a vertical line through the CB; and the length of GZ determines the strength of the righting lever which resists the heeling force of the rig. From this it follows that there are two primary sources of stability: (1) the immersed shape of the hull, a shallow, broad-beamed monohull having greater form stability than a deep and narrow one, and a multihull much more still – its 'straddle' stability, as reflected in the steep initial rise and high peak values of the multihull stability curves. Step aboard a small monohull and its gunwale naturally dips, whereas a multihull would hardly move; (2) ballast or 'pendulum' stability, which is dependent on the height and location of the CG relative to the waterline – below it on a ballasted keelboat, above it on a multihull. At small angles of heel, it is form stability which characterizes the 'stiffness' of the boat. But as the angle increases, pendulum stability takes over as the dominant influence on the righting moment – which is why the keelboat remains stable for so much further into the heeling arc.

The way in which the centre of buoyancy CB moves in relation to the CG is shown in fig 4.5. When the boats are upright, no heeling force is generated; the weight acts downwards through the CG, and the displacement upwards through the CB, one vertically above the other. As wind pressure heels each boat, CB shifts to leeward and produces a righting force proportional to the distance GZ, which resists further heeling, and the boat is once

more in equilibrium. With increasing windspeed and angle of heel, GZ lengthens, until it reaches a maximum beyond which it begins to decrease, and the boat becomes less and less stable as it approaches the point of vanishing stability. Beyond this, the CG will move beyond the point Z, the righting force will become negative, and the capsize will be completed.

Note that although at the point of maximum stability, the tri's angle of heel is greater, its righting arm is longer than the cat's, due to its wider overall beam; and both are more stable at this stage than the monohull. But with increasing angle, GZ shortens quickly on both multihulls, whereas the monohull remains stable well past 90°. Note also how lowering the CG would increase the stability of all three boats. A similar effect is obtained by shifting the crew's weight to windward, normal practice on monohulls and dinghy cats, and a useful means of increasing the sail carrying ability of larger multihulls too, particularly when racing.

It must be appreciated that these diagrams, and the corresponding GZ (stability) curves in fig 4.6, only illustrate the hydrostatic principles. They cannot, of course, take into account the random rolling effect of wave slope and superimposed waves; or of the dynamic strike forces, which can at one moment add to, and at another subtract from the boat's own rotational momentum. Similarly, they make no allowance for the sudden decrease in stability which accompanies the apparent loss in the weight of the boat as it begins to plunge from the crest of a large wave – the roller coaster effect; or for the dissimilar and constantly varying immersed volumes of the bow and stern sections of the hull as it

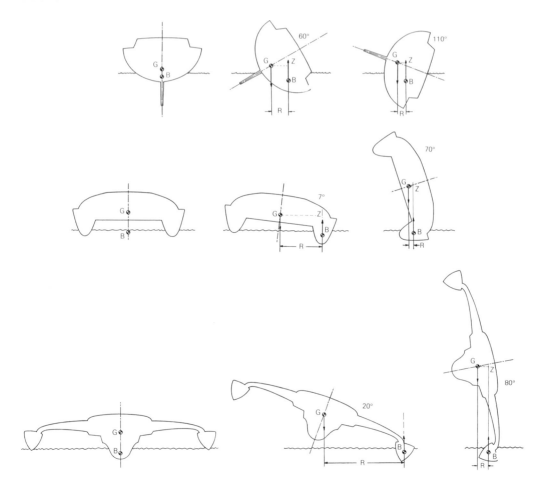

Fig 4.5 *The change in the relative positions of the centres of gravity (G) and buoyancy (B) on a typical cruising monohull, catamaran and trimaran with increasing degrees of heel. The resultant effect on the righting lever (R), proportional to the distance GZ, is indicated at the respective angles of maximum stability, and at a point close to the angles of vanishing stability for each boat. It shows why the monohull heels so readily compared with either of the multihulls, but retains its stability through a much wider range of angles.*

pitches and rolls. Nor are they concerned with the wind forces acting on the rig, hulls, and the undersides of any decked areas.

The righting moment, a boat's *static* resistance to heeling, is simply the product of GZ and the weight of the boat. Typical com-

parative values for all three configurations are shown in fig 4.6 throughout a range of heeling angles. As the angle is increased from zero so the righting moment and the resultant stability of the boat rises to a maximum value. From this point, any further heeling reduces the righting moment, sailing becomes risky even in racing – dangerous when cruising – and sheets or traveller must be eased in order to reduce the downforce of the rig. It can be seen that the cat is initially 'stiffer' than the tri up to its peak at around 7° of heel, whereas the tri's stability continues to increase as far as 20°. The monohull, in contrast, heels much more readily, but remains stable long after both

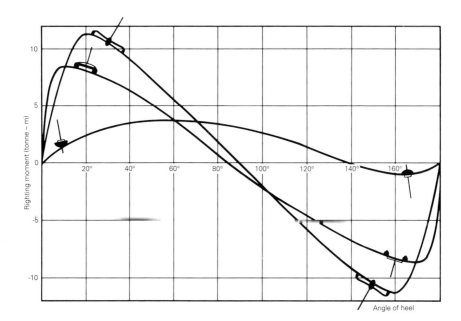

Fig 4.6 *Stability (GZ) curves for typical modern 10–11m (35ft) monohull, catamaran and trimaran cruisers. The righting moment represents the boat's static resistance to heeling, the area under each curve the total energy required from wind and waves to roll that boat to the point of capsize, and the area above each negative curve the corresponding energy needed to right the boat after it has capsized. It can be seen that it takes some 50% more energy to roll the cat over, compared with the monohull, and in the case of the tri, nearly 70% more; but the monohull can safely heel to a much greater angle. Conversely, the area above each negative curve shows the corresponding energy needed to right each of the boats. Wave action alone is often enough to roll a monohull upright, but it usually takes a crane to lift the negatively stable multihull back on to its feet.*

multihulls have passed their angle of vanishing stability.

The area under the curve of positive stability represents the total amount of energy required to capsize the boat in smooth water, and it is much reduced by waves which can supply some (and occasionally all) of that energy. Once inverted, multihulls become negatively stable and remain afloat upside down, assuming they are built of buoyant materials or are provided with buoyancy compartments, while most monohulls (with the notable exception of the very wide, shallow-hulled I.O.R. racers and maxi-raters which derive their stability from their flat sections and also tend to stay inverted) are barely stable while they are upside down and either roll back, or roll right over and recover, provided of course that they have not taken in too much water. This is illustrated by the area under the curve of negative stability, which is a measure of the energy needed to right the boat after it has capsized – very little for the average monohull (wave action might be sufficient) –

but very large in the case of a multihull, more often than not requiring the use of a crane.

Wave action

Stability curves are useful for comparative purposes at the design stage, but they are of not much more than academic interest once you are sailing, and it must again be emphasized that capsize becomes virtually inevitable long before the righting lever reaches zero.

The curve might appear to indicate that at a certain angle, more than half the theoretical stability remains. But in the wind and sea conditions that have heeled the boat this far – the short, steep breaking seas of coastal waters and estuaries being the most dangerous – one big wave alone can supply the rest of the energy needed to turn the boat over; and a trimaran is more vulnerable to this type of wave action than a catamaran. As we know, a tri naturally heels more than a cat, even in light winds and smooth water, because its floats are carried high enough to minimize their immersion (and drag) under these conditions, and being smaller and less buoyant than the hulls of an equivalent cat, they depress further under load. It is the wider beam of the tri that gives it the better *static* stability. However, looking at both boats as contour-following rafts (fig 2.10), it can be seen that, geometrically, a wave crest will lift a tri's main hull higher above its lee float than it will one hull of a cat above the other, because of their relative spacing (few, if any, tris having twice the overall beam of a same-sized cat). So the tri, even with high-buoyancy floats, will be thrown over to a larger angle than the cat, and is consequently more vulnerable to dynamic capsize action – only partially offset by its superior weight distribution and the reduced pressure on its sails. Well designed and competently handled multihulls, with their ability to slip sideways away from wind and wave strikes, can invariably survive the most severe weather conditions. But with either configuration, the risk of capsize, however remote, begins to increase as soon as the stability curve starts to approach its peak; so for peace of mind it is as well to ease sheets, reduce sail, or alter course well before reaching this point.

Survival compartments

Before leaving the subject of capsize, it is as well to consider what can be done to make life easier in the event of the unthinkable actually happening! On a micro that has, for example, been raced too enthusiastically, it is just a matter of sitting on an upturned hull and waving for a lift home, or a tow. But any medium-displacement, offshore cruising boat, as distinct from some of the lightweight cruiser-racers, should be provided with a survival compartment in which the crew can live for days on end, or even weeks, while awaiting rescue. Yet although this is a requirement of which designers are well aware, it seems that it is seldom called for by the client, and to date relatively few boats incorporate it.

It is perhaps not generally appreciated that although there will be plenty of air to breathe, the great surges of water sloshing to and fro through the partially submerged hulls will rapidly dislodge any loose contents and flush them out into the sea. We can safely assume that the boat won't sink, because virtually all multihulls are nowadays either built of buoyant materials such as wood or foam sandwich, or have a number of sealed buoyancy compartments; often both. So all that is needed is the means of quickly converting a section of the accommodation, such as an aft cabin, into an upside-down survival compartment, with no apertures other than an escape hatch above the inverted waterline, and a reasonably watertight door that opens outwards. In addition to its everyday furnishings, the compartment should contain the emergency stores and equipment, provision for rigging temporary cots or hammocks, and a pump.

If such a compartment is not provided, it

should be a fairly simple matter to engineer one without any major expense or structural alteration. It is, however, largely unnecessary in some light displacement boats – such as John Shuttleworth's 'Tektron' series – because these are designed to float, if inverted, on their buoyant crossbeams, with the accommodation space barely submerged. The only essential provision against capsize in such boats is an escape hatch in each hull or – as in the 18m (60ft) Joubert/Nivelt cruising cats – a fishing hatch in the sole of the bridgedeck saloon which doubles as an exit skylight. The undersides of the hulls should also be provided with strategically placed grab handles, or even jackstays, to prevent escapees from being washed off the smooth and slippery bottoms.

The alternative to passive acceptance of an upside-down existence is to try to right the boat. In the absence of a crane, about the only way to do this is to seal off and deliberably flood sections in the bows or sterns, so that the boat rotates; and subsequently to pump them out, after letting go the mast and perhaps flooding the over-centre crossbeam, in order to complete the recovery. (See also page 107.) The principle of self-righting has been successfully demonstrated but never used, as far as is known, in a real life situation at sea.

Keels and centreboards

A number of cruising cats and most of the beach boats have no centreboards or any other form of keel, other than a vestigial skeg towards the stern, simply relying on the lateral resistance of their vee sections for their ability to sail to windward. The majority, however, have shallow keels under their rounded hulls

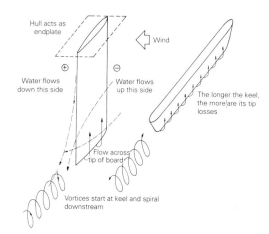

Fig 4.7 *Keel tip losses. (left) Water from the high pressure (leeward) side escapes to the low pressure side of a daggerboard, reducing its effectiveness. As the crossflow is swept aft by the mainstream, it spins the adjacent flow into a coiled vortex, increasing the drag on the board, before spiralling downstream. (right) A keel with a low aspect ratio offers a wider chord across which the water can flow, to the increased detriment of lift/drag ratio.*

to bite into the water and resist leeway. Such keels form a good solid base to dry out on, do not intrude on the accommodation and can also, as on the Prout cats, be used for water storage, the tanks forming a double bottom and at the same time keeping the weight low down in the hulls. Both configurations provide good directional stability when running fast or surfing, making life easier for the helmsman. They will safely sideslip when the boat is heeled in heavy weather, with very little tendency to trip; and there is nothing to break or become jammed, or get forgotten in the heat of the moment. But it is accepted that neither can be quite as effective as a centreboard for windward performance. Prouts even go so far as to offer the performance-orientated owner, who is prepared to accept the additional cost and complication, the option of pivoting centreboards, housed in a watertight box inside each of the fixed keels.

When a boat is under way, with the wind exerting a side force on it through the sails, it travels crabwise through the water in a combination of forward movement and leeway. This causes the hull, and its keel if it has one, to develop a hydrodynamic side force in the opposite direction, in the same way that an aircraft wing develops lift. This is why an aerofoil-shaped fin is so much more efficient than a flat plate for a keel or centreboard (and the same goes for a rudder). The higher the fin's aspect ratio – its depth in relation to its fore-and-aft length – the greater its lift to windward for a given wetted area and skin friction, the most efficient shape being elliptical rather than straight-sided.

It also develops less induced drag. This is caused by vortices, the corkscrew-like currents which are formed as the water escapes under the bottom of the keel, flowing from the region of pressure on the lee side to the opposite (suction) side. This end leakage can be reduced by raking the fin forward, producing an upwash which is confined by the hull acting as an endplate. A forward-raked centreboard has the added advantage that, as it is partially raised for offwind sailing, its centre of pressure moves aft, which improves the handling. But such geometry is not widely used, due mainly to its propensity for collecting weed and debris. The volume of crossflow also varies with the length of fin presented; much less can flow under the short tip of a centreboard than across the considerable length of a longer, shallower fin – one reason for the use of endplates in the form of wings on the bottoms of monohull keels, and recently tried on one or two shallow-keeled cats to sharpen their windward performance. The wings were added only to the inner side of each keel so as not to introduce the risk of tripping – for unlike a leeward centreboard, the wing cannot be retracted. The result was a slight improvement in pointing ability, but not enough to justify

Fig 4.8 *Cruising cats with fixed shallow keels, such as this Edel Cat 35, combine good accommodation with a much higher performance than is generally realized.*

fitting them on a production basis.

Not only are shallow-keeled hulls prone to making more leeway than centreboard boats, but they are at a disadvantage when beating to windward in rough offshore conditions, when the surface becomes aerated and a keel needs to reach down into denser water to get a grip. However, this is to some extent offset by their ability to resist stalling – and hence losing their lift to windward – at higher angles of incidence than a high aspect ratio fin, so that they tend to be less sensitive to the constantly changing directional attitude of the boat in a rough sea. Their increased resistance to turning, which gives them the directional stability that is so beneficial when running, inevitably makes them somewhat slower to tack than a boat that can pivot round its board. Nevertheless, by shortening and deepening the keels (as in fig 2.3), performance and handling move quite close to that attainable with a centreboard, at the expense of some increase in minimum draught. Many of the latest cruising designs feature such an arrangement, the rugged simplicity of fixed keels being undeniably attractive to anyone not looking for the ultimate in speed.

A centreboard and its casing have to be very strongly built to withstand the side forces acting on them in strong winds, and their position is critical to the balance of the boat. When a monohull heels, the CE (centre of effort) of its rig moves to leeward. This produces a turning moment, proportional to the distance between CE and the CLR (centre of lateral resistance) of the hull, that acts against the drag of the hull and tries to skew the boat up into the wind. The designer corrects this luffing tendency in two ways: primarily by ensuring that the immersed volumes of the hull at

bows and stern remain balanced when it is heeled; and by placing the keel a certain distance – around 7–10% of the waterline length – aft of the CE, leaving just enough 'weather helm' for directional stability, and to give the helmsman a feel of the boat when the sails are correctly trimmed without it becoming heavy on the tiller – for corrective rudder wastes energy (not only the helmsman's) by causing drag which slows the boat down. If he doesn't get his sums quite right, or – more likely – the sailplan is altered, excessive steering loads can often be tuned out by altering the rake of the mast.

The matter is somewhat different for a multihull, although correct sail balance is still important. With its smaller angle of heel, not only is there much less leeward movement of the CE, but the centre of buoyancy (CB) moves out further than the CE as the displacement transfers to the leeward hull or float – and with it, the CLR. This tries to drag the boat round to leeward, and has to be counteracted by locating the centreboard on or just forward of the rig's CE.

Most catamarans have a board in each hull, so the balance can be adjusted if necessary under varying conditions. Cats are normally sailed to windward with both boards fully down; and they are left down for reaching, except in strong winds, when the leeward board is partially or fully raised, depending on the conditions, so as to ease the strain on it and to reduce the risk of tripping. Both can be retracted on a run, when they are not needed, to reduce drag. A similar procedure is followed with a trimaran's single board.

There are two basic types of board: the daggerboard, which slides up and down in its casing, and the pivoting centreboard, which

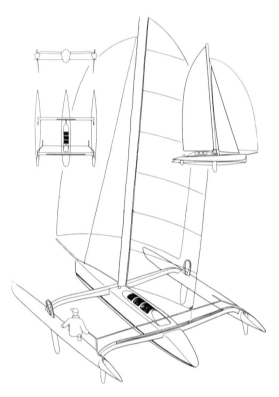

Fig 4.9 *Daggerboards in the floats of a racing trimaran – a Formula 28 design by Nic Bailey and Jack Michel (UK).*

damage than would be likely with a daggerboard. Nevertheless, daggers are the more widely used type in all multihulls, because of the better support and lesser hull stress provided by a tall casing when the board is lowered.

The board cases in a cat are usually offset to one side of either hull, so as to minimize their intrusion into the cabin and are therefore nearly always of the dagger variety. They are either carried on the outboard sides and angled inwards, so as to provide an element of lift when pressed sideways; or inboard, where they are more accessible to the crew in the cockpit. In some of the latest cruising boats, the use of a single deep daggerboard in one of the hulls only has shown no loss of windward performance on either tack, compared with twin-boarded boats, and provides additional space in the other hull – although it must be remembered that cruising cats are not usually designed to fly a hull. For the same reason, they are seldom fitted with asymmetrically shaped boards, because of the inconvenience of having to raise the windward board and lower the other each time the boat is tacked. A further alternative, adopted by Derek Kelsall for many of his designs, is to install a single large board (and rudder) in a central pod between the hulls. In all three locations, the exit slots are kept clear of the hull centrelines, so that they are less liable to become jammed with beach stones when drying out. Some earlier designs avoided this by providing a large gap around the boards, but this results in a lot of unnecessary turbulence and drag, and the boards tend to thump from side to side and spoil the peace of a quiet sail. Instead, the cases should be a reasonably close fit, and the exit gaps bridged by neoprene or similar seals.

swivels around a bolt at its head. The latter has three advantages: it occupies rather less accommodation space, fitting in snugly under the cabin table (assuming the hull is beamy enough to accept one, as in a trimaran) instead of running up to the deckhead; its CP moves aft when it is partially raised for running; and in theory it can hinge up if it hits the bottom. In practice it doesn't always do so in a small boat, because in many installations it has to be held down by a control line to prevent it from floating up in light airs, when there is very little sideways pressure to prevent it from doing so. And when there is, such as when beating or reaching in strong winds, it usually won't move, except from a heavy impact; but then at least the board and its casing will sustain less

In place of a trimaran's single centreboard, cabin space can be saved by placing one in each float, canted inwards for lift and asymmetrically sectioned to improve windward performance – which indeed they do, and without the need to 'swop' boards when tacking, because of the trimaran's natural angle of heel. However, assuming the boards are of the dagger variety, they may project beyond the beam when raised, which creates problems when coming alongside; and without a lengthy run of control lines through numerous blocks, they require a crew-member out on the floats to operate them. On the whole the snags of this arrangement, which is used on the majority of racers, largely outweigh its advantages for a cruising boat.

Rudders

These are another important area of design detail, for in the case of performance boats with lifting centreboards, the rudders should preferably be retractable too, either by lifting vertically or by pivoting up, with reserves of structural integrity, the stresses on them being much greater than in the case of monohulls. This is not only because speeds are higher. A multihull, lacking the momentum of a heavier boat, may stall while tacking in difficult conditions, and sail backwards down a wave, when the resultant load on the rudders can be enough to damage them or even to wrench them off, unless they are sufficiently strongly built. For best performance – i.e. to develop their turning force with the minimum of drag – they should also be elliptically shaped, as in the case of centreboards. Aspect ratio should be at least 2:1 for a spade rudder below the hull, and 3:1 or more for a transom-hung rud-

der which is subject to losses from air–water interference and 'ventilation' – sucking in air on the leading edge. This can to some extent be avoided by sloping the rudder aft a few degrees, and/or by fitting a 'fence' in the form of an endplate on the rudder just below the waterline.

They should also have some provision for fine tuning, in order to give the helmsman a comfortable amount of feel through the tiller. This is governed by the distance between the axis of each rudder and its centre of pressure CP – the greater the distance, the heavier the helm becomes. It can be counterbalanced by positioning some 10–15% of the blade surface ahead of its axis. But a completely balanced rudder, with its axis running right through its CP, lacks any feel, making it difficult for the helmsman to sense when the sails are wrongly trimmed, and may develop flutter, because CP varies with angle of attack.

A problem can arise with swing-up rudders – more so on micros than on big boats – in holding them down at high speeds, without making the pivots so stiff that the blades cannot kick back when necessary. Some form of positive lock is essential, because they have only to be forced back a short distance by the waterflow to effectively freeze the helm – which can be alarming if you suddenly find yourself in a traffic situation before realizing that your rudders aren't where they should be. The big advantage of the vertically lifting blades is that their CP remains constant whatever their position, so the boat can be sailed in shallow water with them partially retracted; but they should also be able to release backwards in the event of grounding. This can in some cases be difficult to arrange, especially on the larger boats, where a section of the hull

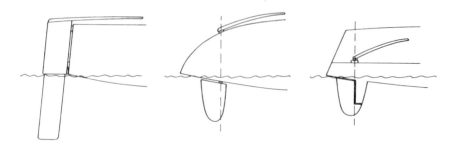

Fig 4.10 *Rudder shape and balance. (left) An unbalanced rudder, of the type used on many small multihulls, canted aft to reduce ventilation. (centre) An elliptical fully-balanced spade rudder, pivoting on its stock, and (right) carried on a fixed skeg.*

must slide up or swing back with the entire rudder stock assembly – a complex piece of engineering that is understandably avoided on many production boats on the grounds of cost. No such problems or complications arise on boats with fixed, low aspect ratio keels. Their rudders need only to match the shoal draught of the hulls, either in the form of a balanced spade, strong enough for beaching; or hinged on a full-length skeg, which makes a sturdy installation with protection from accidental grounding, although it usually prevents the rudder from carrying any balance area.

Most cats have a rudder at each stern, their tillers normally being cranked slightly inwards towards one another, so that the inside rudder turns more sharply than the outside one, which is theoretically steering around a wider radius, as in the case of a car's front wheels.

However, whereas this is essential in order to avoid unnecessary scrubbing between a car's tyres and the road, the friction between the rudder blades and the water is so comparatively slight that Ackermann geometry, as it is called, only really becomes necessary on wide-beamed cats, where the difference in the turning circles of the inner and the outer hulls is significant. The actual tillers, cranked or straight, are linked by a crossbar which can be grabbed from anywhere in the cockpit, with short tiller handles or with universally-jointed and sometimes telescopic extensions which allow the helmsman to steer from either side bench, or from the cabin tops of a small cat. For most trimarans a single rudder is sufficient, since it remains almost fully immersed even when the boat is heeled. However, some of the larger Formula racers, which spend much of their time flying two hulls, feature an additional rudder on each float, in some cases supplemented by a 'canard' steerable foil near the bows, in order to balance the boat when reaching under a big asymmetric spinnaker.

Sails and sail forces, aerodynamic drag, apparent windspeed and angle, rigs, masts and rigging

Moving on from design areas below the waterline to those above it, the primary one from a performance aspect is of course the rig, and to a lesser extent the aerodynamic form of the boat as a whole; for although, as we have seen, this can become a significant contributor to overall drag at the high speeds of which most multihulls are capable, some of it is produced by the sails themselves.

How sails work

From the results of wind tunnel and water channel studies of the airflow around sails and solid foils, we can reproduce its behaviour on paper by drawing what are known as streamlines, representing the various paths taken by the air. Where these lines get closer together, the air has to speed up to pass through the smaller areas; and where they get wider apart, the air slows down. Each speed variation is accompanied by a corresponding change in pressure, in accordance with Bernoulli's Equation which tells us that they are inversely related: as speed increases, pressure drops, and vice versa.

Figure 5.1 shows a central or 'stagnation' streamline dividing the air passing either side of a sail, and bending the freestream to leeward as it senses the approaching luff. The result of this 'upwash' is that as the streamlines divide, those passing round the lee side rapidly become squeezed together, as the air speed

increases and its pressure drops sharply. Meanwhile the windward streamlines have opened out, though comparatively lazily, with a correspondingly modest deceleration and

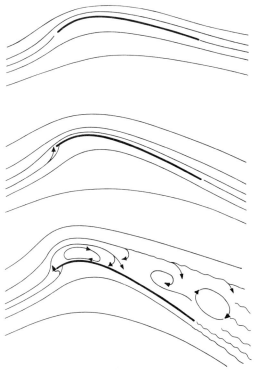

Fig 5.1 *Central 'stagnation' streamline divides air passing either side of sail. Streamlines on the leeward side of sail become closer together, depicting accelerating flow and falling pressure, while windward streamlines open out as flow decelerates and pressure rises. (top) Sail at 25°; moderate lift. (centre) Sail at 35°; maximum lift, flow still attached. With further increase in angle, the airflow will begin to separate from the sail in the region of maximum camber, but will re-attach downstream without appreciable loss of lift. (bottom) Sail at 45°; stall has set in, with reversed flow vortex inside separation 'bubble', random eddies and large turbulent wake. Severe loss of lift and increase in drag.*

pressure rise in the flow. By the time the two streams reach the leech, they have gradually readjusted themselves, so that their speeds and pressures begin to coincide, and they mingle downstream with equally spaced streamlines. But their general direction has been changed compared to that of the freestream ahead of the sail, which results in an equal and opposite reaction (Newton's Law), the overall thrust on the sail being proportional to the mass of air and the angle through which it has been diverted, most of it from the suction on the lee side and only a small proportion from pressure on the windward side. This can be strikingly demonstrated at the kitchen sink by dangling a spoon between finger and thumb and turning on a tap. As the back of the spoon is brought close to the stream of water, it will suddenly be drawn towards it as the flow is accelerated and the pressure drops.

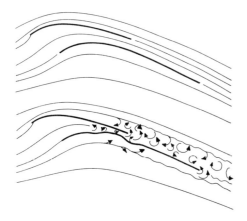

Fig 5.2 *The slot effect of setting a headsail.*
(top) Reduced pressure gradient across mainsail allows it to be sheeted in closer, increasing its power. Jib also develops more lift than it would without a mainsail because more air is being directed around its lee side. (bottom) Too small a slot; over-sheeted jib backwinds the mainsail and spoils the flow.

STALLING

This thrust varies with the angle of attack of the sail, starting at zero when it is free to weathercock at no incidence, and increasing as the sail is sheeted in to the optimum angle. Beyond this, as the suction along the lee side drops increasingly rapidly towards the leech and the pressure gradient becomes correspondingly steeper, the hitherto smooth 'laminar' flow starts to separate from the after surfaces of the sail in a jumble of rotating eddies and vortices, to the detriment of drive. As the angle is increased still further, the separation point moves forward and the flow becomes more and more turbulent until finally the sail is completely stalled and has lost the last of its lift.

SAIL INTERACTION

So far, we have only been considering a single sail – call it the mainsail. Setting a jib ahead of it (fig 5.2) and creating a slot between the two sails dramatically alters the shape of the streamlines, which is why most boats really come alive as the headsail is hoisted. Now the upwash to the main in turn increases the angle of the jib upwash, with the two stagnation streamlines spreading further apart. The effect is firstly that, contrary to popular belief, airspeed is actually reduced in the initial part of the slot, rising again towards the jib leech to much the same as it would have been without the slot. But the reduced pressure gradient allows the boom to be sheeted in closer, with a consequent increase in power, before the mainsail flow begins to separate. At the same time, because of the wider local apparent wind angle, more of the airflow is directed around the lee side of the jib, with a correspondingly large drop in pressure, and an increase in lift.

If the slot is left too open, by under-sheeting the jib, much of its effect is lost as each sail tends to act independently; too narrow, and the over-sheeted jib dumps its airstream on to the lee side of the main and backwinds it. A small degree of backwinding near the luff is perfectly acceptable, provided the airflow remains attached across the rest of the sail, but too much causes turbulence and loss of lift. Correctly trimmed, each sail complements the other. Only at extremely high speeds, and correspondingly small apparent wind angles, does the jib become more of a hindrance than a help.

SAIL FORCES

Figure 5.3 depicts the pressures, above atmospheric on the windward side, below atmo-

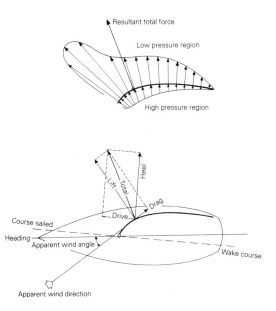

spheric to leeward, acting at various points along a sail, the length of the arrows representing the amount and direction of the forces being exerted on it. For convenience, they can be combined into a single resultant arrow approximately perpendicular to the mean chord of the sail, and acting through the centre of effort of the sail – or the effective CE of the rig where more than one sail is set (fig 4.4). This represents the total aerodynamic force exerted by the sail, and it can in turn be considered as having two principal components: a driving force in the direction of the boat's course, and a much larger heeling force at right angles to it and to the mast, producing leeway and trying to heel the boat over. It is strongest when sailing somewhere between close-hauled and close reaching, depending on the boat, touching a maximum of around four times the driving force. As the wind frees and sheets can be eased, the heeling force becomes less severe, drive increases rapidly, and the boat picks up speed.

The total force can also be resolved mathematically into a crosswind or lifting force at right angles to the apparent wind, and another acting directly downwind and representing the drag of the sail. The higher the lift/drag ratio, the greater is the drive of the sail and the less the harmful heeling force and its effect on leeway; and the wider the range of angles through which high L/D ratios can be sustained, the greater is the all-round efficiency of the sail. It varies not only with the angle of incidence but with the shape of the sail, including its aspect ratio – the higher the better, as with keel shapes – and with the way in which it is set and trimmed by the crew, who can regulate its angle, the depth and shape of its camber, and the amount of twist to suit the

Fig 5.3 (top) Pressure distribution over the sail surfaces under conditions of attached flow, showing how most of the lift is developed on the lee side of the sail, and is concentrated close to the leading edge. The large arrow denotes resultant total force, acting through the centre of effort. (bottom) Relationship between the driving and heeling forces produced by the sail, and its lift/drag ratio.

wind conditions, by adjusting the sheet and traveller, and the tensions of the luff and foot.

It is important to appreciate that the smaller the area of the sails – as for example when reefed, or in the case of an under-canvassed boat – the less is their drive in relation to the overall parasitic drag of the hull and rig, and the boat will consequently be unable to sail as close to the wind. This can sometimes become embarrassingly obvious when trying to beat off a lee shore under reduced canvas.

The precise way in which sails work is a fascinating, complex, and from certain aspects still a controversial subject. For those interested, some recommended reading is given in Appendix 1.

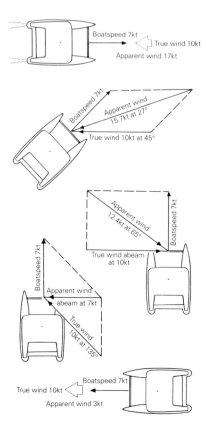

Fig 5.4 *Variations in the strength and direction of the apparent wind with the boat's heading.*

Apparent wind

The wind acting on a moving boat is known as the apparent wind, and is composed of two vectors: true windspeed, and boatspeed. Travelling directly into the wind – as when motoring – has the effect of adding the speeds together: e.g. true windspeed 10 knots, boatspeed 7 knots, apparent windspeed 17 knots. Running downwind, one is subtracted from the other, so the crew will now experience only 3 knots across the deck. Throughout the range of headings in between, the apparent windspeed and its direction will vary between the two extremes, as determined by the vector diagrams (fig 5.4). These show that, except when the true wind is dead ahead or dead astern, the apparent wind is always forward of the true wind; and when beam-reaching or close-hauled, it has a higher velocity than the true wind. A good boat will beat to weather at 30° or less to the apparent wind, but still only tack through 80° on the compass. Conversely, as the true wind comes aft, the apparent wind decreases; and with the true wind well aft, it only requires a small change in its true direction to make a large change in apparent wind direction.

To complicate matters, the true windspeed increases with its height above the sea, where it is slowed by surface friction, the windspeed difference between sea level and the masthead of even a micro being of the order of 30%, and more with taller masts. Consequently the apparent speed is also greater at the masthead than at deck level, which in turn increases the apparent angle towards the top of the sail. This variation is accommodated by allowing the sails to twist from foot to head (fig 5.5), the object being to present a constant angle of

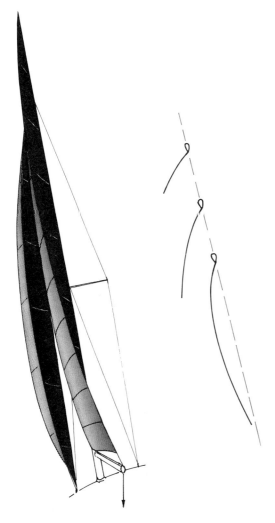

Fig 5.5 *(left) Twist in the mainsail and jib, viewed from astern. Pulling down the boom would tighten the leech and reduce the twist. (right) Mainsail shape near the head, in the middle, and near the foot.*

entry to the wind all the way up. But because the wind 'senses' the presence of the boat as it approaches it, the freestream is already lifting as it reaches the hull topsides, and in consequence is already accelerating; so that the actual speed difference between deck level and masthead is less than is generally believed – probably no more than 10%. Indeed, under most conditions the sails, if left to themselves,

will twist more than is necessary, and need to be restrained from doing so by mainsheet or vang tension, and correct positioning of the headsail sheet lead block.

Hull air drag

To the unavoidable drag of the sails must be added the aerodynamic resistance, or parasitic drag, of the rest of the boat. It will be appreciated that when sailing with the wind aft of the beam, aerodynamic drag acts forwards, and is in fact beneficial to boatspeed; the bigger and blunter the shape the better, downwind. But as the boat comes round on to the wind, the drag acts increasingly in opposition to reduce the speed; and since windward performance is all-important, it pays to minimize parasitic drag wherever possible in the design, especially bearing in mind that it varies as the square of windspeed. Nothing much can be done in this respect as regards the rig, other than to specify an efficient sailplan and to keep an eye on the size of the mast section and the various bits of rigging, all of which add to drag.

The profiles of the hulls, cabin tops and other superstructure can, however, be stream-lined to good effect, the first essential for good performance being to reduce their areas as much as possible. It has been calculated that adding a bridgedeck saloon to a typical open-decked 10m (33ft) cat can increase its parasitic drag by as much as 25% and its angle through the tack by 10° – and by more in bad weather, a serious penalty when sailing upwind in a gale, when pointing ability from the reefed sails will already be reduced.

Even open decks offer a certain amount of windage, so except for a section of solid deck-ing in the cockpit area between the cabin

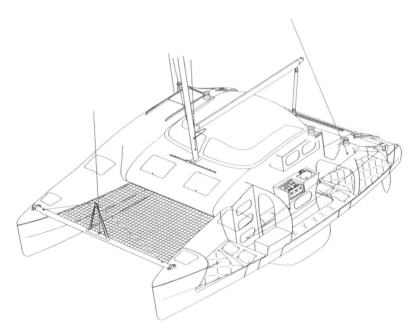

Fig 5.6 Hull air drag minimized by streamlining the decks and superstructure on the Clyde Cats 'Cheetah'.

hatches, possibly extending as far forward as the main (mast) beam, the space between the hulls of a small open cat is best covered by a porous polypropylene trampoline, which is light in weight and comfortable to sit or lie on, while freely letting through the wind (and water!). Larger boats will be solidly decked in this area so as to incorporate proper seating and helming positions. If the main beam itself is a deep box or girder section, it not only keeps some of the wind and spray off the crew but is better able to resist the mast compression loads than a tubular spar of the same weight. It can also form part of a handy deck locker, or on big boats tankage for additional water storage in harbour. But it must of course be provided with a streamlined leading edge fairing to help smooth the otherwise turbulent airflow behind it. Across the bow area, an open mesh of polypropylene webbing can be fitted to improve visibility when picking up a moor-

ing – and further reduce windage; nylon netting is better still, provided it is replaced at regular intervals as a safety precaution, because it deteriorates from exposure to sunlight. The majority of 'accommodation' cats, on the other hand, have bridgedeck cabins forward of the mast, so the solid decking is usually continued right up to or near the bows, to provide a comfortably firm footing for anchor and headsail handling, as well as drained locker space for warps and fenders.

On all but the largest cruising trimarans, solid wing decks represent extra weight and drag that is best avoided. There is no doubting their convenience as an extension of the cabin top for fore-and-aft access and as a lounging area; they also represent some reserve buoyancy, and provide additional accommodation space in some of the larger boats. But when the boat is hard pressed, wind under the weather decking tends to increase the angle of heel still further, and the lee deck can take a thumping from the wave crests. This is avoided by using trampolines or netting between the main hull and the floats, with narrow 'walking boards' carried on the crossbeams if a more solid footing is preferred for crew movements. The beams on a small tri are seldom large enough in section to cause much drag, but on larger boats their resistance and the effects of wave impact on them should be minimized by fitting aerofoil-shaped fairings on their leading edges, strongly made and well fixed, because they take a considerable battering in heavy weather.

In considering what other steps can be taken to reduce drag, it is important to appreciate that when sailing, the wind is never blowing from straight ahead. It is the projected profile at around 30° to the boat's heading that is presented to the wind and will benefit most from streamlining. Accordingly, sharp corners such as deck edges can with advantage be rounded off and the cabin tops radiused and curved to blend in with the decks and topsides to form, as far as possible, a smooth uninterrupted oval shape with the hull bottoms (see figs 2.3 and 5.6). Unfortunately this encourages rather more water to sweep over the decks when the boat is being driven hard, and makes it easier for anyone to slip off accidentally; but on a fast boat this may be considered a relatively small price to pay for the gain in performance. High-crowned, rounded or elliptical foredecks (including the floats of a tri) also reduce the risk of pitchpoling by presenting as streamlined a bows-down shape as possible, with a correspondingly less sudden increase in drag, compared with flat decks, if they submerge.

The airflow should also be provided with a clean exit, so that the boat does not drag a turbulent wake along behind it. For those who place comfort and security ahead of performance, however, an externally-flanged joint between hull and deck, capped with a rubbing strake, not only serves to deflect much of the water but gives external access to the bolts securing the guardrails, where these are fitted, and provides a toe-hold where they are not. For others, interested in flying a hull, it is further worth noting that parasitic drag – as well as wetted surface friction – drops sharply as the hull leaves the water and allows the air to flow smoothly under it, instead of turning it abruptly upwards as it meets the topside.

Rig

Just as a multihull's speed, light weight and upright stance influence the design and disposition of its hulls, so the rig must be able to suit a combination of operating conditions that seldom if ever apply to monohulls. As it happens, a multihull is so easily driven that in light weather it will sail reasonably well with almost any sort of rig, and a number of boats – mostly the older ones – are to be seen happily cruising around with what appear to be quite unsuitable sails.

Many different configurations have been tried on multihulls at one time or another, with varying degrees of success, including both ketches and schooners with junk, gaff and sprit sails. On monohulls, all three of these shapes are superior to the Bermudan when the wind is aft of the beam, because of their broader high-level profiles and larger drag, which is then acting in reverse. Such benefits are nullified, however, on a multihull as soon as its high speed draws the apparent wind forward until the boat is reaching, or even close-hauled.

There are some interesting exceptions to

the 'Bermudan rule'. One is the Pacific crab-claw sail, which is shaped like the delta wing of very high speed aircraft, although it dates back to ancient times (p. 8). Tony Marchaj's wind tunnel tests showed that it can actually generate more power than a low aspect ratio Bermudan on nearly all points of sailing, notably on a reach, when its driving force is almost double that of the Bermudan rig. This, he explains, is because in addition to its normal lift, the ultra-low aspect ratio foil produces 'vortex lift' from the suction of the spiral coils of air rolling rapidly above each of its leeward edges, and growing larger as the angle of incidence increases. Since the air in these helices is moving faster than the foil through the air, its pressure is lower, hence the lift. In

its present form the crab-claw is too unwieldy for most yachting applications, but a current series of back-to-back tests on a micro-cat may lead to its further development.

An interesting rig that has become a feature of the Wharram cats is based on that of the traditional Dutch barge. It features a short curved gaff carrying the head of the mainsail, which has a deep luff pocket that wraps round a tubular mast, in the manner of a sailboard rig, to reduce leading edge turbulence and the usual mast wind shadow; and a loose foot which can be either boomless for sheer simplicity, or held out and down by a diagonal wishbone, so as to control both twist and camber; both incidentally avoid the risk of head banging. Like the boats it graces, this rig is both

Fig 5.7 *Loose-footed, boomless mainsail on a Wharram 'Tiki 26', with luff pocket surrounding the mast and short gaff supporting the head of the sail.* (Photo: Domon Sails)

picturesque and purposeful, though without
any pretence to sharp performance, and reefing is apt to produce a rather baggy bundle of
sail in the absence of a conventional boom.

Another application of luff-pocket sails is
Dick Newick's adaptation of the Ljungstrom
rig for his own live-aboard trimaran schooner,
Pat's, which features a pair of rotating,
unstayed masts, the forward one wrapped by a
two-layer sail which can be opened like a clam-
shell for downwind sailing, doubling its area.
Reefing and furling is done by simply rotating
the masts, and partial rotation is used as the
means of varying the sail camber (p. 106).

For optimum performance a purpose-
designed rig is required, but this is not to say it
has to be complicated. For most multihulls,
there is still nothing to beat a simple
Bermudan sloop layout, because it has proved
to be generally the most efficient and easily
handled over the whole range of heading
angles, and particularly to windward, the most
critical region. For top performance the
mainsail should be loose-footed, as with the
majority of dinghy cats, so as to allow the maximum amount of control over its fullness by
use of the clew outhaul. Nor is there any need
to split the sailplan into several smaller units
for ease of handling (except on some of the big
cruising boats which are often rigged as cutters
and occasionally as ketches), because the two
primary sails are usually small enough to be
easily manageable – even for single-handing
when necessary. And by restricting the size of
the jib to slightly less than 100% of the
foretriangle area – i.e. so that it does not project aft of the mast – and sheeting it to an
athwartships traveller just forward of the mast,
the boat can also be made self-tacking (more
on p. 101).

Fig 5.8 'Northern 11', an 11m (36ft) fast cruising cat
designed by Malcolm Tennant (New Zealand). Note
the diagonal wishbone boom which controls both twist
and camber of the loose-footed mainsail and the non-
overlapping headsail.

A notable exception to the conventional
sloop layout is the easily recognizable Prout
sailplan, characterized by a very small mainsail
('minsail') set on a mast just ahead of the cockpit, where the halyards are easily reached, and
a large roller-furling genoa, supplemented by a
self-tacking staysail. The consequence of
stepping the mast so far aft is that the angle of
the forestay is noticeably shallower than normal, with the result that the genoa develops
more than the usual amount of lift (with, of
course, correspondingly less forward drive and
hence some slight loss of performance). The
combination of this lift with the narrow Prout
sterns helps to prevent the lee bow from burying, and has proved to be an effective and very
reassuring safety feature of these boats.

Fig 5.9 'Northern 11' at speed downwind, with
spinnaker set from short bowsprit.

Apparent wind angle

On the fastest racing boats, the two sails normally comprise a very large mainsail and a
skinny little jib whose primary purpose in
strong winds, apart from satisfying the official
requirement for a storm jib, is to help tack the
boat – in marked contrast to most monohull
racers, whose genoa is usually the powerhouse

of the sail plan. Nearing their maximum
speeds of well over 30 knots, these greyhounds
are not only sailing into a permanent gale, having added most of their own speed to that of
the true wind, but they draw the apparent
wind so far forward that they are obliged to sail
exceptionally close to it – within 20° or less,
with correspondingly close sheeting angles –
in order to make good as high a speed as possible in the direction of the true wind, which is
probably blowing from around 40°. The result
is that whereas a jib usually helps the mainsail
to perform when hard on the wind, under the

highest speed conditions it cannot be sheeted in closely enough to be effective without backwinding part of the mainsail or wingmast, and is often removed or rolled up. Only in rough water, when the boat needs to be sailed more fully to keep going through the waves, or at lower windspeeds, is the jib brought back into use. A similar sailplan is used on the latest racing micros, although these boats can usually carry their jibs right up to their top speeds of around 20 knots. The final limit of speed to windward is reached when the airstream is drawn so far forward that the boat simply cannot point high enough. It follows that only a close-winded boat can be a really fast one, since so much sailing time is necessarily spent in beating to weather.

Sail areas

In arriving at an optimum sail area, aside from the various measurements and sail proportions by which its rating is assessed for racing, a compromise has to be reached between an under-canvassed boat, which is invariably rather dull, and the need for frequent reefing and unreefing on an over-canvassed one whenever the wind strength changes – which soon becomes tedious. The aim should be to have enough sail area for the boat to be fun to sail in 8–10 knots of wind, while remaining stable without reefing in windspeeds of up to about 15 knots. Multihull sails should also be cut much flatter than those for a monohull, to suit their higher operating speeds, and in the case of a cruising boat's genoa, to compensate for forestay sag at the increased loadings.

A further reason for adopting the large mainsail/small jib combination is that, as we know, when going for top speed in racing, a multihull needs to be sailed with its windward hull – the main hull in the case of a tri – flying just clear of the water, so as to minimize drag. This delicate balance is achieved by easing the mainsheet, or better still its traveller in the gusts, so as to quickly dump the excess heeling force. A big headsail cannot be played in this way, because freeing its sheet only makes it fuller, without inducing enough twist to reduce heeling.

Roach

As we have seen, the efficiency of a sail increases with its aspect ratio – which is another way of saying that the longer its leading edge, or luff, the more power it can generate for a given area. The problem with a very tall sailplan is that not only is its CE correspondingly high, which affects transverse stability, but the momentum of a long and heavy mast encourages pitching. Neither of these considerations means so much in a ballasted monohull, which heels more readily to spill the wind and whose mass and full lines resist pitching.

The solution adopted for high-performance multihulls is to gain mainsail area by means of an accentuated roach – the curved leech profile projecting beyond the straight head-to-clew diagonal – which can add a third or more to the overall size of the sail, and provides a more efficient, semi-elliptical shape, with less drag and more power than a straight leech (for example see fig 5.10). It also places much of the increase high up, where it derives maximum benefit from the wind gradient without the need for an excessively tall mast. It does of course raise the CE, but this is offset to some extent by the fashionably tiny jib, carried

Fig 5.10 *High-tech sails on a wingmasted micro, designed and built by Derick Reynolds (UK). Note the large amount of roach on the mainsail, full length battens, and the tiny jib.*

low down on a fractional forestay and – if necessary to restore stability – by an increase in beam.

Full-length battens

A large roach has to be adequately supported by battens, and these invariably run full length from leech to luff. Full-battened mainsails have a number of other advantages over their traditional forerunners, and following their development and success in multihull racing, it is not surprising that they have become so popular for use on cruising boats, including monohulls. First and foremost is the improve-

ment they bring in ease of stowing or reefing, particularly when combined with the use of lazyjacks, which are loops of line running under the foot of the sail and suspended from twin topping lifts rigged from the aft end of the boom to a point about two-thirds of the way up the mast, or preferably taken out a few centimetres along the spreaders. By drawing the sail out as it is lowered, and transferring some of its weight aft, the long battens allow each fold of sail to be gathered in by the cradle of jacks, and stacked evenly on top of the boom, instead of flopping down on to the deck or enveloping the struggling crew. Another main advantage over a 'soft' sail is that it does

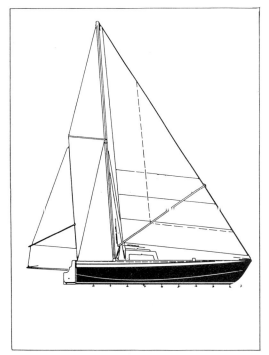

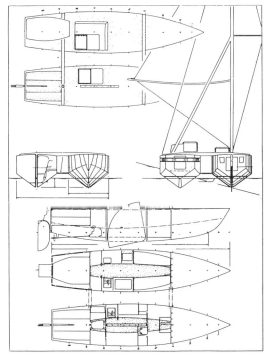

Fig 5.11 *And now for something completely different! American Phil Bolger chose to ignore convention with this thought-provoking design for a home-build plywood cruising cat. He reasons that a modest overall breadth produces a less jagged stability curve, as well as making it reasonably compact for berthing. Masts, with simplified rig, engine, centreboard and working area all in starboard hull; domestic accommodation only in port hull. It may look rather odd, but why not?*

not flap and flog while being hoisted or reefed, or when it is feathered during a gust. The absence of the noise and general commotion that usually accompanies these operations is much appreciated by any nervous newcomers to sailing, and with the loads spread more evenly, the life of the sail is undoubtedly prolonged. Efficiency is also improved, because the shape is largely predetermined and better controlled, especially in light airs when it is normally difficult to retain an aerofoil profile. The tension on each batten pocket is adjustable with lacings or by webbing straps and buckles – or in some state-of-the-art boats,

with miniature screwjacks. The forward end of every batten should be directly supported by a mast slider, or by a ball-bearing car, so as to resist the very considerable forward thrust without distorting the sailcloth.

Unfortunately, the very stability of a full-battened sail makes it difficult to 'read', so that telltales, a short distance back from the luff and along the leech, are an essential guide for the helmsman who would previously have looked for signs of flutter, or undue lifting in the region of the luff, to indicate that he was pinching up too close to the wind. Also on the debit side, a full-battened sail is more prone to chafe than a short-battened soft sail, is heavier to hoist – though not noticeably so in micro size – and costs around 20% more.

Spinnakers

Spinnakers are particularly affected by the large changes in apparent wind angle that are experienced on a multihull. In a light breeze on a dead run, which is the slowest point of sailing, as soon as the spinnaker is set, the helm is usually eased to bring the wind off the stern. The speed jumps as the wind draws forward, and when racing – or cruising in a hurry – the boat is then tacked down the course in a series of gybes so as to maximize VMG (velocity made good) towards the destination (see page 165). A very flat-cut spinnaker or a cruising chute is also effective for reaching in reasonably light winds, since it can be designed to drive down to as little as 40° apparent angle. However, when starting off with a moderate-to-fresh breeze well out on the quarter, the apparent wind will quickly be drawn on to the beam, and may become so strong that the helmsman will be obliged either to bear away and slow down, or even to drop the spinnaker before he blows it out.

Because of the multihull's wide overall beam, these sails can be used without a pole by leading their tacks to the two bows, or out to the floats; or when reaching in a trimaran, to the main bow and downwind float. A popular alternative is to use an asymmetric spinnaker, with its tack carried clear of the forestay and jib on a 'prodder', or hinged bowsprit – an idea borrowed from the Formula 40 boats for which it was originated, and which effectively increases the overall length of the boat without altering the actual hull measurement on which its class eligibility is based.

Fractional rig

Instead of running up to the crane at the masthead, the fractional forestay is attached part way down, usually between one-quarter and one-eighth of the mast length from its head. This not only reduces the size of the headsail, which makes the handling of a large genoa or spinnaker less of a struggle; but with less sag in the shorter forestay, its windward performance is improved. At the same time, total sail area is maintained by increasing the size of the mainsail, the reduced overlap allowing the main to be eased out further without being backwinded or stalling, at the same time decreasing the heeling and leeway forces and reducing weather helm. The fractional rig is also more efficient than the masthead layout at high speeds. For these reasons, it has become the automatic choice for performance multihulls, leaving the masthead rig for those cruising-orientated owners who don't mind sacrificing a little performance for the security of a standing backstay and simpler rigging, as will be discussed later.

Self-tacking headsail

Either type of rig can include a self-tending jib, which has proved an invaluable labour saver for the short-handed sailor, especially when it is set on a roller-furling forestay. As mentioned earlier, the sail is usually sheeted via a traveller car which runs on a track across the deck immediately ahead of the mast, so that the sail tacks itself as the boat is put about. A further advantage of using a non-overlapping jib, *provided it is of sufficient area*, is that it makes for more efficient windward sailing, because it can be sheeted in further, which improves the pointing, while off the wind the main can be let out further without backwinding, to improve both the drive and the balance of the boat, until reefing becomes necessary.

The sail is trimmed with either a single sheet, or a pair port and starboard, using separate lines from the car to control its travel and hence the angle of the sail, and to enable the jib to be backed when necessary – as when heaving to, or to help swing the boat's head across when tacking in difficult conditions. Twin sheets can also serve to position the traveller instead of using control lines, though usually less precisely, because if they should be heavily tensioned when the boat is tacked, the traveller may tend to stop short of its correct position along the track.

In the interests of simplicity on the smaller boats, the traveller and its track can be replaced by a wire span – or even dispensed with altogether, the sail then being sheeted through a central deck block via a barber hauler which is used to pull the clew outwards for reaching, and to prevent it from lifting. On trimarans, where the track can seldom be made long enough to suit offwind sailing, barber haulers should be rigged from the jib clew out to the floats to serve as vangs. Although seldom seen on multihulls, the foot of the jib can also be supported by a boom and tensioned with a clew outhaul, as in a traditional club-footed staysail. With such an arrangement, the sail is quiet and well behaved when running, because it doesn't keep collapsing and filling again. It can either be with a quick-release tack and slab-reefed like a mainsail, or the fore-end of the boom must be hinged on a pedestal and the clew carried on a ring or track so that it can slide forward as the sail is rolled up.

Standing rigging

Because of the reasonably short length of the average micro or cruiser mast – around 10–13m (30–40ft) compared with the awesome 25m (80ft) spars of some of the big racers – it needs no elaborate network of spreaders and shrouds to keep it 'in column'. But because a multihull heels so little in a gust, there can be a considerable strain on its rig – as much as double that of a monohull, and even more on a

Fig 5.12 7.3m (24ft) 'Strider Club', designed by Richard and Lilian Woods and built by Fantasy Yachts, Plymouth, England. A trio of these simple, low-cost micros day-sailed to Russia and back in the summer of 1989, covering some 3,000 miles (4,800 km) in 100 days.

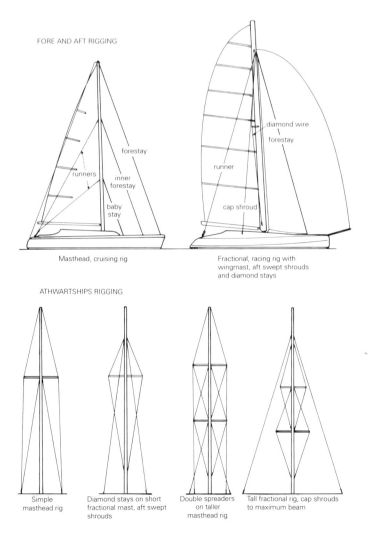

FORE AND AFT RIGGING

forestay

runners

inner
forestay

baby
stay

Masthead, cruising rig

diamond wire

forestay

runner

cap shroud

Fractional, racing rig with
wingmast, aft swept shrouds
and diamond stays

ATHWARTSHIPS RIGGING

Simple
masthead rig

Diamond stays on short
fractional mast, aft swept
shrouds

Double spreaders
on taller
masthead rig

Tall fractional rig, cap shrouds
to maximum beam

Fig 5.13 *(above) Fore and aft rigging.*
(below) Athwartships rigging.

cat than on a tri. This can to some extent be compensated for by leading the upper (cap) shrouds out to the maximum beam possible, preferably to the floats of a tri, to minimize the compression loads on the mast support. The mast in its turn is traditionally prevented from bending sideways like a banana, by means of lower shrouds. However, these tend to prevent the headsail from being sheeted in at a sufficiently narrow angle for windward

working at high speed, and on high performance boats they are usually replaced by one or more sets of diamond stays, fastened back on to the mast instead of leading down to the deck.

The longitudinal staying of a masthead rig is straightforward, but it limits the amount of roach that can be carried by the mainsail without the need to partially lower it to clear the backstay every time the boat is tacked, or to sail reefed whenever short-tacking becomes necessary. Some long distance racers are configured like this, because for them tacking

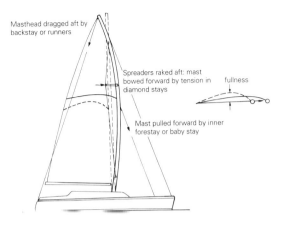

Fig 5.14 *Flattening the mainsail by bending the mast.*

is comparatively infrequent. But it is obviously quite impracticable for most purposes, so a masthead rig is generally only used in conjunction with a modest amount of roach.

There is no such restriction on fractional rigs, because in the absence of a masthead forestay the cap shrouds, which are attached to the mast near the forestay, can be angled aft so as partially to triangulate the forestay loads, with the slight attendant disadvantage that forward movement of the boom is restricted by the shrouds. The result is that the mainsail is liable to chafe when running, and extra care is needed when gybing, to avoid broken battens. The cap shrouds are usually supplemented for racing and heavy weather cruising by running backstays ('runners'), the upwind one being tensioned on each tack (and the other released) via multi-part purchases, to provide additional support against the drive of the mainsail, and to keep the forestay tight.

Mast rake – the amount by which it leans forwards or backwards – can be altered by adjusting the rigging screws on the forestay and backstay or aft shrouds, in order to vary the amount of standing helm. Forward rake moves the CE of the sails forwards and

decreases the amount of weather helm, and vice versa.

Mast bend

Whatever the rig, the centre of the mast must be prevented from bending aft in stong winds, since this not only makes the mainsail fuller, increasing both the heeling force and weather helm, but at the same time it slackens the forestay, producing more belly in the headsail, to the detriment of pointing ability and the performance at the higher windspeeds.

On a fractionally rigged boat, dragging the top of the mast aft by tensioning the backstay, or using an additional pair of runners leading to a point near the masthead if the mainsail carries a large roach, induces it to bow forward in the middle. This draws the fullness out of the sail, as the luff moves further away from the leech, effectively flattening it and depowering it as necessary to suit a freshening wind (fig 5.14). The rig is as quickly powered up again by releasing the tension on the backstay or runner. This is a particularly useful facility in gusty conditions, up to the point when the slower process of reefing becomes necessary. A similar effect can be produced on a masthead rig by using a tensioner on a babystay or an inner forestay leading from somewhere around the middle of the mast down to the foredeck area. Other means of draught (camber) control are explained later.

Storm jib

Where no permanent inner forestay is fitted, the addition of a temporary one also turns a sloop into a cutter for the purpose of setting a storm jib. A temporary stay is best attached to the mast about one-third of the way down from the permanent forestay, and led via a tensioning lever, block-and-tackle or muscle box to a strongpoint at deck level (represented by a crossbeam or a wire bridle on a cat) and at an equivalent distance aft of the bow. This gives the storm jib a snug inboard position from which to balance a heavily reefed main or a trysail, and avoids having to use the permanent forestay, which may be occupied by a rolled-up genoa. When not in use, its lower end can be released and stowed against a shroud.

Rotating masts

A normal mast, despite its aerofoil shape, leaves a turbulent wake except when the wind blows from straight ahead, which it never does when you are sailing. The efficiency of a mainsail can be considerably improved by allowing the mast to rotate until it assumes the correct angle of attack relative to the apparent wind. It then provides a smooth entry for the airflow across the leading edge of the sail and its heavily cambered forepart, where much of the drive is developed. For high performance boats, the complications of a bearing under the heel of the mast, and rigging points that allow it to rotate within wide limits, have

Fig 5.15 *Wingmasts, as designed and produced by UK specialist Nick Barlow. The wood/epoxy masts are suitable for home construction, with plans available from the designer. The composite moulded masts are much more complex to build, but are stiffer and lighter. In this respect they outperform aluminium construction, being some 40% lighter, but they cost around 25% more because they are hand-built.*

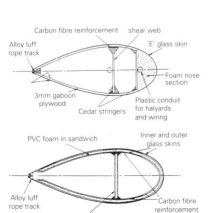

8m trimaran wingmast with curved trailing edge (see text). Note how boom compression loads on mast are avoided by supporting gooseneck on mast baseplate

Mast rotated by baseplate acting as spanner

on the whole proved well worthwhile; but opinion on their suitability for cruising boats, except in the hands of a very experienced crew, remains divided.

Masthead wind direction indicators and tricolour navigation lights cannot, of course, be used without some form of control linkage running up the mast, or an electric servo system to prevent them from turning. Except on the simplest dinghy cat installations, where the mast is freely rotated by the airstream, its angle relative to the boom is usually adjusted by control lines or webbing linking the boom to a 'spanner' projecting from the mast. Pre-bending the latter, by tensioning the diamond stays which are arranged to face slightly aft, then allows the area of mainsail below the forestay attachment point to be either flattened or made fuller by respectively under- or over-rotating the mast. On some of the high-tech racers, rapid and precise control of mast bend and sail shape below the forestay is also achieved by means of swinging spreaders which are moved in the fore-and-aft plane by hydraulic rams, aft to flatten the sail, forwards to increase power (fig 5.14).

On Dick Newick's innovative schooner *Pat's* (p. 96), the unstayed masts are lens-shaped, the amount of bend and the resulting variation in sail camber being controlled by the degree of rotation. These masts are very stiff when the sail pulls directly on their major axis, but bend when they are rotated to put the sail on their minor axis, making the sail flatter the harder it blows.

Wingmasts

The principle of rotation is carried a stage further with a wingmast, whose chord (depth) is extended to form a significant part of the sail's drive-producing area (fig 5.15). Resembling the wing of a high-performance glider, and 'steered' either by the spanner control lines or, in some of the latest big-boat installations, by an inner wheel at the main helming position, it is an extremely powerful device when set to the correct angle; but it can have a devastating effect on performance if it is not. A large wingmast can also be very dangerous in a gale, because of course it cannot be reefed, nor can it effectively be 'feathered' in gale force winds, when heavy seas constantly alter its attitude. Even with all sails down, it will continue to drive – at over 12 knots on a typical maxi-racer; a number of capsizes have occurred in this way. The aim therefore should be to select the smallest possible wingmast area that will provide an efficient leading edge. It can then be used as a stormsail.

A further potential problem occurs when the boat is moored and unattended. Although a wingmast can be locked in the fore-and-aft position, where it cannot develop any effective forward drive as long as the boat is secured alongside a dock, locking becomes intermittently ineffective as soon as the boat is free to swing. On a mooring, therefore, the mast should either be lowered, or allowed to weathercock – in which case some form of hydraulic damping, or a Y-shaped spoiler hoisted in the luff groove, is essential to prevent it from oscillation, which can quickly become so violent as to destroy it. A wingmast also requires more effort to use, and is more vulnerable and less tunable than a simple flexible mast, which for these reasons is still preferred by many of the long-distance racing skippers, and for the vast majority of cruising boats.

Nor is a wingmast particularly suited to fore-and-aft bending for the purposes of mainsail flattening, although surprisingly even the huge deep-chord spars of some racing multihulls are routinely distorted in this way by brute force hydraulics. Provided, however, that the section is fairly shallow it can, as mentioned earlier, be bent from the diamond stays without resorting to excessive tensions. Alternatively, it can be bowed sideways by differential tensioning of the lower shrouds each time the boat is tacked (which must be rather tiresome).

On the plus side, a wingmast can be very effective in controlling mainsail twist. A small amount of twist, we know, is needed to suit the variation in wind angle with height; but twist increases with aspect ratio, and it becomes a major problem on tall rigs. It can be largely overcome, as it is when mast bend is induced, by curving the trailing edge of the wingmast, so that as its leading edge is turned to face the wind, its trailing edge sticks out and drags the mainsail into a matching curve with minimal twist.

In an ingenious method of camber adjustment devised by Austin Farrar, who wrote the foreword to this book, each full-length batten is attached to a mast track slider by a small hinged gooseneck with a limited angle of swing. This allows the batten to swing to a line which blends in to the lee side of the mast on each tack. Turbulence on the other side is relatively unimportant. (As Farrar puts it, you have only to watch the underside of a bird's wing – the windward side – to realize that the bird isn't bothered about it either.) When the mast is over-rotated, additional camber is induced into the sail as the fore ends of the battens are bent by the goosenecks, which

have come on to their stops. In addition, a sealing strip on the luff of the sail engages with the mast track and closes the gap between mast and sail to prevent air leakage, the strip springing out again when the sail is reefed or lowered. Alternatively, fairing flaps can be attached to either side of the mast to streamline the airflow on to the sail.

Further important benefits of the wingmast are that it can be home-built in wood and epoxy for a fraction of the cost of buying an alloy or composite spar; it can be given sufficient buoyancy to prevent the boat from inverting after a capsize; and on some of the latest designs with wingmast options, there is also provision for temporarily releasing the upper shroud and hauling in on the lower one, so that the boat can be righted when lying on its side. Another interesting idea, which is being evaluated in the United States by Dick Newick, is to allow the mast to be heeled to windward after the manner of a windsurfer, by mounting its base on an athwartships sliding track.

Reefing and furling gear

Of the various methods of reefing the mainsail, by far the simplest and most widely used is the slab system, in which the luff reef cringles are hooked down at the gooseneck and the clew cringles are hove down on to the boom by reefing lines. This basic system is easy to operate on micro cats, where crew access to the mast is unrestricted and safe in rough weather, and on the Prout boats, whose masts are stepped so far aft as to be within easy reach of the cockpit. On most other cats and on trimarans, additional lines can be run to the luff reefing points and led, together with the

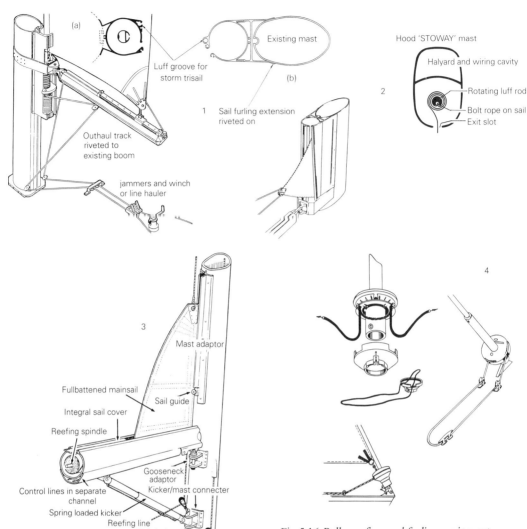

Fig 5.16 *Roller reefing and furling equipment.*
(1) Typical mainsail luff roller systems for fitting to
existing masts (a) Goiot (b) Easyreef. (2) Cross section
of Hood Stoway mast. (3) Sailtrainer in-boom system
allows the use of fully battened main with roach.
(4) One of Hood's jib furlers, using an endless reefing
line led to a cleat or a two-way self-tailing winch or
line hauler.

main halyard, back to the security of the cockpit. Reefing then becomes a quick single-handed operation, which can be further simplified by running a single line through a series of blocks to pull both corners of the sail down on to the boom at once. But unless the angles and the number of directional changes along the line can be reasonably restricted, friction through the blocks becomes excessive, and for this reason a twin-line system is generally preferred. Lazyjacks, even without the

benefit of full-length battens, take much of the remaining hassle out of mainsail handling.

A labour-saving alternative method of reefing or furling is to roll the sail and its battens round the boom – like the jacks, another traditional concept that has been revived and brought up to date. The idea is simple: you simply rotate the boom with a handle at the gooseneck in order to reduce the sail area. Unfortunately, it doesn't give such good control over the reefed sail as the slab system, because the battens seldom roll down parallel with the boom, and the fullness of the sail, combined with the angle of the leech, tends to roll the sail forwards into a creased bundle with insufficient foot tension. The sail must also be cut without roach, or preferably with a slightly concave leech; and unless the foot runs precisely at right angles to the luff, the boom needs some sort of padding in its after end to achieve a neat roll, and tape instead of rope luff reinforcement so as to avoid bunching around the gooseneck. It also requires the kicking strap to be disconnected before reefing, or replaced by some other form of vang to hold down the boom and control twist in the sail. These disadvantages apart, it is a quick and easy way to reef or stow the main, and its simplicity has been a blessing to short-handed sailors.

The latest systems feature a specially fabricated boom supporting a tubular spar round which the sail is rolled, both the boom and the rolled up sail being covered by an outer casing. Even with this equipment, however, it is difficult to adjust foot tension to set the right shape for the reefed sail – although full-length battens help to maintain this tension – and the angle between the boom and the mast has to be held at precisely 89–90° to allow the sail to roll evenly and without bagging, requiring delicate adjustment of the vang and topping lift, or the use of a special strut kicker.

The third method is to roll the sail, which is then loose-footed, vertically round its luff on a tubular spar, which gives good control over

shape, and quicker furling than the boom system, because it rolls along the long side of the sail. The spar is mounted either behind the mast – aerodynamically as well as aesthetically unattractive, but fairly easily fitted to an existing mast and accessible in the event of a snarl-up; or in a streamlined fairing riveted on to the after face of the mast – a more elegant arrangement that also prevents the spar from bowing under load without placing it under strong tension, which tends to distort the mast in the open system; or best (and most expensive) of all, inside it, requiring an entire new and specially extruded mast. Like in-boom reefing, a mast system is hard to beat for sheer convenience and for short-handed sailing, providing instant power control just by winding the sail in or out with a winch – or pressing a button on the electrically driven versions. But it has its drawbacks: it adds weight up the mast, raising the centre of gravity as the sail is furled; it cannot, of course, be bent to control the draught of the sail; it precludes use of long battens, which means that the sail can have little if any roach and must in consequence be taller for the same area, with a taller and correspondingly heavier mast (or a longer boom, which is seldom practicable); in the unlikely event of a jam, there is no way of reefing or lowering the sail, which could be embarrassing, to say the least; and like boom rolling, it is rather costly. Nevertheless, luff reefing is well suited to large cruising boats, where the loss in mainsail area can be recovered by using a larger genoa.

In-boom reefing has the advantage of keeping the weight low down and of using a fully battened, roached sail, with the ability to drop it in an emergency independently of the reefing system. Either system of furling avoids one of the most physically demanding chores on a big yacht – lifting and dragging the heavy, slippery folds of the mainsail into a tidy harbour stow.

For headsail reefing, there is a straight choice between using several sails of different sizes to suit the wind strength – the traditional way, but hard, wet work in rough weather; or a single headsail hanked to the forestay, with slab reefing – foredeck work again; or forestay roller furling and reefing, which is now almost universally used on cruising boats and on many ocean racers too, because the multihull's immediate increase in boatspeed, following quite small increases in true windspeed, causes such a rapid change in apparent windspeed that continual alterations to the sail area are needed in order to drive the boat efficiently. Furthermore, these are done from the safety of the cockpit, instead of having to go forward to an exposed position for every sail change, and the expense of the system can be offset against that of a wardrobe of three or more alternative headsails.

Against the convenience of being able to respond instantly to changing conditions, by simply pulling in or paying out a control line, must be offset a slight loss in sail efficiency due to the presence of the luff spar and the thickness of the cloth rolled round it; and to the increasing fullness of the sail as it is furled. The latter can be minimized by having tapered foam pads sewn into the luff, and on the more up-market equipment by rolling the centre of the sail first so as to flatten it, with the head and tack following on independent swivels. In the case of a micro, care is needed to avoid kinking the luff spar when it is lowered for trailering, and it must be adequately supported while in transit. On the smallest boats, the problem can be avoided by using a flexible plastics extrusion in place of the torsionally stronger aluminium spar needed for most headsails.

Deck gear

An important requirement of a roller headsail is that its sheet lead should be readily movable fore and aft on a traveller and track as it is furled and unfurled, so that the sheet continues to pull at the correct angle to the sail. This is found by sighting an imaginary line from the centre of the luff across to the clew and on down to the traveller. A very high cut sail, with equal foot and leech lengths, needs no adjustment to its sheet lead, because as it is rolled up, its clew moves along a line at right angles to the forestay, so that the angle of its sheet remains constant. But such a sail is limited in area and has an unnecessarily high CE. For best performance and maximum area, the foot of the sail should lie close to the deck and the sheet fairlead must be moved forward as it is furled. However, the 100% deck hugger can collect quite a lot of ocean in heavy weather; and it is also a considerable inconvenience in close-quarters sailing because it severely restricts forward visibility, so a compromise shape is preferable if neckache (or the need for a crew member stationed in the bows) is to be avoided.

Looking at sheeting angle from a different viewpoint, i.e. from above, we have already seen that it needs to be very narrow for correct jib trim and an acceptable tacking angle at high apparent windspeeds. The precise geometry varies, of course, with the design of the boat and its sails, but the object should be to position their tracks well inboard, so that on the fastest boats they make an angle of only six

Fig 5.17 *Full width radial mainsheet track on a home-built 'Searunner' 7.6m (25ft) trimaran, designed by Jim Brown (USA). The track for the self-tacking jib can be seen just forward of the mast.*

to eight degrees with the base of the forestay, and no more than 15° or so on a cruiser. Some state-of-the-art racers are fitted with additional tracks athwartships to adjust the angle when sailing off the wind, but it is much simpler to rig barber-haulers, in the form of a block and tackle from each hull or float, to pull the sail clews or the sheets outboard as necessary.

So far as the mainsail is concerned, the vertical angle of the boom and the consequent shape of the sail can be controlled in two ways. The boom can be held down in the traditional manner by means of a vang (kicking strap) linking it diagonally to the base of the mast. It

requires a powerful tackle, lever system, or hydraulic strut to exert the necessary force at such an unfavourable angle and at so relatively short a distance along the boom, so the fittings and their attachment points need to be very robust. A vang strut can also be used conveniently to replace the topping lift by supporting the boom while reefing or stowing the sail. But with a high aspect ratio rig in strong winds, vanging imposes severe compression loads on the mast at the gooseneck; and the boom, unless it is massively engineered and correspondingly heavy, will flex upwards, opening the leech and allowing the sail to twist. So vangs are seldom fitted on high performance multihulls.

Instead, the mainsheet track is made as long as possible, running the full width of the boat and preferably – though not essentially – radiused, with the mast as its axis. (The track on a cat is usually straight, because it is mounted on the aft crossbeam.) A wheeled or recirculating ball traveller on this track enables the boom, and with it the entire sail, to be trimmed in or out relative to the centreline of the boat to suit the apparent wind, while maintaining constant – or in the case of a straight track, nearly constant sheet and leech tension and a corresponding degree of twist. (A monohull has, of course, to rely on its vang, because of the relatively short track possible within the confines of its beam.) A further benefit of a long track is that power when beating or close reaching can be controlled, and the boat kept balanced, by playing the traveller. When, for example, the apparent wind draws aft in a gust (as it usually does), it is quicker and safer to feather the sail in this way than to dump the mainsheet or luff the boat. In Formula 40 racing, for example, the mainsail is seldom reefed, the degree of hull flying being dependent on the skill (and courage) of the crew, the mainsail leech being powered and depowered by fine adjustment of the mainsheet, with instant and more extensive control of power being in the hands of the traveller trimmer. If the track is not long enough to restrain the boom when it is squared off for running, it can be supplemented by a preventer strop or tackle, rigged forward of the track and as far outboard as possible between boom and deck or float; but it must be capable of being released quickly.

This is not to say that any sort of mainsheet track is essential in a conservatively rigged boat, where performance is not a prime consideration. For the sake of simplicity on some small boats, such as the Strider Club, the mainsheet tackle is permanently secured amidships, with perfectly satisfactory results.

The siting of most other deck gear, such as headsail sheet tracks, turning blocks, jammers and winches, depends very much on the leads permitted by the shrouds and other obstructions, and the geography of such features as the crossbeams and the cockpit, the centre cockpit of some trimarans posing particular problems in this respect. For out-and-out racing boats, the choice and positioning of the hardware and the ergonomics of operating it take precedence over anything else at deck level, and to a certain extent influence the above-water shape of the hulls. It is when cruising requirements and creature comforts have to be taken into account that compromises have to be reached on deck layout.

As in so many of the interlocking aspects we have been considering in the overall make-up of a boat, much of the designer's skill lies in clearly defining the purposes for which it will be used and the owner's likely requirements, and then in striking the right balance between wishful thinking and real life essentials. The most successful designs are invariably the finest compromises.

Auxiliary engines

To begin with, it is important to define the purposes for which engines are required. Come to that, do we want one at all? It depends, of course, on the type of boat. An off-shore cruiser may occasionally be required to motor for long periods while on passage. If he has a schedule to maintain, her skipper will tend to use the engine whenever the wind falls light, or to motor sail if headed, and he will nearly always rely on it for berthing and manoeuvring in harbour. On a micro, how-ever, the total amount of engine running dur-ing an entire season probably won't amount to more than a few hours. Many small-boat owners sail for months without once using their engine – assuming they have one: some determined purists don't even carry a motor on board, preferring to rely on a pair of oars, or a sweep, a handy anchor and their own exper-tise, as did all the early yachtsmen. But nowa-days there are occasions, even on a micro, when engine power becomes more of a neces-sity than a convenience. As well as giving you the freedom to navigate in confined waters, it is a safeguard against any embarrassing moments in a busy shipping channel should the breeze die suddenly. In very light airs, motor-sailing can be both economic and effi-cient. Running the engine even at tickover revs will increase the apparent wind strength suffi-ciently for the sails to fill and start driving the boat, which will then accelerate and point higher as it feeds on its own wind. Then, too, there's heavy weather to consider, whatever the size of the boat. Suppose you are close-hauled, probably reefed, with the rig unable to develop its maximum drive and with short, steep head seas trying to stop the boat dead in the water or butting the bows off to leeward. Running the engine will help to keep her moving ahead, pointing higher and making less leeway. At times like these you might find yourself in serious trouble without a reliable auxiliary.

A multihull's power requirements are sur-prisingly modest, compared to those of an equivalent keelboat. An engine big enough to push an 8m (26ft) ballasted monohull up to its top speed of 6 or 7 knots would be rated at around 20–30hp, but its not inconsiderable weight would only represent a comparatively small proportion of the total displacement. A multihull, being so easily driven, needs much less power at those speeds but hates weight. To drive it up to its maximum – in the case of a high performance multihull, two or three times that of the monohull – would require such a powerful and heavy lump of machinery that its sailing performance would be ruined, and it would become just a motorboat. So for high speeds, we must rely on the wind.

Indeed it is only too easy to overestimate the size of engine to suit a multihull. Experi-ence has shown that a single 10hp motor with a good sized propeller will drive most 35–40 footers (10–12m boats) along very nicely in reasonably calm conditions, with 20–30hp – or at the most, twin twenties in a big cat – giving a reassuring reserve for headwinds and lumpy seas, and an easy 8 knots or so cruising. Twins have the added advantage of safety in the event of one engine playing up or refusing to start, dual battery charging facilities in case an alternator should give trouble, and quite exceptional manoeuvrability with the two propellers so far apart. For small, lightweight boats such as micros, a 4hp outboard has proved to be perfectly adequate for most purposes and able to push most of them along at a comfortable 6 knots, with 6–8hp producing an additional knot or two and a reserve for headwinds. Bigger than that in a micro, and the engine is very unlikely to justify its extra weight and cost.

A useful formula for calculating the approximate speed of a multihull under power is

$$V = \sqrt{\frac{L \times P}{\Delta}}$$

where V = speed in knots
L = load waterline length in metres
P = horsepower
Δ = displacement in tonnes

It is primarily the multihull's limited load-carrying capability, and to a lesser extent its hull shape, that narrows the choice among what at first sight might seem like a bewilderingly wide range of alternative types of installation: diesel or petrol (gasoline), outboard or inboard – and in the latter case, conventional shaft drive, vee-drive, hydraulic transmission, fixed saildrive leg, or a lifting outdrive, some types of which can also be steered for extra manoeuvrability. All have been used in multihulls, but some designs are unduly heavy, and weight is a very important consideration in deciding which to go for – jet (pumped water) drives are used on some of the larger boats, but they are not only heavy but somewhat inefficient at low boatspeeds.

DIESELS

These are the natural choice for a cruising boat, except for the lightest ones, on account of their long life, fuel economy and dependable starting. The smallest inboards develop around 10hp and weigh 80–100kg (about 200lb) including their sterngear or drive leg with 20–30hp being the usual power range for the larger boats. This class of engine is a very good proposition for cruising cats with bridgedeck accommodation, using one of three alternative drive systems:

(1) One engine and straight shaft or saildrive leg in each hull. *For:* excellent manoeuvrability, twin engine reliability. *Against:* drag of leg through the water, even with a folding or variable pitch propeller, difficulty of clearing a fouled propeller, noise in the accommodation, weight and cost.

(2) Single engine in sound-deadened casing in the cockpit, driving via a lifting and usually steerable leg. *For:* no drag when sailing, good accessibility, single engine weight and cost. *Against:* some noise in cockpit, steering control not quite as effective as twin propellers.

(3) Single engine in cockpit, driving hydraulic pump connected to propulsion motors and drive legs in each hull. *For:* twin propeller manoeuvrability, single engine

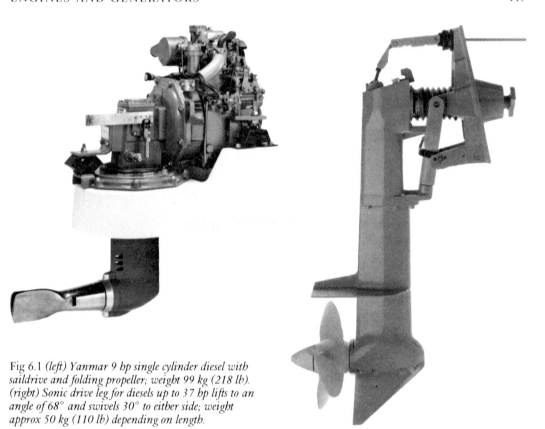

Fig 6.1 *(left) Yanmar 9 hp single cylinder diesel with saildrive and folding propeller; weight 99 kg (218 lb). (right) Sonic drive leg for diesels up to 37 hp lifts to an angle of 68° and swivels 30° to either side; weight approx 50 kg (110 lb) depending on length.*

weight and cost. *Against:* some loss in overall efficiency, hydraulic noise (whine) in most installations and engine noise in cockpit, drag of legs and difficulty clearing them.

Small diesels have also been installed by some cruising-orientated owners in their trimarans – even in one or two micros, whose comparatively roomy main hulls provide the engine-room space lacking in the slimmer cat of the same length. But for any high performance multihull, as distinct from a long distance cruiser, a petrol outboard motor is invariably the best choice, despite certain inherent disadvantages.

OUTBOARD MOTORS

Points in favour of an outboard are its light weight, simplicity, relatively low cost, quietness compared with a diesel, and the ease with which it can be lifted clear of the water when sailing. This is essential in any fast boat, in order to avoid the drag of the propeller and drive leg, which becomes significant over about 6 knots even with the prop spinning freely in neutral, and can take the edge off the light-airs behaviour of a micro at boatspeeds as low as 3 knots. An outboard motor has the further advantage of being portable for maintenance or winter storage ashore.

The chief drawback of a small two-stroke motor in the low power band we are considering, apart from an occasional reluctance to start, lies in its small, high-revving prop, which at low boatspeeds wastes much of the available power just digging a hole in the water instead of converting it into useful thrust. A larger and slower turning prop is much more efficient, but the combination of this, with the necessary lower gearing and the slower-running four-stroke motor is available in only a very few models, such as the Yamaha 10hp. Although at 45kg (100lb) this is too heavy for a micro, it is only half the weight of a 10hp diesel, and when properly insulated makes a beautifully quiet and smooth running engine for the larger boats, with electric starting and remote controls.

CAVITATION

The inefficiency of a small prop on an outboard motor while it is busy trying to get the boat moving is often aggravated by cavitation, which is mainly caused, in the lower-powered installations we are concerned with, by air entrainment when the blades are working too near the surface. A long or extra-long shaft version of the engine helps to avoid this, at the expense of some extra weight, without having to mount it so low down that it is dunked by every passing wave. Although outboards are reasonably waterproof and unaffected by rain or spray, it is best to keep the water off them as much as possible. Wherever it is mounted, the engine is liable to catch the occasional crest. On a small boat, a simple protective pod or fairing will shield it from most of them; larger boats can house the engine in a ventilated well with a sound-insulating lid.

Intermittent cavitation is nevertheless difficult to avoid with any stern-mounted motor if the boat is pitching heavily in a seaway. To cater for these conditions, the long driveshaft can be supplemented by mounting the engine on vertical rails or a parallelogram type of bracket that allows the engine to be either lowered below its normal position, or raised clear of the water. An alternative solution, for a catamaran, is to bring the engine some distance forward into the cockpit area so that vertical motion is substantially reduced, and to mount it on a crossbeam – if necessary an additional one – or in a deck console, with space to swing or slide up. An interesting alternative for open bridgedeck cats of suitable size is to carry an inflatable dinghy between the main and aft crossbeams, hoisted to deck level when not in use as a tender. To propel the cat, the stern of the dinghy, with its outboard suitably tilted, is lowered into the water, leaving the bows to push against the main beam. When installing in this area, however it is done, care must be taken to ensure that the prop is working in clear water and not in any transverse wave pattern between the hulls; and that it is not starved of solid water in the troughs. Wherever it is located, a single engine steered with its tiller, and on larger boats, remote controlled twins, provide an excellent means of manoeuvring the boat ahead or astern at low speeds when the rudders are ineffective.

This is more difficult to arrange on a trimaran where most of the narrow transom is swept by the rudder, requiring a mounting bracket on one side of the hull or on an after crossbeam. An offset position poses no problem provided the engine tiller can be reached by the helmsman. On a centre-cockpit boat, however, remote control push-pull cables are needed, simple enough to connect to the throttle and gearbox linkages, but sometimes involving awkward cable runs to the engine tiller. Low speed manoeuvring with a fixed and offset engine is still possible, though it takes good judgement and a fair amount of practice.

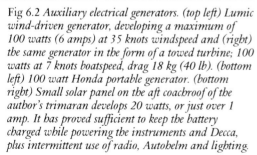

Fig 6.2 *Auxiliary electrical generators. (top left) Lumic wind-driven generator, developing a maximum of 100 watts (6 amps) at 35 knots windspeed and (right) the same generator in the form of a towed turbine; 100 watts at 7 knots boatspeed, drag 18 kg (40 lb). (bottom left) 100 watt Honda portable generator. (bottom right) Small solar panel on the aft coachroof of the author's trimaran develops 20 watts, or just over 1 amp. It has proved sufficient to keep the battery charged while powering the instruments and Decca, plus intermittent use of radio, Autohelm and lighting.*

Any outboard motor benefits from being run at regular intervals, if only for a few minutes, and preferably under load (in gear). This also serves as a precautionary check on starting reliability. These engines are very robust and require little maintenance; bad starting is about the only fault that is likely to occur – and then invariably at the wrong moment.

Generators

The electrical system on a multihull is basically no different from that on any other boat, except for the necessarily longer run of wiring between the hulls of a cat. The subject is regularly discussed in the yachting press and is well documented in specialist books, so it needs no further coverage here. Except on micros, however, the generous amount of space below decks invites the fitting of rather more in the way of domestic and navigational equipment than might otherwise be the case. The small generators on outboard motors only provide 4–6 amps during the short periods for which they are normally run. And even though most inboard engines have powerful alternators (typically 55 amps), they are not always – seldom, if the skipper is more interested in sailing than in motoring – run for long enough to keep the batteries fully charged. Some form of auxiliary generator is usually needed, if they are not to be periodically taken ashore for charging – which is only practicable for light-weight batteries on small boats. The following notes may be helpful in deciding which type to install.

The alternatives are:

1. A portable petrol-engine driven set. These are compact, clean, quiet (most of them –

certainly much quieter than any diesel) and capable of restoring the voltage on a depleted battery in a few hours. The smallest Honda weighs just 8.5 kg (19lb) and delivers around 100 watts for battery charging (6 amps), with a total of 300 watts at 230 volts AC for small power tools and domestic appliances (but be extra careful when working afloat or near water). The alternator on your diesel will probably deliver 50 amps or more for battery charging, but its noise is liable to keep the off-duty crew awake on passage, and you'll also be unpopular if you run it for long periods in harbour.

2. A windmill generator, which can be left rotating while the boat is unattended; but with a fan diameter of some 750mm it is, for reasons of safety as well as aerodynamic drag, best removed when sailing. Typical output in 20 knots windspeed (Force 6) is 70 watts (4 amps), it weighs about 6kg (13lb), and charging starts at 5–7 knots. Since moorings are usually chosen for the shelter they can offer, conditions are not always ideal for windmill power.

3. A water-driven generator, either bracket-mounted, or using a towed rotor with the alternator attached to the pulpit. Weighing some 12kg (26lb), these can deliver as much as a small petrol-engined set at 7 knots boatspeed. They naturally cause significant drag when sailing – say 18kg (40lb) when charging at 6 amps – and when the boat is moored the tidal flow has to exceed 3 knots before they can begin to charge.

4. One or more solar panels, which are passive, silent and maintenance free. A typical panel measuring about a metre by half a metre will deliver 50 watts (2½–3 amps) in bright sunlight, less than half that output on a cloudy day. That may not sound very much, but bear in mind that charging is continuous throughout the hours of daylight, regardless of wind and tide. With an average European summer output, for example, of 100 ampere-hours per week, a single such panel – or even a smaller one – can usually balance the battery drain from the instruments, and the intermittent use of lights, radio, autopilot and navaids, with additional panels being necessary for winter or heavier usage of these services, plus engine starting and for running such items as a refrigerator, stereo, and pressure water system.

7 CONSTRUCTION

Boatbuilding materials and techniques

We have examined the design and performance parameters that determine the shape of a multihull and its rig. In this section, we take a look at the materials used in its construction and the various ways they can be applied, either by professional builders or in your own back yard. This is not the place to tell you how to build a boat (though it may perhaps encourage you to do so). There are a number of excellent specialist books on the subject, if you want to go into it more thoroughly. But an understanding of the basic anatomy of a boat is more or less essential if it is to be sailed sympathetically, and it helps in troubleshooting any faults that may develop, and in assessing damage repairs.

The primary reasons for building a boat, instead of buying one, are either that the design you want is not available off the production line, or that you want to save money, or both; and perhaps the idea of DIY on such a noble scale attracts you. Indeed, there is so much to enjoy about building a boat that it is not surprising that some people prefer building them to actually sailing them; and at the launching of a new boat, there can be no one prouder than the person who has created her with his own hands. Setting sail in a boat that you have built yourself is a dream that has been shared over the years by countless aspiring sailors, and many have succeeded in this.

However, a boatbuilding project must be recognized at the outset as a major undertaking that should only be embarked on with a certain degree of caution. It requires patience, perseverance, and not a little courage – for even a micro can seem like a monster in the building shed. The worst mistake is to choose a design which is too big for the budget in terms of labour or finance. Too ambitious in either respect, and it may have to be finished off in a hurry with cheap, shoddy materials and fittings; or worse still abandoned, incomplete and probably unsaleable.

Be under no illusions about the economics of a DIY yacht by the time it is ready for the water. Somehow the saving is always rather less than one had hoped for, even allowing for the 'free' labour, which normally represents more than half the total cost of a completed hull. Given a succession of first-timer's mistakes in budgeting on materials and hardware, with the latter costing as much and often considerably more than the hulls themselves, or even in underestimating the size of the building shed and its heating bills, the project can sometimes end up nearly as expensive as a factory-built equivalent. Nevertheless, with the huge sigh of relief at the end of what has probably felt like a mammoth task, and the enormous satisfaction and sense of achievement as the boat takes to the water, the misgivings and frustrations, even the aching back are soon forgotten. And anyway, much of the uncertainty and hassle can be avoided when the building plans are accompanied by a comprehensive set

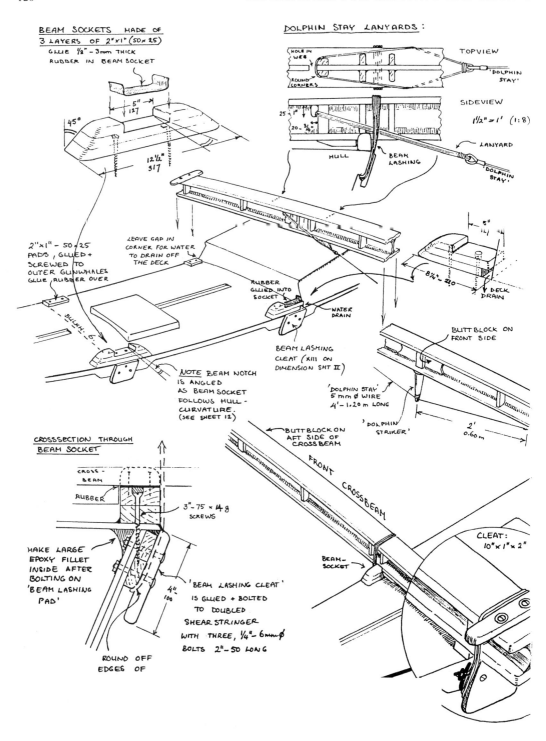

Fig 7.1 *Much of the hassle of building a boat at home is avoided when the plans are accompanied by a comprehensive set of instructions. These are typical of James Wharram's.*

of instructions from the designer, with explanatory illustrations of awkward or important details, and a materials shopping list.

So if you cannot find an off-the-shelf boat that suits your requirements as well as your pocket, then home building is well worth considering, especially in the case of multihulls, for which the choice of production types is still very limited. It is estimated that four times as many people build their own multihull as buy a professionally built one.

For those who have never tried their hand at boatbuilding before, or have serious doubts about their capabilities – or like most of us simply haven't the time or the resolve, both of which are needed in plenty – there are several other ways of getting afloat, although they cost more. You could hire some labour to help with the difficult bits and shorten the time scale – or if you can afford it, to work with you throughout the entire building programme; or more expensive still, go out and buy professionally built hulls, or the mouldings that comprise them, and do the rest yourself. Even this should cost substantially less than the company product, provided you buy in everything at the right price.

It can be very encouraging if you get to know other home builders in your vicinity. Talking over your proposals and sharing one another's problems helps to keep you motivated, especially at times when it's all beginning to look too difficult and you are in danger of losing heart. If a number of you get together, you can also generate quite effective purchasing power, and there are some national associations with the same objectives that may be well worth joining.

Whichever route you follow, the same ranges of materials and techniques are avail-able. They must be as strong and as light as possible, within the constraints of cost; the construction must be stiff, to resist deformation under the loads imposed by a powerful rig and by wave impact, and it must retain its strength over many years of hard use without weakening through flexing and fatigue. Steel and ferro-cement are too heavy for multihulls; and aluminium construction is not only expensive, but in the thin plate needed on a small boat to minimize weight, it tends to sag between the ribs and soon takes on a 'hungry horse' appearance, besides being vulnerable to puncture from rocks and even beach stones. So for all but the really big yachts and commercial ferries, for which aluminium is ideal, the choice lies between wood in its various forms, reinforced plastics, or a composite construction.

Wood

Timber is the original boatbuilding material, and for many still the best. It is comparatively inexpensive, if you exclude the heavy hardwoods such as teak, it is readily available, simple to shape and fabricate, and satisfying to work with. It is also without question one of the stiffest of all structural substances for a given weight, while its strength-to-weight ratio and fatigue resistance are surpassed only by the most exotic and expensive of space age materials. What is probably better known about wood is its susceptibility to rot and moisture absorption, and its dimensional instability; but these traditional weaknesses are nowadays preventable by using an epoxy resin treatment, best known of which are the WEST System pioneered by the Gougeon brothers in the USA and now in worldwide use, and a similar range of materials developed in the UK by S. P. Systems.

MECHANICAL PROPERTIES

Wood is a complex organic material composed mainly of cellulose in the form of tiny elongated cells or hollow needles of fibre, cemented together like bundles of reeds by a sticky substance called lignum. The cells, which are in turn made up of even smaller fibres (and so on, down to the cellulose molecules) run vertically in the standing tree, giving all timber its major strength along the grain. Another group of cells, known as rays, extend radially outwards from the centre of the tree to the bark, and these determine the lesser strength across the grain, typical ratios being 15:1 for hardwoods and 30:1 for softwoods. This is why wood splits more readily along the grain, and why you would never dream of putting up a shelf with the grain running across it. If strength is needed in both directions, then two or more layers of wood are used with their grains running across one another, as with the frames and planks of a traditional wooden hull, and in plywood.

MOISTURE CONTENT

Cellulose on its own is heavier than water, with a specific gravity of about 1.5, although as dry wood it floats, because much of the volume of wood is taken up by the cell cavities and the pores in the cell walls. These are partially full of water when a tree is felled; and while the green log begins to season, the fibres themselves remain saturated until all the free water has evaporated from the cavities. The wood has by then dried to its fibre saturation point, which is around 25% moisture content, but although it looks and feels dry and is much lighter, its qualities as an engineering material are still mediocre.

It is from this stage that further drying causes dramatic physical changes in the wood. It begins to shrink, and the strength and stiffness of its fibres increase rapidly as they lose their moisture content, until this reaches equilibrium with the humidity and temperature of the atmosphere that surrounds it. Drying to 10% moisture is a practical level at which to maintain an equilibrium, and this produces load-carrying and strength increases in the order of 60–70% from the saturated state, while extreme drying to 5% moisture can actually double both the end crushing or compressive strength, as well as the bending strength of most timbers, and triple it in some. So it is easy to see that the drier the wood, the stronger and lighter the boat.

The trouble with wood is that without special treatment, its properties change with the weather, notably in the way that quite small variations in the level of humidity cause it to swell or shrink across the grain as the fibres absorb or expel moisture through their pores. This dimensional instability, which seldom occurs evenly and often varies between adjacent pieces of timber, in turn leads to warping and splitting from internal stresses, and to leaks.

ROT

Wood is also susceptible to decay by fungal growth which destroys the fibres and turns timber into a weak and crumbly sponge. It has been said that more wooden ships were lost through rot than through all the storms and naval battles of recorded history. For the fungi spores to exist and cause decay, they need oxygen and warmth (ideally 25–30°) and the

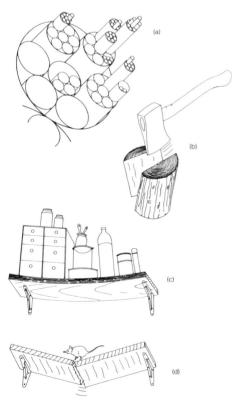

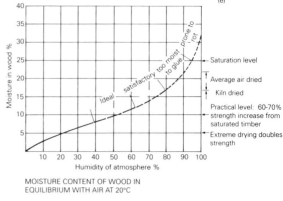

Fig 7.2 *The basic characteristics of wood.*
(a) Diagrammatic representation of the composition of wood and the disposition of its cellular fibres, showing why (b) timber splits more readily along the grain, and why (c) shelves are stronger with the grain running lengthways than (d) across it. (e) How the moisture content of wood and its suitability for boatbuilding varies with atmospheric humidity.

Saturation level

Average air dried

Kiln dried

Practical level: 60-70% strength increase from saturated timber

Extreme drying doubles strength

prone to rot

too moist to glue

satisfactory

Ideal

Moisture in wood %

Humidity of atmosphere %

MOISTURE CONTENT OF WOOD IN
EQUILIBRIUM WITH AIR AT 20°C

wood must be at or near saturation point. Neither very dry nor totally submerged timber is likely to rot, hence the survival of so many ancient wrecks; and seawater actually kills any spores it can reach, which is why fishing boats and similar craft used to be periodically sunk for 'pickling'. The problem while the boat is afloat is that not only must the water be kept out of the woodwork, which is not too difficult nowadays with modern paints and glassfibre to provide a sheathing, but every nook and cranny must also be protected from atmospheric moisture in order to keep it stable, as well as to prevent rot.

Epoxy resin

Without super-efficient ventilation, the humid atmosphere of a warm cabin, supple-mented by evaporation from wet crew and sails coming below in foul weather, condensation from the galley area, and possibly from a little bilge water, can quickly generate a destructive 100% humidity. The only sure way to keep the moisture vapour away from the wood is to coat every piece of it with a protective film of a suitably formulated resin. This may sound tedious, but in fact it is a quick and perfectly straightforward process, provided the manufacturer's instructions on mixing and application are followed scrupulously.

Conveniently, the same resin in various slightly different forms is used for all the bonding and gap-filling operations, mixed with a filler to make a paste for reinforcing fillets at high stress joints, and to provide a hard, durable surface which can be painted or varnished where necessary – for example, to shield it from sunlight, which degrades it. Saturating the wood with resin has the additional benefit, particularly for softwoods, of increasing its compressive strength; and by distributing the loads on each joint over a much larger area than would be possible with mechanical fastenings such as screws or bolts, the integrity of the structure is guaranteed, with every joint being stronger than the parts that comprise it.

A wonder material it certainly is, but epoxy's disadvantages should also be recognized. First, there's the health risk. Epoxy requires strict handling precautions, such as the wearing of plastic gloves, and good ventilation because the hardeners and solvents used in the epoxy mixtures are sensitizers and irritants, and their fumes are toxic. So is the dust from subsequent sanding, face masks being essential for this part of the operation. It is said that as many as 30% of builders become permanently sensitized to epoxy, despite these precautions, and a few people are naturally allergic to it.

Like wood, it needs a warm, dry working environment while it is curing, in order to ensure a good bond. And it is very expensive, accounting for anything up to half the materials cost of a wooden hull. There are other far less expensive adhesives, such as resorcinal and the urea-type glues which are simpler to use and non-toxic, and much more tolerant of working conditions. But few of them have epoxy's gap-filling capability, so that they require correspondingly higher standards of workmanship; and like paint, which is similarly water resistant but not totally impervious, they cannot form the essential vapour barrier around wooden components.

Framing

Most of our contemporary boatbuilding techniques have evolved from the traditional frame-and-plank system that has served shipwrights for hundreds of years. It starts with a rigid building base, or strongback, built from baulks of wood accurately levelled and squared on the building shop floor. Two timbers run the length of the future boat, and about ten more are fastened squarely across them at intervals corresponding, for convenience, to the stations on the hull plan. If the floor is in good condition the strongback is unnecessary, each frame instead being supported and precisely aligned on a pair of legs, which should preferably be chocked to the floor to prevent them from sliding about.

Attached to them keel uppermost – because for ease of working, boats are mostly built upside down – are the transverse frames which are shaped in outline to represent the hull cross-sections at each station, with the stem and sternposts standing up at either end. Instead of the closely spaced oak frames of the old, heavily planked vessels, today's wooden boats need only basic plywood formers, notched to accept a series of longitudinal ribs – the stringers – and an inner keel running like a backbone across the tops of the frames.

What happens next depends on the method of construction that is to be followed.

Plywood

The simplest way to plank a hull is to use plywood. It comes in big, handy sheets, usually 144 × 122cm (8ft by 4ft). It is not inclined to warp, and since it has the same strength in both directions, it doesn't matter which way it is cut. Top grade marine ply is expensive, but well worth using for a high quality boat; exterior grade is considerably cheaper and perfectly adequate for low cost projects. The sheets are cut to shape and either bonded or tacked to the frames and stringers, depending on whether the frames are serving only as moulds, to be removed later when the hull is turned over – in which case cheap chipboard may be used instead of ply – or left in place as structural bulkheads. Since in this type of application, plywood of the necessary thickness can only be bent in one plane, longitudinal planking with large panels, labour saving though it is, restricts the shape to the straight vee or the multi-chined hull. Alternatively, a series of panels can be laid vertically from keel to sheerline and bent across the frames to produce a gently rounded vee. The hull is then coated on both sides with epoxy, and given an external sheathing of epoxy-saturated glass cloth for protection against abrasion and to reinforce the joints. Polypropylene cloth is a cheaper and lighter alternative, but it is softer and less durable than glass.

When planning the work programme, it is important to bear in mind that it is far easier and quicker to fabricate all major items such as bulkheads, centreboard cases, locker sides and berth supports at the workbench, precoat them with epoxy, and install them before planking begins, rather than have to make innumerable journeys to the interior of the hull via a ladder. Glass-sheathed ply is also used (as an alternative to sitka spruce) for small boat rudders and centreboards, carved from the solid to the required aerofoil section, or in the case of larger boats applied as a thin fairing skin over a box or I-section, also made of ply, which resists the transverse buckling

loads. Wingmasts are frequently built in this way, and so too can crossbeams, with their web framing extending into the hull or float bulkheads, so as to distribute the loads over large areas of planking and framing.

DEVELOPED PLYWOOD

Of all the ways of producing a hull or a trimaran float, this is by far the quickest, because it needs no initial framework or moulds of any kind. Often referred to as the 'stitch-and-glue' method, it consists of making a pair of symmetrically shaped flat panels, stitching them together along the keel with copper wire, and opening them out to the designed angle. Then just insert a few frames and presto – instant boat. It's as simple as that. Well, almost.

Looking at it again in slow motion, the process still appears quite straightforward, but there are certain constraints on its use. The first is in the overall shape of the boat, because compounding a sheet of plywood entails bending it in two dimensions – hence the term 'tortured' or 'persuaded' ply used to describe this process – so there is a limited range of hull types for which it can be used. Their shape is determined by their rocker profile and deadrise or keel angles; and unless they are of basic vee-form, their size is limited to around 8m (26ft) by plywood thickness, because 5mm is about the maximum gauge that can be used with any marked degree of compound curvature. One of the best known examples of a developed plywood hull is the Olympic Tornado cat.

The process begins by joining up several sheets of ply with scarfed or butt-strapped joints to make two rectangular panels of the necessary length (slightly more than that of the boat), placing them on top of one another, and cutting out a pair of identical hull panels to the required profile shape. (Alternatively flat panels made of glass-reinforced plastic, described later, can be used instead of plywood.) These are precoated with epoxy, wired or fastened together with nylon webbing along the line of the keel, opened out to the correct angle and bonded with epoxy puttee and glass cloth. The sides are then bent up into the shape of the hull and clamped or strapped together – or in the case of a production boat, pushed down into a jig – while the bulkheads, stringers, beams and deck flanges, stem and sternpost or transom are added.

A benefit of this method is that very little fairing is necessary, because the plywood compounds naturally into a very fair curve, with few if any of the bumps and hollows that have to be filled and sanded in most of the other processes.

Laminated hulls

Wood laminating is often still referred to as 'cold moulding' to distinguish it from the hot moulding process that was necessary with the earlier glues. Compared with plywood skinning, laminating is considerably more labour intensive, but it is one of the alternatives for building designs involving compound curvature, free of the limitations of developed plywood. The stringers themselves must be spaced more closely than for plywood planking, in order to define the shape more accurately, and much thinner ply is used, the first layer being stapled diagonally across the framework in narrow, flexible strips edge-glued to one another. The more severe the curvature, the narrower the strips have to be,

ranging from about 5 to 15cm (2–6in). Because the curvature is also compound, each strip must first be tapered towards its ends for it to butt up without a gap in the middle, a laborious process known as spiling. This is followed by a second layer on the opposite diagonal, cross-laminated with staples and epoxy on to the first. Alternatively, the strips may comprise single veneers, usually no wider than 3mm, which bend easily over the severest curves; but great care is needed with the first veneer to avoid sagging or ripples between the supporting framework. The direction of the grain is then varied with each succeeding layer, leading to a strong and resilient semi-monocoque capable of withstanding loads from any direction. It is still reinforced by the framework, most of which will remain *in situ*, unless the skin is to be built up to such a thickness as to be virtually self-supporting. Removing all but a few major frames and stringers then leaves a beautifully clean and unobstructed interior, although significantly heavier than the fully framed, thinner skinned boat.

The same hull can, of course, serve as a mould on which to lay up a number of identical wooden shells – in which case all the interior framework and joinery must be installed after the mould is removed – or as a 'plug' on which a female mould is built for the production of plastics hulls.

Fig 7.3 *(a) Frames, stringers, bulkheads and centreboard trunk for a multi-chine mainhull and port float of a 'Searunner' 25 trimaran. (b) Sheet plywood planking on a vee-hulled Wharram cat. (c) The constant camber system of building a complete hull from a small mould. (d) The stitch-&-glue method. The two hull sides are wired together along the keel, and then opened out to receive the bulkheads. (e) Laminating a hull. Veneer strips are stapled to the stringers and edge-glued to one another. Successive diagonal layers of veneers are then bonded on with epoxy.*

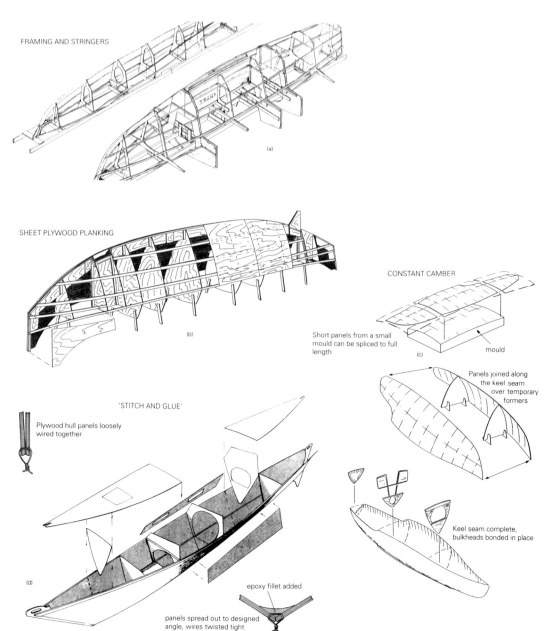

FRAMING AND STRINGERS

(a)

SHEET PLYWOOD PLANKING

(b)

CONSTANT CAMBER

Short panels from a small mould can be spliced to full length

mould

(c)

Panels joined along the keel seam over temporary formers

'STITCH AND GLUE'

Plywood hull panels loosely wired together

Keel seam complete, bulkheads bonded in place

(d)

epoxy fillet added

panels spread out to designed angle, wires twisted tight

LAMINATED HULL

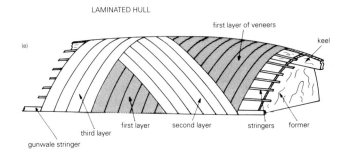

first layer of veneers

keel

(e)

first layer   second layer   stringers   former

third layer

gunwale stringer

As with a sheet plywood hull, the outside, and particularly the bottom, may be given a protective sheathing of glass cloth, although it is not strictly necessary for strength. Some prefer not to incur this additional weight and cost, or to use a lightweight cloth which allows the topsides to be varnished rather than painted, so as to show off the beauty of the natural wood. Even the best varnishes, however, have a shorter life than paints because, despite containing UV shielding materials, they gradually degrade in sunlight and therefore require more frequent maintenance.

CYLINDER MOULDING

Using an innovative combination of tortured ply and laminating techniques, cylinder moulding allows a hull to be turned out in about a tenth of the time it takes to laminate one. As in a developed plywood hull, a pair of panels, cut to the same perimeter shape, are joined along the keel and folded into a boat shape. But in this case, the panels are already curved in one direction, having been made one after the other on a simple mould comprising a row of identical plywood formers shaped to the profile of the hull mid-section.

The process begins by covering the mould with a thin sheet of polyethylene to form one side of a vacuum seal. Next, sheets of thin plywood (normally 3mm), scarfed in batches with an angle grinder, are laid side by side on the mould, with their face grain orientated along the lines of the greatest bending stress, tacked top and bottom, and all their mating surfaces are coated with epoxy. (No spiling is necessary, because the curvature is in one direction only.) This is quickly followed by two or three more layers, depending on the size of the boat; a skin thickness of 9mm from three layers would be

normal for a micromultihull, 12–15mm for larger boats. Split polythene tubes are then laid on top of the workpiece at strategic intervals to serve as air channels (or alternatively, bubblepack, or a special perforated breather fabric), the polyethylene sheeting is draped back over the workpiece, the edges are taped together to form a bag, and the air is extracted with a vacuum pump, which keeps the laminations pressed firmly and evenly together while the epoxy is curing. (An ordinary commercial vacuum cleaner or refrigerator compressor will do the job.) Heat from overhead radiant lamps helps to speed the process and ensures a good cure. The resulting half-hull panels are trimmed to the required profile, joined at the keel, pulled together at bows and stern, and supported the correct distance apart at deck level with a temporary flange. Bulkheads and stringers are then inserted lightly, so as not to deform the skin which is now held in a 'fair' curve, and all surfaces are coated and glassed where necessary.

CONSTANT CAMBER

There are some restrictions with cylinder moulding on the shape and type of section that can be produced. Constant camber is a technique perfected by Jim Brown, his partner John Marples and designer Dick Newick that allows greater freedom in hull design. The essential difference from cylinder moulding is that the CC mould and the panels taken from it already have compound curvature, and hence need no torturing to assume their final shape, although overall the process is somewhat slower. The mould itself must be fully skinned, but it can be comparatively small – between half and one third the length of the hull is sufficient – so the panels can if necessary be built in a controlled indoor environment in the winter, and assembled outside in the summer.

The mould has a constant cross-section, hence all its frames are identical, only their height being varied to produce the necessary longitudinal curvature, and it is sheathed in plywood like a laminated hull to present a smooth, firm working surface. The panels are also formed in the same way, from several cross-laminations of narrow veneer strips epoxied to one another and vacuum-bagged down on to the mould. However, because of the constant cross-section, no individual spiling is necessary, all the strips being identical and pre-cut in batches from a template. Two or three panels are then joined up to make the full length and cut to perimeter profile; and finally what are now two fully shaped half-boats are fastened together and completed in the usual way.

The choice of hull shapes is further extended in a similar but much more complex technique known as variable camber. As the name implies, a single master mould offers a variety of camber sections, so that boats and panel parts of differing characteristics can all be built on the mould by selecting the appropriate area on which to work. With such a wide range of shapes present on the one mould, this process also lends itself to computer assistance in producing co-ordinates – offset measurements – for accurate placement of each set of laminates. But it represents a much larger investment than the simpler types of mould, and such a powerful tool can only really be justified for a big multihull, or to build a number of different boats on a professional basis.

Fig 7.4 *A 31ft strip planked hull taking shape in amateur builder Pat Webb's 32ft garage. The completed catamaran cruiser, which was designed by Richard Woods, achieved 18 knots on the day she was launched.* (Photo: Bailey)

STRIP PLANKING

Using the normal system of transverse framing, but with few if any stringers being needed, the hull is planked from bow to stern with narrow strips of a lightweight, stable wood (Western red cedar is the best) edge-glued together with glass cloth and epoxy inside and out to provide sufficient panel stiffness, and to resist impact damage as well as abrasion, cedar being too soft and vulnerable without it, despite its epoxy coating. For larger boats, veneers can be laid diagonally over the strip planked hull, which then supports them like a mould, resulting in an exceptionally strong and rigid monocoque with a minimum of interior obstructions. The cedar sandwich, as with the other forms of sandwich constructions described later, has one major advantage: it provides a considerable degree of both sound and thermal insulation, whereas ply and laminated hulls are inclined to act as a sounding board for the noise of the waves, and need to be lined to avoid condensation. The strip planked hull also provides more positive buoyancy in the event of flooding, and will float like a cork even when totally waterlogged. (The 'solid' wooden boat would be partially awash under these conditions, unless it were provided with watertight compartments, which are usually located in the bow and stern areas under the bunks – although as a multihull it would not, of course, be in any danger of being dragged under by a heavy keel.)

Moulded plastics

Glass-reinforced plastics, or GRP as it is commonly called, is the combination of materials most frequently used in the commercial production of small cruising craft, and the cheapest – provided that a sufficient number of hulls are taken off the moulds, because these are expensive pieces of tooling. Unlike the moulds used in laminating timber, they are female in form, having themselves been moulded in GRP from a wooden 'plug' (usually derived from another hull as mentioned earlier). Accordingly they are reinforced on the outside to keep them rigid, with the materials being applied to the inside of the mould. They also require a high standard of surface finish, free of any ripples or blemishes, so that this can be imparted directly to what will become the outside of the boat, without the need for any filling or polishing.

Even without the expense of a suitable mould, solid GRP – as distinct from the foam sandwich described later – has certain other drawbacks. Unlike timber, it is not 'user-friendly' and it is also relatively heavy, so it lacks positive buoyancy. It is a poor thermal and sound insulator, and its indifferent panel stiffness has to be corrected in key areas by additional ribs and stringers, adding weight to an already heavy structure. But it is basically simple to produce, and lends itself particularly well to commercial manufacture.

The process consists basically of first coating the mould with a release agent to prevent the new GRP part from sticking to it, followed by a coating of a pigmented, thixotropic resin known as a gelcoat, which will form its outer skin. As soon as this has partially cured – the term used to describe the chemical reaction between the liquid resin and the hardener which is added to it – one or more layers of polyester-saturated glass cloth are applied, according to the wall thickness required, being worked firmly on to the mould with a hand

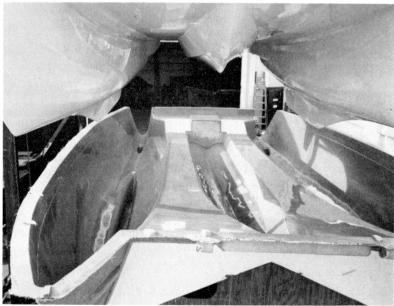

Fig 7.5 *One-piece hull and bridgedeck assembly of a Prout 'Snowgoose 37 Elite' being released from the mould. Note the highly polished mould surface and the correspondingly high standard of finish on the hulls.*

roller, and left to cure.

Composite construction is often referred to as if it were some new high-tech method of boatbuilding. In fact it is one of the oldest.

Back in the Bronze Age they were stretching animal skins over basketwork frames for their coracles and kayaks, and *Cutty Sark* was built with wood planking on her iron frames. Nowadays synthetic resins have joined wood as one of the primary groups of materials in small craft construction, with other manufactured substances being added for reinforcement.

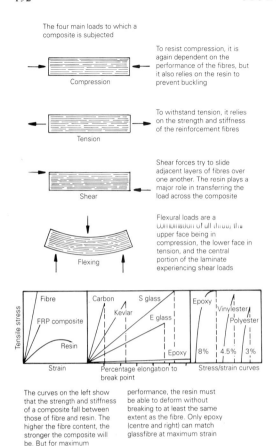

The four main loads to which a
composite is subjected

To resist compression, it is
again dependent on the
performance of the fibres, but
it also relies on the resin to
prevent buckling

Compression

To withstand tension, it relies
on the strength and stiffness
of the reinforcement fibres

Tension

Shear forces try to slide
adjacent layers of fibres over
one another. The resin plays a
major role in transferring the
load across the composite

Shear

Flexural loads are a
combination of all three; the
upper face being in
compression, the lower face in
tension, and the central
portion of the laminate
experiencing shear loads

Flexing

The curves on the left show
that the strength and stiffness
of a composite fall between
those of fibre and resin. The
higher the fibre content, the
stronger the composite will
be. But for maximum

performance, the resin must
be able to deform without
breaking to at least the same
extent as the fibre. Only epoxy
(centre and right) can match
glassfibre at maximum strain

Fig 7.6 *Behaviour of a composite panel and its
components under load.* (Figs 7.6, 7.7 and 7.8 based
on information supplied by SP Systems Ltd)

REINFORCING MATERIALS

Foremost among these is stranded glass in
many different forms, ranging from low-cost
mats of chopped glass strands which give bulk,
and hence stiffness, without adding very much
strength, to a variety of woven and knitted fab-
rics whose filaments are aligned in specific
patterns, such as triaxial, with corresponding
and predictable strength characteristics, and
uni-directional cloths, where the majority of
the fibres run parallel, so as to give maximum
longitudinal strength. Most GRP boats are
built with a combination of chopped strand
mat and woven glass fabric, in which the glass

itself can be of two grades: the normal E-Glass,
which was originally developed for electrical
circuit boards, and the more expensive S-Glass
('S' for structural) which has 25% more
strength and 35% better impact resistance.

For top level racing boats, where weight
saving is vital, glassfibre is often replaced by an
aramid fibre trade-named Kevlar, which is half
the weight and three times as strong as glass –
and five times the price; and in areas of the
greatest stress, such as crossbeams and rigging,
by carbon fibre which is as strong as light alloy
in compression, twice as stiff as Kevlar, and
unfortunately no less than ten times the price
of glass. The same materials can of course be
equally well applied to high-tech wooden
boats; sinews of carbon, for example, are
often used in the construction of wooden
wingmasts. For convenience, the umbrella
term fibre reinforced plastics (FRP) is nowadays used to cover all three types of laminate.

Aside from their high cost, however, these
exotics have other drawbacks. Carbon fibre is
extremely brittle and vulnerable to impact,
and Kevlar is weaker than glass in compressive
strength. So they are also combined into
hybrid cloths, such as Kevlar/carbon and
glass/Kevlar, to optimize their mechanical
properties. Another state-of-the-art technique
is the use of 'pre-preg' cloths. These have been
passed through a bath of resin and hardener
dissolved in a fast evaporating solvent, con-
veyed through a hot air drying tower, and
stored in a fridge ready for use. They are
subsequently laid over the mould and vacuum
bagged, and the entire hull is cooked in a huge
oven until the resin has cured. The cost of such
facilities is considerable, but it enables fibre-
to-resin ratios to be accurately controlled –
essential for minimum weight and maximum

strength – and greatly reduces labour costs in laying up.

RESIN TYPES

There is a choice of resins too, on a rising scale of cost and performance, orthophthalic polyester being the cheapest and easiest to use. (Incidentally, it is not the resin that gives a freshly moulded boat its characteristic smell, but the styrene solvent.) Next comes isophthalic polyester, 50% more expensive, but more resilient and with better resistance to water (see under 'Blistering'). Then there's vinylester, stronger and more water resistant still, but more than double the price of ortho-polyester. All three behave in the same way chemically, and begin to cure following the

addition of a tiny amount (1–2%) of a catalyst to start the polymerization process. And finally there's epoxy, five times the price of ortho-polyester but far superior in every other respect, notably in its resistance to water degradation as well as in its adhesive strength. Instead of a catalyst, epoxy requires a large proportion of hardener to start the reaction (from 20% to as much as 50%, depending on the particular product) and this hardener forms part of the final polymer. The use of epoxy allows composites to be produced with very high fibre-to-resin ratios, making them much stronger and lighter than is possible with the other resins, but it is still too costly to be considered as a universal replacement for them. Somewhere in the middle of the scale of toughness, water resistance and cost is SP Systems' modified epoxy Epacryn, now specified by the Royal National Lifeboat Institution for its rigid lifeboats and by a number of commercial boatbuilders.

BLISTERING

The main reason for acceptance of additional cost in a series produced boat is epoxy's good resistance to water penetration and the resultant blistering, which remains the most persistent and aggravating problem of polyester resin construction, affecting possibly as many as one in three of all boats under five years old, and an even higher proportion of older ones. What happens is that unless the hull is either built with epoxy resin, or thoroughly coated with it near to and below the waterline, the gelcoat absorbs moisture, and an aqueous solution builds up in the small voids which can occur in the laminate unless the strictest precautions have been taken during manufacture – and sometimes even then. As a result,

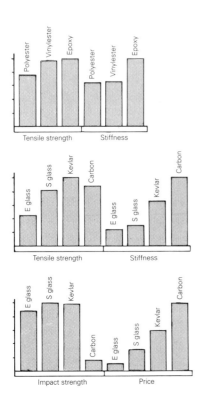

Fig 7.7 *Mechanical properties of the fibres and resins used in composites.*

osmotic cells develop under the gelcoat, pressure builds up and blisters form and burst, leaving the skin heavily pockmarked and weakened. Laminates made with Epacryn are actually guaranteed against osmosis for ten years by its manufacturers, which is bound to improve the resale value of the boat, although it does inevitably increase its initial cost, by around 2%.

Sandwich construction

The basic principle of sandwich construction is to separate two load-bearing skins with a lightweight core material. In a sandwich panel flexing under load, one skin will be under compression and the other in tension, and it follows that the further apart they are, the stiffer the panel will be. In fact, the stiffness of a laminate is proportional to the cube of its thickness, and the purpose of the core is to increase the thickness of the panel without adding significantly to its weight. Typically, a 3mm FRP skin on either side of a 15mm core creates a much stiffer skin than would 6mm of solid FRP, without being much heavier. Unfortunately the weight advantage of a sandwich diminishes with the size of the boat, because for strength reasons skin thickness cannot be scaled down proportionately, so unless Kevlar is used, a micro can end up heavier than if it had been built of plywood.

Nevertheless this type of construction has a number of other advantages over solid FRP. The first is that instead of a highly finished mould, it is only necessary to use temporary frames covered with closely spaced longitudinal battens as the male former. The sheets of core material are draped or bent over it, and the outer skin applied, filled and faired – quick

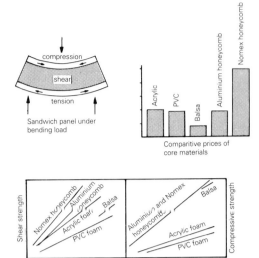

Fig 7.8 *Behaviour and comparative prices of sandwich core materials.*

to say, but in reality involving much tedious trowelling and dusty sanding for the finish to approach that obtained from a good production mould. The hull (or deck component) is then turned over, the framework removed and the inner skin applied, followed by the bulkheads and accommodation items. Conversely, the core material can be applied to the inside of a moulded but thinly skinned FRP shell, or to a tortured ply or laminated wooden hull, followed by the inner skin and interior structure.

As well as stiffness and light weight, and hence positive buoyancy, sandwich laminates provide excellent sound and thermal insulation, helping to avoid condensation in cold climates, and in summer preventing the worst of the sun's heat from soaking through the deck to the interior accommodation. The majority of commercially produced boats with solid FRP hulls incorporate sandwich decks for this reason.

Looking at the other side of the coin, unless the outer skin is so heavy as to largely nullify the strength-to-weight advantage of sandwich construction, it is more vulnerable to impact damage, and somewhat more complicated to repair than a solid laminate, especially in the sharply curved areas. As might be expected, the materials themselves cost around 50% more than for solid FRP, although, surprisingly, they are hardly any more expensive than epoxy-saturated plywood and glass cloth. The core and skin must also be a reasonably good chemical match to ensure a strong and permanent bond; there have been a number of cases of the core delaminating from the skin, due to flexing of panels subjected to heavy pounding from head seas. And the positioning of all fittings needs, if possible, to be planned well in advance, because hardware can develop high local stress concentrations which must be dispersed throughout the adjoining structure. Whereas the fittings on a plywood deck are simply through-bolted to wooden pads which spread the load, a sandwich deck would crush when the bolts were tightened, so the core in the region of each fitting must either be replaced by a plywood insert (doing this after the boat has been built entails cutting away the outer skin and core, bonding in solid blocking and reskinning); or by bonding an FRP plate on to the skin to spread the load.

CORE MATERIALS

Because it lies between one skin in tension and the other in compression, the core is subjected to shearing forces, and its most important property is therefore its shear strength and stiffness. It must also, because it is protected only by a comparatively thin skin, be able to withstand a reasonable amount of compressive loading.

The most widely used core material is PVC foam, which comes in sheets of various densities and thicknesses, and under several trade names such as Airex, Divinycell and Termanto. It is highly resistant to impact, so it makes a good composite partner for carbon, which is not. A good example is a moulded foam sandwich wingmast, in which carbon fibres carry all the primary loads, and unidirectional glass the shear and transverse loads. The result is great structural integrity and an exceptionally high strength and stiffness to weight ratio. PVC foam can readily be bent cold over gently radiused surfaces, or if it is required to follow more severe curves, softened with a hot air gun or infra-red lamp. For this reason some types are unsuitable for decks exposed to the sun, end-grain balsa wood being the best material for this application.

Balsa is also superior to PVC foam in its compressive and shear strengths, and is half the price. It is available in the form of small, closely spaced squares of the wood, mounted on a light scrim backing of open weave FRP which can be draped over quite acute compound curves; or for single curvature, in panels or narrow strips sandwiched between hardwood veneers. Balsa's drawbacks are that it is at least twice as heavy as foam, and can become heavier still by absorbing large quantities of resin along its grain during lamination – and water too, if the skin should later be punctured, whereas PVC foam with its closed cells is virtually non-absorbent. Despite its great compressive strength, balsa is also vulnerable to impact, so it should not be used under a thin skin in areas where it might get dented, with consequent delamination.

Among the other core materials are cedar, heavier than balsa and not available in end-grain mats, but much stiffer when used as strip planking. Then there's acrylic foam, strong, stiff and stable, but difficult to form on to curved surfaces; and polyurethene foam, which is more brittle than PVC and liable to deteriorate at the skin interface, causing delamination. But PU foam is also available in aerosol cans as a liquid which expands into a foam, useful for filling large voids such as double skins and small watertight compartments, and in the bows to provide a crumple zone in the event of collision. However, despite being theoretically unicellular, it can become a waterlogged liability if exposed to prolonged water leakage, and is virtually impossible to remove without cutting open the affected areas.

Finally, there are the honeycombs which have originated from the aircraft industry and provide very light, stiff laminates with tremendous strength in compression. But their very small bonding surface area, which is restricted to the very edges of the honeycomb walls, requires great care when applying the epoxy resin, to ensure adequate adhesion to the skins. They are made either of aluminium, or from Nomex, which is an aramid paper. Aluminium honeycomb costs no more than PVC foam and is stronger in shear, but it will deform permanently on impact; and since the FRP skins are resilient, delamination follows as it does with balsa cores that have been thumped; and there is always the danger of corrosion in a marine environment. Nomex is the strongest of all the core materials for its weight, completely stable and reasonably resilient, but alas, at three times the price of the others, its use is mostly confined to the big budget boats.

Kit panel system

Because the male former needed for sandwich construction can alone entail as much work as building an entire wooden boat up to the planking stage, and the filling and fairing routine is equally time consuming, a greatly simplified building system has been pioneered and developed, by designer Derek Kelsall. It requires only rudimentary framework, produces a high standard of surface finish, is quick to build and is so straightforward that it can be used by complete novices.

The hull shapes that can be built with it must, however, be designed to avoid compound curvature as the boat is assembled from a kit of flat and single curvature panels. All of these are prefabricated on a mould table, which is simply a boat-length table (or half, if space is short) made from kitchen-type melamine-faced chipboard, on to which the panels are laid up – and in the case of sandwiches, vacuum bagged. When they are taken off the table after curing, they have acquired the melamine's mirror finish, and need no further surface treatment. They are also sufficiently flexible to be sprung to a gentle radius, but where sandwich panels such as deck and coachroof need any substantial amount of curvature, the inner skin is not bonded on until after the panel has been bent to shape. The panels are finally assembled against a set of temporary frames which pull them into the required cross-section, their mating edges are joined with lengths of radiused moulding which have been made on a separate jig, and the fitting of the internal structure and furniture, most of which has also been made on the

(a)

(b)

Fig 7.9 A 15.8m (52ft) cruising cat built using Derek Kelsall's kit panel system. (a) Sandwich panels assembled against temporary frames, with a small FRP moulding forming the bottom section. (b) The completed hulls, ready for launching.

mould table, proceeds in the normal way.

A favourite approach to such a project, as with the constant camber method, is to spend the winter months making the complete kit of parts indoors in an extended garage or work-shop, and to assemble the boat outside under a polythene shelter during the summer. The resulting hulls are extremely roomy, reason-ably easily driven, and contrary to what might be expected from a collection of flattish pan-els, do not appear at all slab sided.

High volume hulls such as these cannot be expected to have the performance of an ultra high-tech racing shell, built using some of the other techniques we have been examining, but regardless of cost, which more often than not is borne by commercial sponsors. For greater latitude in design, without disproportionate investment of time and money, it often makes sense to mix the methods, bearing in mind that a mirror finish is only needed on the topsides, the bottom usually being covered in antifouling paint and the decks with a non-slip paint or other material. For example, one economic way to build a good, fast boat is to use flat panels of foam sandwich for the topsides, a comparatively small moulding of solid FRP from just above the waterline downwards, puncture resistant and shaped for optimum performance; and any convenient combination of balsa sandwich mouldings and flat panels for the deck and coachroof assemblies.

Even on dream budgets, though, there are limits to be observed in the quest for the ultimate light weight and stiffness. Not so long ago, a certain well-known maxi, built from the most exotic materials under the guidance of a specialist design engineer, suffered a major structural failure of her side decks in an area where a pair of tactical compasses had hurriedly been installed by the crew just prior to the start of the race. The engineer's response, not surprisingly, was that you don't just cut a hole in your mast without first consulting the firm that made it. Unlike the cruisers or cruiser-racers we are concerned with, top level racing boats are deliberately stressed close to the limits of structural safety; and they behave impeccably only so long as they are operated and sailed accordingly. They are highly sensitive machines, totally unsuited to everyday yachting. But then, as one of their owners remarked, you wouldn't go shopping in a Formula One racing car.

8 ROAD TRAILERS

Legal requirements, mechanical features, rigging and launching the boat

With your boat on a trailer you are free to choose your cruising ground, attend events far from your home port, and to use it as a caravan *en route*, to say nothing of off-season storage in the security of your own garden. Trailering adds enormously to the freedom of sailing, although unfortunately the notion of total mobility is often oversold. Treat with caution any manufacturer's claim that his micro can be sailing within half an hour of arrival. One or two highly engineered designs actually can; but half a day is usually more realistic, with the same again for retrieval and loading. Unless you are fortunate enough to have a team of experienced helpers, the idea of making a return trip inside a weekend is better in theory than in practice, the assembly and rigging time

Fig 8.1 *'Firebird' in the Alps, a trailer sailer used as a caravan while* en route *to the holiday cruising area.*

being something of a lottery dictated by the way in which the hulls are fastened together and the arrangements for raising and lowering the mast. The type and layout of the trailer can also contribute to this, but its major influence is on the safety and pleasures – or worries – of the road journey.

In Europe prior to October 1983, when the EEC regulations came into force, the laws covering the use of light trailers were vague and contained a number of loopholes that left the user, and sometimes the police, in some confusion, allowing many unsafe car-and-trailer combinations out on the roads.

The law on your trail

The regulations can vary in detail between one country and another – and in the USA, even between neighbouring states – but they are

mostly similar in principle, with strict limitations on maximum weight, width and towing speed, and specifications governing the braking, coupling and lighting systems. The figures quoted here apply at the time of writing to Britain and the EC, and are fairly typical of those in other countries, but you should check the regulations covering your proposed trailering areas in case of any differences. Remember that it's always your responsibility, and not that of the firm that supplied the trailer, to ensure that it complies with the local laws. The police have the authority to stop and examine a trailer if they have any reason to suspect that it may be insecure, overweight or incompatible with the towing vehicle. It makes sense to obtain a copy of the regulations from one of the motoring organizations or a national

yachting authority such as the RYA in Britain, consult the car handbook, and unless you are certain of the weight of your boat (including its contents) and its trailer, visit your local weighbridge before towing them any further.

Fig 8.2 *The CC 26, designed by John Marples (USA) for amateur construction in wood by the constant camber method. It folds in the same way as the F27.*

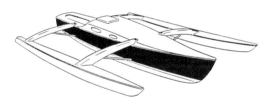

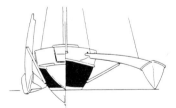

Speed and size constraints

Taking the simplest regulation first, the almost universal speed restrictions while towing a trailer are 60mph (96km/h) on motorways and 'split' highways, and 50mph (80km/h) on all other roads unless, of course, some lower limit applies, such as in built-up areas. On a long journey, you can usually reckon on averaging at least 35mph (say 55km/h), excluding overnight sleeping.

Size is also a fairly straightforward matter, especially since micros are designed for trailering, with the regulations in mind. The maximum 'normal' width of a trailer being towed by a car or a light commercial vehicle is 2.3m (7ft 6in), but since in many countries (including the UK) the load is permitted to project one foot (305mm) either side of the trailer, the boat including any projections can measure up to 2.9m (9ft 6in) wide. Nevertheless, in order to be on the safe side, and to be acceptable as universally as possible, the majority of production boats are built to a 2.5m limit in Europe, and generally 8ft 6in in the USA. Wider loads require two clear days' notice to the police, which is often impractical. While still on the subject of projections, any sharp ones (such as an outboard motor) that might constitute a danger to pedestrians or other vehicles in an accident, must be protected by a reinforced cover.

Length seldom presents a problem either, for although the general rule is that a trailer and its load must not exceed 7m (23ft), excluding drawbar and coupling, dispensation is given for an 'indivisible load', which a boat is considered to be; so in practical terms, 9m (29ft) is usually allowable without any raised eyebrows. There is no legal limitation on

height, but if the top of your load – usually the mast – is much more than about 3m (say 10ft) off the ground, you may occasionally find yourself in trouble with a low bridge or filling station roof, so watch out for them. Incidentally, make sure your rudder(s) and centreboards are locked up and the tiller tied to one side; and it's a good idea to put a lashing round the retracted jockey wheel – it might otherwise work loose and drop into contact with the road.

Weight and brakes

Although two-wheeled trailers are perfectly legal and capable of accepting the weight of a micro, the extra cost of a four-wheeled type is more than justified by its superior stability and convenience of handling. Unless the gross laden weight of the trailer is less than 750kg (1650lb), as would be the case with a dinghy or beach cat, it must be fitted with brakes on all wheels, including a handbrake for parking. On any trailers built since April 1989, these brakes must incorporate an auto-reversing system which pulls one of the shoes away from the drum when the wheel rotates backwards, as when the trailer is being backed. (Without auto-reverse, the driver must get out of the car and set the reverse catch to prevent the overrun linkage from applying the brakes.) When the trailer is parked facing uphill, a spring energy store attached to the handbrake pulls the brake lever further on, overriding the auto-reverse which would otherwise release the brakes.

The brakes are also required to be at least 50% efficient. This is very difficult to measure, and in practice about all you can do is check that they really seem to assist the braking of the rig, and that you do not feel the trailer pushing the car.

The ultimate limiting factor in towing is, of course, the weight of the load, and in this respect the unballasted multihull shows to advantage over a monohull trailer-sailer, whose lifting keel necessarily adds 30–40% to its weight. The car handbook will specify the maximum permitted tow weight and trailer

nose weight. Some cars can tow rather more than their own kerb weight – a few four-wheel-drive vehicles over twice as much – other models less, depending on their design and weight distribution. For example, a relatively heavy 900kg (1980lb) micro on a 400kg (880lb) trailer would be within the capabilities of most rear-wheel-drive cars of 2 litres and above. The lighter the load in relation to the permitted maximum, the easier the driving will be. Front-wheel-drive cars have rather less traction for towing, especially on steep gradients where the weight distribution shifts off the front wheels and on to the back ones.

There is no legal requirement governing trailer nose weight, but it should always be positive. You can measure it on a bathroom scale. For stable towing, roughly 5–10% of the total weight should be on the coupling ball. Nose weight can be adjusted by shifting a few heavy items, such as an anchor or the outboard motor, fore and aft in the boat. Too little

Fig 8.3 The 'Somersault 26' by Dick Newick (USA). The four short crossarms fit into tapered sockets on mainhull and floats. Cruising for two, daysailing for four, 20 knots capability, series production in FRP by Outrigger Boat Co., Chicago.

weight will result in snubbing and fishtailing, too much may result in loss of steering under hard braking; either can make the towing uncomfortable and possibly unsafe. It is also important that a four-wheeled trailer should tow in a level attitude. If the coupling is too high or too low, it will throw a large proportion of the weight on to a single axle, much to the detriment of handling and braking, at the same time overloading two of the suspension units and causing uneven tyre wear. The problem can be overcome by relocating the tow hitch, or by fitting a drop plate on the towbar. Above all, don't overload the trailer. Besides being illegal, overloading is the most frequent cause of accidents, and could also invalidate your insurance.

Couplings

The travel of the coupling when the tow vehicle decelerates and the trailer tries to over-run it, is linked to the rod that actuates the trailer brakes. The spring overrun couplings that were used for many years are still legal, and are undoubtedly robust and reliable, but hydraulically damped couplings provide better control and are nowadays mandatory on all new trailers. Also attached to the handbrake linkage of the coupling is a breakaway cable, its other end being looped around the towball or clipped on to the tow vehicle, so that if the coupling should fail or jump off the towball, the cable will pull the brakes on.

Tyres

The load capacity of any tyre depends on its pressure, load and speed. Never use agricultural or industrial tyres designed for slow-moving vehicles. Any tyre unfit for use on a car, whether from damage, wear or type of construction, is equally unfit for a trailer; and as with cars, you shouldn't mix radial and cross-ply tyres on the same axle, or if twin axle, on the same trailer. It's generally best to fit

Fig 8.4 *Detail of dovetail crossarm attachment to hulls of the all-plastic* Podcat. *Edges knock down spray, and holes provide attachment points for blocks and lines.*

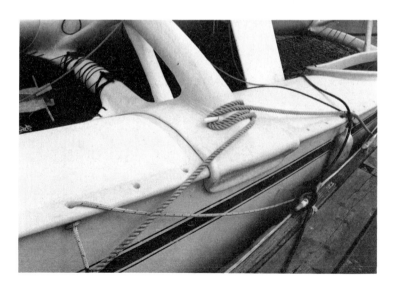

the same type of tyre to both car and trailer, and to observe the trailer manufacturer's recommended tyre size, although neither is mandatory. But maintaining the correct tyre pressures is an actual legal requirement and is liable to be checked by the police if they should stop you.

Lights

The regulations concerning the positioning of the various rear lights and reflectors are similar

Fig 8.5 *Telescopic trailer for an 8m (26ft) 'Strider'. Assembly and launching are possible singlehanded, easy for two.*

to those for a car and are somewhat complex. If your trailer is not already fitted with lights, it's simplest to go out and buy a ready-made lighting board incorporating the tail, brake, fog and number plate lights, direction indicators, and a pair of reflective triangles – rather than trying to fit one up yourself. The board is best carried on an extending frame on the trailer, but it can alternatively be fastened to the stern of the boat, and it should be detachable, terminating in a waterproof plug and socket as high above the ground as practicable. You will also need white front lights near the outer edges of the boat as a width warning to oncoming traffic, a pair of orange

reflectors on either side of the trailer frame, a 'long load' reflective triangle hung on the masthead where it overhangs the stern of the boat, and a heavy duty flasher relay, together with a bulb failure warning lamp on the fascia panel.

Aids and accessories

There are two devices that can make towing safer and more enjoyable (or less of a hack, depending on your attitude).

Spring assistors

The rear ends of cars, particularly those with soft suspension, will drop appreciably when the trailer nose weight comes down on the hitch, and the suspension may even bottom on an undulating road. Load levellers, in the form of auxiliary hydraulic struts, can be fitted to maintain the suspension in near normal trim as the trailer tries to depress it. (In fact, the Citroën hydraulic suspension self-levels, but it's about the only one that does.) Alternatively, coil or rubber spring assistors can be inserted either side between suspension and bump stop, or hard PVC rings can be fitted on coil springs to inhibit their compression.

Stabilizers

Tail wagging is an all too common occurrence, caused by excessive speed, buffeting from crosswinds or overtaking trucks (boats present quite a bulky profile high up on their trailers), incorrect weight distribution, or wrong tyre pressures. Braking only makes it worse, and can lead to jack-knifing. The correct response is to gently decelerate until the oscillation damps out naturally. The tendency to snaking can largely be eliminated, however, and its amplitude if it does start can be controlled, by means of a stabilizer, which comprises either a friction or a hydraulic damper unit bolted to the car's towbar, with an adjustable operating arm leading back to an attachment point on the trailer. This has the effect of resisting any relative angular movement between the two vehicles.

Other useful accessories

- Locks on tow hitch and spare wheel.
- Wheel clamps for when trailer is parked.
- Trolley jack capable of lifting trailer + boat.
- Spare wheel-bearings and the tools to fit them.
- Purpose-made triangular wheel chocks (better than bricks).
- Front tow hitch on the car (makes manoeuvring easier).
- Strong trailer mudguards to climb on.
- Ladder for access to the cockpit.
- If not already on the boat, a chemical toilet for roadside stops.
- Ball jockey wheel, or twin wheels, for soft ground or beach.
- Electric trailer winch for fingertip control.
- Docking arms to help guide the boat on if the trailer is submerged.

Trailer types

A conventional type of boat trailer is suitable for most trimarans, whose crossbeams and floats are either removed (two people can easily lift one) and stowed on chocks beside the main hull, or hinged inwards alongside it – in which case the boat is stable enough to be launched, motored around, docked or moored with floats still retracted.

The trailer itself may be equipped with a system of easy-loading rollers, typically comprising two sets of 16 rubber rollers which cradle the main hull. Each set is mounted on a swivelling crossmember which pivots transversely, and each individual pair is free to

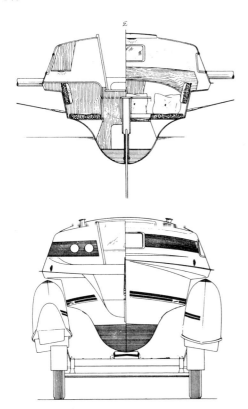

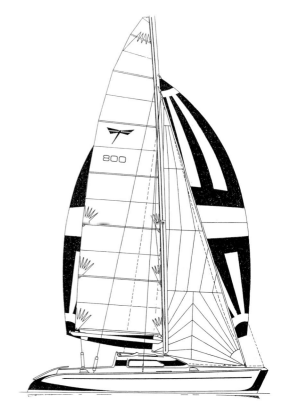

Fig 8.6 *8m (26ft) 'Dragonfly' by Quorning Boats (Denmark). Roomy little cruiser, competitive racer, stows neatly on simple 2-wheel trailer. The latest version, and its big sister the 31, have swing-in floats on the John Westell principle.*

pivot fore-and-aft. This not only enables the rollers to follow the exact shape of the hull and to spread the load evenly, but by allowing the boat to roll off the trailer and be winched back on to it at a steep relative angle, it keeps the precious wheel-bearings out of the salt water.

Another option is a separate 'piggyback' launching trolley, dinghy style, which runs the boat off the trailer and into the water. It can be provided with buoyancy tubes so that it floats, making it particularly easy to position prior to recovering the boat, which is then simply pulled ashore, up the ramp, and on to the trailer.

A cat trailer has to cater for a pair of full-sized hulls. The more elaborate types support these on a telescopic framework which allows them to be dragged apart for assembly while still on the trailer (and on some cats the crossbeams themselves are also telescopic). The mast is usually carried between the cabin tops on brackets, preferably with rubber rollers, at either end of the trailer – or in the case of a trimaran, on a transom crutch and forward pulpit – with most of the overhang above the roof of the tow car and as little as possible projecting behind the boat. Pad the mast well where it touches anything, and tie the rigging wires to it at intervals, otherwise they can chafe.

The most economical and trouble-free form of cat trailer, however, is a simple flat-bed of the type used for transporting cars, the

Fig 8.7 *Seeing double: this unstayed biplane rig on 7m (23ft) 'Aztec' hulls usually turns a few heads. The boat is fast, easy to trail and launch, but somewhat tricky to tack.*

hulls being stowed beside each other on individual wheeled chocks, the cockpit decking on its side between them, for assembly and rigging near the water's edge. It doesn't matter that these chocks get submerged; the trailer itself stays high and dry.

Stepping the mast

Provided that the raising and lowering equipment is properly engineered – and that you check carefully to see that there are no power lines for the mast to touch on its way up – this need not amount to the hair-raising experience that some first-timers expect. The essence of the process is not to rush it, and to keep continuous control of the mast.

Its heel will normally be hinged by hooking it under a baseplate, which prevents it from slipping, and on a trimaran (or a monohull) this must be raised sufficiently above deck

level for the lowered mast to clear the cabin top or other projections. Both objectives can conveniently be met by means of a sheet-metal box or three-sided bracket known as a tabernacle, in which the mast pivots on a hinge bolt. It has also to be restrained from swinging sideways, either by a helper on either side hanging on to the shrouds, or by arranging for their bottom toggles to be located in line with the mast pivot, so that they can maintain a constant tension throughout the 90° arc.

The raising and lowering is done either by taking the trailer winch wire to the masthead and winding the handle, or by using a three-part tackle between the trailer and the end of the forestay or a halyard, in each case with a strut, such as a spinnaker pole or the reversed boom, inserted between the hoist and the mast so as to maintain the pull at an effective angle. Both the lifting and the steadying can be accomplished simultaneously – and single-handed – by means of a wooden or aluminium A-frame, its feet hinged on either sidedeck and its apex hitched to the forestay or halyard. Dutch canal sailors, who frequently need to

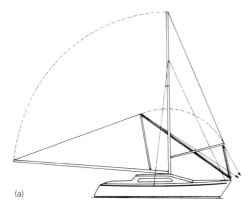

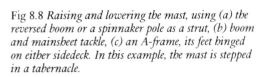

Fig 8.8 *Raising and lowering the mast, using (a) the reversed boom or a spinnaker pole as a strut, (b) boom and mainsheet tackle, (c) an A-frame, its feet hinged on either sidedeck. In this example, the mast is stepped in a tabernacle.*

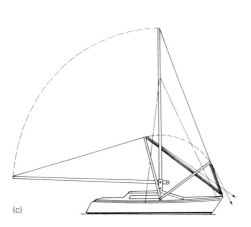

(a)

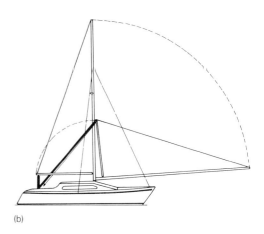

(b)

(c)

lower and re-raise their masts when passing under the many bridges, have an A-frame permanently mounted on their foredecks, but yours would normally be stowed on the trailer. An ingenious and particularly secure alternative is to combine the use of a raising strut with an A-frame whose feet are mounted aft of the mast pivot, with its apex carried on a slider in the luff groove of the mast.

Launching tips

- Check that the centreboard is still cleated in the fully 'up' position.

- Remove the trailer lighting board if it's liable to be dunked, and make sure the socket is capped.
- Warm wheel-bearings suck in water. If they are to be submerged and you can't wait for them to cool off, dowse them with a few buckets of fresh water.
- If you haven't gone to the expense of a multiple roller system or a launching trolley, consider the alternative cost of having the boat craned in and out, to avoid immersing the trailer.
- If you are a considerable distance from the dock or a mooring, start the engine as soon as it's in the water, so that you can back off when the boat floats.
- If you can make fast to something near by, take a stern line out to it, especially in an onshore breeze or a crosswind, which may otherwise blow the boat sideways back on to the ramp.

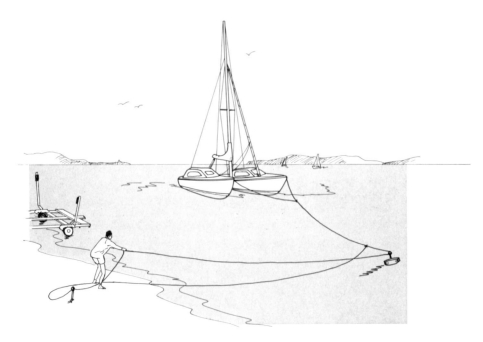

Fig 8.9 *Temporary mooring. A sinker, pulley block and a long line gets the boat offshore quickly after launching, and is useful for beach picnics on a falling tide.*

- Alternatively, use the dinghy to lay your own temporary mooring in the form of a heavy (say 30kg/65lb) flat-bottomed weight or 'frape' – not an anchor, if there's any possibility of its fouling other lines – with a stand-up block attached to it. Through this block is to run a long line, with its ends brought ashore, taken round a post or through another block fastened to a stake above the tide line, and tied together. A painter from the boat is then made fast to the frape line, and as soon as it has been launched it can be pulled out into deep water and left moored while someone parks the car and trailer. Do not, of course, rely on the sinker to hold in any sort of a blow, and be sure to allow enough scope on the painter for the depth at high water. When not in use, the line is best kept coiled up in something like a washing basket, from which it can run out freely.

- The same system works well for picnics ashore, the weight being dropped in the appropriate depth of water and the line paid out as you motor or drift astern on to the beach, and the boat pulled back out after the crew has disembarked. It saves launching the dinghy, or even getting your feet wet if the bank is steep to.

Procedures in cruising and racing, and heavy weather tactics

Because everything tends to happen faster on a multihull, sailing one to the full requires rather more basic skill and a higher standard of seamanship than with a monohull. The principles are the same, of course, but they sometimes have to be applied differently and often more rapidly to get the best out of the boat. It is not that multihulls are necessarily any more difficult to sail in leisurely fashion than the others – indeed many people find them easier – but they are a different breed and need to be sailed in a different way. It also takes a higher level of sustained concentration, quicker reactions, and better anticipation to sail one really fast and still remain within sensible safety limits, especially in heavy weather.

To anyone used to monohulls, the most noticeable differences on first acquaintance with a multi are the way it heels so little when you step aboard, its stiff and upright sailing stance, the vivid acceleration in a breeze, and how quickly way is lost the moment the breeze drops or the boat is brought head to wind; and that for much of the time the wind seems to be blowing from forward of the beam, whatever its direction when you left the mooring.

Apparent wind

It takes some getting used to, this business of the apparent windspeed and direction, and also the rapidity with which it can change as a consequence of the lively acceleration and high boatspeed potential – more noticeable, naturally, on a lightweight racer than on a heavier cruising cat. As we have already seen, the faster a boat goes, the more apparent wind it generates and the further ahead that wind will appear to be. On a breezy day, you will often be close reaching or even close hauled, even though the true wind is abaft the beam. Any further rise in speed will then cause the boat to be headed. You respond by bearing away, the boatspeed increases even more and the whole process is repeated as the boat 'feeds' on its own wind. It needs a certain amount of skill and experience to take advantage of this phenomenon without ending up headed in the wrong direction.

Instead of constantly playing the sheets and helm to take account of every variation of the wind, you may be quite content to jog along and take things easy, but you should remain continually aware – at least subconsciously – of where the wind is coming from and its strength; and stay alert. If the weather should turn squally, frequent sail trimming and heading corrections will become more important. It could happen, for instance, that after momentarily drawing ahead in a lull the apparent wind swings aft as the boat slows down, and if the sheets were not eased, or if you did not luff up, you might find yourself with sails pinned in just as the next gust hits you – from abeam. Conversely, if the breeze were suddenly to pipe up, the apparent wind would again draw aft and the boat would be over-sheeted until it had time to accelerate, or you luffed.

The effect of gusts

In puffy conditions on a monohull, not only are the changes in the apparent wind smaller in comparison and more gradual, but a gust will only lay the boat further over, the wind's energy being absorbed as she heels and effectively reduces the sail area while she gathers speed and gets back on her feet. For the performance multihull, with centreboards lowered, and largely prevented from heeling by the broad beam, so still presenting the full sail area to the wind, there is only one way to go and that is forwards, as rapidly as inertia will allow. If the sails should be seriously over-sheeted at the time, producing unnecessarily large heeling forces instead of maximum drive, not only will acceleration be sluggish, but if you happen to have left reefing a bit late and are already over-canvassed, the boat may approach the limit of stability. This is the condition necessary for flying a hull in a racing boat, the knife-edge balance being maintained by skilful playing of sheets and traveller (more about this later) but it should otherwise be avoided at all costs.

The good news is that when hard pressed, a modern lightweight multihull will usually forgive a bit of over-sheeting, and pick up speed quickly enough to restore the balance, and the shallow-keeled cruiser will simply skate sideways. But this has been one of the primary causes of capsize among the earlier types of narrow, centreboarded boats. The other is carrying too much sail. It doesn't matter so much on a keelboat; it just slows you down

and gives you a wet and uncomfortable time. Not so on a multi. So for peace of mind, unless you are racing – and even then, unless you are hell-bent on sailing on the limit – always reef early in blustery weather, raise the leeward board of a cat, if she has one, trim the sails continually, and if necessary feather them or gently luff the boat to reduce power at the height of a gust. In other words, 'ease back and enjoy the ride'.

Contrary to popular belief, most multihull capsizes have occurred because the boat was sailed over, not because she was blown over in gale force winds or rolled over by big seas; a number of these accidents have occurred in comparatively moderate winds and smooth water, when the crew were off guard and were caught out by a sudden vicious squall.

Releasing sheets

It makes sense in blustery conditions to keep the sheets and the traveller control lines close at hand, or preferably held so that they can be surged or let fly instantly. A big headsail should already have been rolled up or exchanged for a smaller one, but if it is still set, its sheet should be the first to be released in a gust, in order to relieve some of the pressure on the lee bow and at the same time to disturb the airflow across the main so that its drive is reduced. This is followed by the mainsheet, or preferably by its traveller (more about this later).

Ensure that the sheets are free to run out and are not being sat on or lying in a tangled heap where they can snarl up or catch on something. If using a winch, put the minimum number of turns round the drum that will accept the gust loads without slipping, for if it should do so, the chances are that the tail will jam in the cleat and require a hard yank to release it. This is less likely to happen to a mainsheet with a four- or six-part purchase; some high powered rigs need an eight-part tackle to minimize the tailing loads, usually with a ratchet sheave as well. But then the blocks must be as large and frictionless as possible, to allow the sheet to run out reasonably freely in light weather, despite the number of directional changes it has to follow. These powerful purchases are correspondingly slower to operate and they also involve a lot of extra rope lying about in the cockpit, so it pays to use the simplest system you can without excessive effort. The alternative is a double-ended mainsheet tackle, with one tail for fast sheeting and the other running through additional sheaves for slow, fine adjustment – a very effective arrangement, though still with lots of rope. Beyond this, in terms of mainsail size and power, the sheet has to be winched in, as on the big racers.

Self-tailing sheet winches, those wonderfully convenient labour savers, should never be used in their ST mode in heavy weather, particularly on small boats, because it takes appreciably longer to cast off the locking turn clear of the horn than to jerk the sheet out of a cleat and surge it round the drum. Any undue delay and a hull could be lifting before the excess pressure could be dumped off the sail, whereas on a larger, heavier boat there should be rather more time to act.

The cleats themselves must be one of the quick release types, cam or clam, and never of the traditional double horn variety which are much too slow to use for anything other than halyards or mooring warps. Automatic sheet releases have been used in the past with vary-

ing degrees of success, but unfortunately they cannot always be relied upon. One type operates on the pendulum principle, being adjustable to let go at a predetermined angle of heel – but the pendulum can be fooled if the boat is jumping about in a seaway. The other responds to wind force by releasing the sheet at a preset tension, but it has to be precisely adjusted by trial and error so that the gadget doesn't act prematurely from isolated shock loads, which could become very annoying, or too late, which might be disastrous. Like the unsightly masthead floats that used to add unwanted weight and windage aloft on many a cat as an anti-capsize safeguard – until it was found that they were more inclined to break away when the mast hit the water than to stop the boat inverting – automatic sheet releases are seldom fitted these days. In the last resort – with a riding turn on the winch, for example – the quickest and surest means of release is a sharp knife, which should always be carried in the cockpit, stowed where it is immediately accessible to the helmsman or sheet trimmer.

It is not the intention to sound alarmist with these references to hair trigger responses and the risk of capsize. In reality it is extremely unlikely, and the majority of people sail their cats and trimarans year after year without ever approaching their limits of stability. But it is as well to recognize that the possibility is always there, and to use normal care and common sense to avoid it.

Sailing close hauled

The ability to point high without losing speed is arguably the single most important key to fast sailing on any boat, and on a multihull the most difficult to achieve, because its wide per-

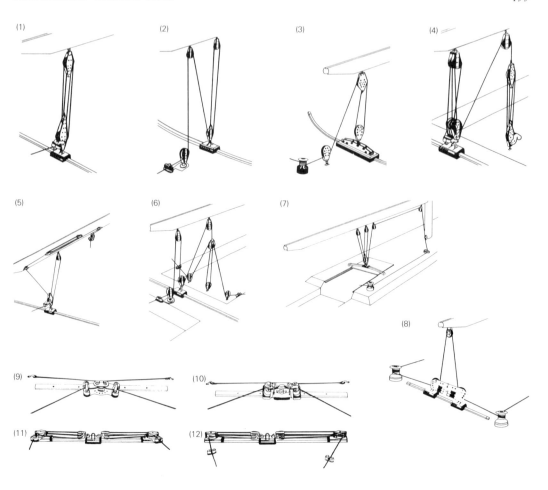

Fig 9.1 *Mainsheet and traveller control systems. (1) Simple four-part tackle for small boats. (2) Tailing mainsheet off traveller allows adjustment without dragging the car to windward. (3) Basic big-boat system with single winch. (4) Dual-purpose mainsheet tackle, 6:1 for fast trimming in light airs, 24:1 for fine tuning and more power in strong winds. (5) Fine tune tackle on the boom avoids tightening the leech as the car is moved off the centreline, and cleans up the cockpit. (6) Double-ended fine tune tackle puts the sheet on the cockpit sides. (7) Popular system on cruising boats leads the sheet round the companionway. (8) Simple double-ended system allows trimmer to sit to windward. (9) Basic traveller control (mounted on a car). (10) Windward sheeting traveller with 3:1 tackle and slider mechanism that allows the car to be pulled to windward without releasing the leeward control line. (11) 3:1 control line tackle with cleats at the track ends. (12) 4:1 tackle with cleats mounted at any convenient location.* (Diagrams: Harken)

formance envelope makes any speed differences due to fine tuning more apparent than on a monohull.

Looking first at sail setting in relation to the ship's head, over-sheeting the jib or genoa is a common fault when beating to windward, for although it may enable you to point higher, it will tend to choke the slot and backwind the main. One of the advantages of a fully battened main is that it will hold its shape better than a soft sail under these conditions. In a good breeze, a small amount of backwinding doesn't much matter, provided the rest of the sail is drawing powerfully, and – more importantly – the tight sheeting of the headsail will help to reduce any excessive weather helm, to the benefit of rudder drag and boatspeed. Conversely, hardening in the main will increase the weather helm and reduce the backwinding, but if you overdo it, you will end up with the entire rig over-sheeted and lacking power. What's more, if you open up the slot too much, it will lose its effect on the airflow across the main (see pp. 89–90). Adjustment of the slot becomes less important as the wind strengthens, but in light to moderate airs it is critical to boatspeed. Another mistake is to pinch up too much in trying to lay your course, especially in light airs or in a seaway, to the detriment of both speed and the amount of leeway the boat will make. The sail luffs may not be quite lifting, but upwind progress will be unnecessarily slow. This applies particularly to shallow-keeled cruising cats, which need to be sailed more fully than centreboard boats to keep their speed up and avoid excessive leeway. Crack the sheets and allow the rig to breathe, bear away a few degrees, and the boat will come to life again.

Once speed is restored, you can experiment by hardening in the sheets again, a little at a time, and try heading very slightly higher without losing boatspeed. The moment it shows any sign of dropping back, ease off a fraction and you should find yourself nicely in the groove, ready for the next wind fluctuation. If it's slight, there'll be no need to touch the sheets; a small helm correction is usually sufficient.

In the very lightest of airs, when you are creeping along with scarcely enough wind to lift the mainsheet off the deck, all trim adjustments must be delicate and finely judged. Give the sails their maximum fullness and list the boat to leeward if you can, avoid any jerky movements about the boat that might shake

what little wind there is out of them, pay close attention to the telltales (explanation later) and restrict helm corrections to the minimum. The crew should be positioned sufficiently far forward to ensure that the transoms are clear of the water; and in a trimaran, depressing the leeward float with the weight of one or more crew-members may also allow you to point up a few degrees by inducing a bit of weather helm without incurring any rudder drag. Under these conditions, you can increase the apparent wind by motor-sailing at low revs, which will not only keep the sails filled, but will enable you to point higher to the benefit of VMG (see p. 165).

In ghosting conditions you can also make use of the tide on some headings, when it is setting against and across the wind, not only to push the boat along but thereby to generate an increase in the apparent windspeed and hence in the drive of the sails. It may pay you to bear away slightly to achieve this. The increase due to 'lee-bowing' may be barely noticeable, but if it gains you a mile during an hour's frustrating drifting, it will have been worthwhile.

Tacking

Any well designed boat will sail to windward without a headsail, and most keelboats will also tack quite normally without one. But some multihulls are difficult to tack bareheaded, particularly in a jumpy sea; being so light they cannot be relied on to carry their way long enough for the bows to swing through the eye of the wind. The surest way of main-only tacking is to first ease the sheet and bear away to get speed up, then head up and sheet in; keep the helm down and ease the sheet as the bows come through the wind to avoid the tendency to weathercock until the head has paid off on the other tack; and then wait for speed to build up again before heading up on to the new course.

A jib or genoa, as well as increasing the boatspeed and hence the momentum prior to the tack, can if necessary be kept sheeted to weather until it has back-filled to help the head round. It should then be brought across and smartly sheeted in on the other side to keep the bows swinging, and before the main has a chance to drive them up again. Given reasonably smooth water, a two-sail tack should always be started from hard on the wind; but with a light micro, if there is a sea running, it may be advisable to let her pay off and get plenty of way on before attempting the manoeuvre. If you see a squall coming, either begin luffing for the tack the moment it hits you and complete it before the gust has passed; or wait, because the wind will usually veer in the gust and might catch you in stays.

If the worst happens, and you find yourself in irons, lying head to wind, all you have to do is let fly the sheets, reverse the helm and wait until you have developed enough sternway to turn on to the new tack. In a crowded anchorage or river, don't be in too much of a hurry to do this. A multihull can be steered astern with precision, so long as she remains nearly head to – indeed, with the appropriate sails held a-back, sailing backwards is a very useful method of close-quarters manoeuvring. With the boom over the same side as the tiller, you can then back on to your new close hauled heading before powering up again, but give yourself plenty of room to pay off until the keels bite.

Heaving to

A variation on the tacking procedure is to put the helm down without touching the sheets, so that the boat tacks and then lies hove-to, with jib a-back and almost stationary at an angle of 40–40° off the wind, fore-reaching at a knot or two, tiller lashed to leeward and centreboard(s) still lowered. This is an invaluable tactic if you want to leave the helm while you put the kettle on, or to wait around at a rendezvous without losing too much ground to leeward. Most multihulls refuse to stop dead in the water like a heavy displacement keelboat will, but they can usually be made to behave quite well by easing the main to reduce its tendency to drive the boat up into the wind, and freeing the jib until it acts as an effective brake without pushing the bows too far off. Some boats will happily heave to with centreboards raised and sheets released, although the sails will flog if it's windy. You will probably have to fiddle around with the tiller to find the best position for it, but this can be done while eating a sandwich.

Anchoring

Because multihulls are essentially lightweight craft, it is important not to weigh them down with long lengths of anchor cable. This applies particularly to micros. Four or five metres of chain is needed next to the anchor to ensure that its pull is horizontal along the seabed, and to withstand abrasion, but the rest of the rode should be of nylon, using at least five times the maximum predicted depth of water during your stay – much more in a blow. Unfortunately the combination of a long, light cable with a shoal draught lightweight boat will make it ill-behaved in a popular anchorage, sheering about with every fluky shift of the wind or sailing up over her anchor, while any neighbouring monohulls, heavier and deeper, and usually lying to chain cables, will remain almost stationary and docilely stemming the tide until they swing at slack water. Leaving your centreboard down will

Fig 9.2 *Lying to two anchors on a bridle. (1) Let go first anchor, fall back and secure second anchor chain. (2) Set first anchor and drop second anchor. (3) Move ahead and set second anchor, being careful not to foul the prop. (4) Drop back on bridle. (5) Watch out for other boats which are probably on single anchors. Keelboats may swing towards you when the tide turns, and a wind across the tide could make matters worse by blowing you in their direction while they remain tide rode.*

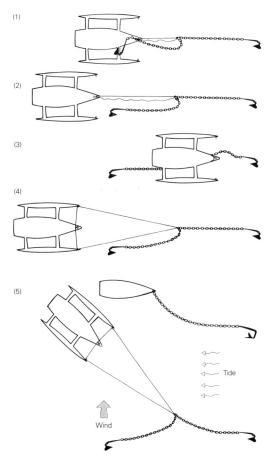

(1)

(2)

(3)

(4)

(5)

Wind

Tide

help to steady the boat, but this is not to be recommended, for fear of snagging your cable, or someone else's.

There are, however, several things you can do to improve the situation, apart from the obvious one of anchoring somewhere else, well away from the rest of the fleet (which you often can do, because of your shallow draught), or of taking the ground there for a quiet and peaceful night. If there is no alternative to the anchorage, try sliding a heavy weight, such as a bundle of chain or another anchor, down the warp on a shackle attached to a retrieval line. This will have the effect of damping the movement of the warp and reducing the surging.

When anchoring – and the same goes for mooring – multihulls always benefit from using a bridle to the hull or float bows, instead of lying to a single central cable. The bridle lines should run from mooring cleats on either bow of a cat, or out to snatchblocks on a tri's float bows (rather than through fairleads, which can cause chafe) joining the anchor warp some distance ahead of the bows, preferably right down at the start of the anchor chain, or the riser of a mooring. The bridle's straightening effect will to some extent restrain the boat from sawing left and right, and will act as a failsafe by doubling up on the warp. On small boats, depressing the bows with some additional weight can also have a stabilizing effect.

Better still, the bridle can be used in conjunction with two anchors to give multi-directional security in changing wind or tide. Their positioning will depend on the conditions; normally they are best laid up and down the tidal stream in a river, or along the prevailing or forecast windpath in an open anchorage. The routine is to drop the first anchor, fall back and shackle on the second anchor chain; then set the first anchor firmly in, drop the second anchor, run forward and set it; and finally drop back on the twin warps of the bridle.

Use of telltales

A windvane, mounted on the masthead or just above deck level ahead of the forestay, provides a quick indication of the apparent wind angle through which you can expect to have tacked after you have picked up speed again, and of your optimum upwind heading. But since this varies with windspeed, a windvane can only serve as a rough guide. By far the most valuable and sensitive aid to sail trim is a set of airflow telltales. These can be made from artificial yarn (not wool, which is too heavy when it's wet) or narrow strips of spinnaker nylon – or better still, short pieces of magnetic tape from a scrap cassette. They should be attached, using self-adhesive cloth patches or waterproof plasters, three or four on either side of the jib or genoa, about 30cm (1ft) behind the luff – say 50cm (1½ft) on a roller headsail, so that they operate in air undisturbed by the luff foil – and spaced out along its length. It helps to have a small window in the headsail in the way of the bottom pair of telltales so that both can be seen simultaneously, which is otherwise difficult unless the sun is behind the sail and silhouetting the leeward one. Mainsail luff telltales are not essential, because the sail itself will tell you what is happening to the airflow around its forward areas, but its behaviour further aft can be clearly indicated by single streamers on the leech between the battens.

The general principle, having got the boat settled on course to windward, is to start with the jib and try to sheet it so that all its telltales stream horizontally, and all begin to lift and dance as the boat is luffed above her optimum heading. If the windward telltales lift first, either you are pointing too high or the sail is too open and you are under-sheeted. Check that you are not pinching, and pull in the sheet until the telltales stream. If the leeward telltales break first, you are sailing too low or the sail is too close. Check that you haven't strayed off the wind, and ease the sheet until those telltales behave. Now luff again slowly. They should all break together, but the chances are they won't.

Controlling sail shape

Still with the jib, if the upper windward telltale misbehaves first, there is too much twist in the sail (see pp. 91–2). The aim is for the luff to be in line with the apparent wind all the way up from tack to head, so in order to reduce the twist you move the sheet fairlead forward. If the upper leeward telltale lifts while the lower ones are streaming nicely – or if the lower windward telltale flutters and the uppers behave – the sail needs more twist: move the fairlead aft. And vice versa.

You can also vary the amount of twist by adjusting halyard tension. The sailmaker builds fullness into a sail by tapering its component panels towards their ends, instead of using parallel-sided strips of cloth, to produce a slight bagginess when they have been sewn together, and he then cuts the luff with a convex curve. Increasing the luff tension by tightening the halyard reduces the twist and at the same time flattens the sail and draws its fullness forward, which is one way of reducing its power to suit increasing wind strengths until it's time to reef. Too tight a luff, though, and you begin to lose pointing ability, besides wasting power. Conversely, easing the halyard increases twist, the camber moves aft and deepens, powering up the sail. You need maximum fullness in light airs, but again you may not be able to point so high; and watch the upper windward telltale for signs of lifting. You also need fullness to power you through rough water, and more often than not, this conflicts with the need to de-power in strong winds, so a compromise setting is called for when it is both bumpy and windy.

A simple way of seeing what effect each control has on the sail is to over-adjust them one at a time, leaving the others fixed. The halyard should normally be tightened only just hard enough to eliminate wrinkles, the setting for maximum camber and light winds. Now over-tighten the halyard until a hard crease appears, the upper part of the sail being drawn almost flat and the leech curling back inboard. Then note how, as you progressively ease the halyard, camber reappears in the head of the sail. The leech opens out and eventually begins to flutter as the position of maximum draught moves aft of centre and tries to drag the boat over instead of driving her. Forty to fifty per cent of the distance back from luff to leech is usually about right.

Next try moving the sheet fairlead fore and aft. Pushing it too far forward will slacken the foot and over-tighten the leech, which will hook in and ruin the flow on to the mainsail; too far aft will produce too much twist and a wide open leech, losing power and spoiling the slot between jib and main. The best results are usually achieved when foot and leech tensions are approximately equal, and this occurs when

the line of the sheet, extended across the sail, meets the luff at or fractionally below its midpoint.

Control of mainsail shape follows similar principles, but the methods are different and more varied. The halyard can be used, as before, to tension the luff and counter the tendency for fullness to increase and be forced aft with increasing wind strength. Tightening the halyard restores the camber to its correct depth and position, but the same effect can be more conveniently achieved by tensioning the Cunningham downhaul. This consists of a line leading up from somewhere near the base of the mast, through a cringle a short distance above the tack and down to a cleat; or a tackle to do the same thing with more power.

Some high performance boats are fitted with halyard locks on their masts, in the form of hooks or latches which engage with a corresponding fitting on the headboards of the main and jib when they are fully raised, so as to eliminate the effect of halyard stretch. The respective downhauls must then be used to control luff tension.

Mainsails are often provided with a leech Cunningham as well, the two together constituting a 'flattening reef'. Fullness can also be varied by tensioning the foot of the sail, using the clew outhaul tackle on the boom – essential with loose-footed mainsails – and by using the rigging controls to induce mast bend (see p. 94). The latter, along with halyard tension, is the most effective means of shaping a fully battened mainsail which, compared to a soft sail, is much less responsive to minor adjustments. Foot tension, for example, only affects the lower panel (except on loose-footed sails), because the camber is to a large extent predetermined by the stiffness of the battens themselves and the degree to which they were tensioned before the sail was raised – the more the tension, the greater the camber, and vice versa.

A rotating mast provides another means of varying the draught or camber, in addition to smoothing the entry of the airflow on to the forepart of the sail. Its setting will depend on the shape of the mast section, the cut of the sail and the batten tension, together with the tension in the diamond stays and the rake of the spreaders, both of which are used to vary the amount of mast bend, and hence the shape of the sail. A typical angle for beating in light airs would be about 30° to the centreline of the boat, giving the mast a pronounced bend to leeward, accompanied by a slight bend forward from the tension in the diamond stays, and producing a deep camber in the sail. In strong winds, the mast might be rotated to 60° or more, resulting in the more pronounced bend being forwards, dragging the fullness out of the sail. Alternatively, above Force 6 the mast angle can either (contrary to normal practice) be reduced so as to spoil the flow and depower the sail; or increased to such an extent that the camber in the top third of the sail is actually reversed, with the middle flat, and only the bottom third driving. Under normal conditions, however, control of mainsail draught must be balanced against the need to set the angle for optimum airflow across the sail, as indicated by the telltales. In practice, you will seldom find yourself overpressed in winds below about 15 knots, or say Force 5, when you'll be thinking of reefing anyway, so you will usually only need to ignore the telltales in heavier airs.

Shaping the mainsail leech is a more positive process than that for the jib, achieved by

POWER CONTROL CHECKLIST

Use of the various power controls, some of which (marked *) are unlikely to be used – or even fitted – on the average cruising boat, but which play an important role in performance sailing and racing, can be summarized as follows.

In light airs or rough water, to set rig for maximum power (at the expense of some speed and pointing ability) – equivalent to selecting a low gear in a car for hard acceleration or hill climbing:

- Ease sheets, traveller(s) up
- Reduce main and jib luff tensions (halyard or Cunningham)
- Loosen masthead runners*
- Under-rotate mast*
- Tighten diamond stays*
- Rake spreaders aft*
- Reduce foot tension (ease main outhaul, jib lead forward)
- Battens fairly tight

In strong winds or smooth water, to de-power rig – equivalent to high gear for top speed:

- Harden in sheets, traveller(s) down
- Increase luff and foot tensions
- Tension masthead runners
- Over-rotate mast (but see text)
- Loosen diamond stays
- Rake spreaders forward
- Battens fairly loose

the simple expedient of pulling down the boom with the mainsheet to adjust twist (assuming no vang system). The angle of the boom and that of the sail as a whole, relative to the centreline, is then set by moving the mainsheet tackle across on its traveller. The objective is for all the telltales to stream aft together, indicating that smooth laminar flow is being maintained along both sides of the sail. If those on the upper part of the sail are flapping about erratically or hiding behind it, there is turbulence on the leeward side, due to its not being angled to match the higher windspeed aloft. This may be because the jib has more of a backing effect on the lower part of the main, especially on a fractional rig, supplementing the natural differential in apparent windspeed with height. In other words, it hasn't enough twist and the leech needs to be opened by easing the sheet and bringing the traveller up to windward so as to maintain the trim. This is usually only necessary in light weather.

If there is too much twist, with the leech sagging open and the boat trying to heel as the wind freshens, you correct it by simply letting the traveller down to leeward and correspondingly hardening the mainsheet. In anything of a breeze, the sheet should be pulled in as tight as you can get it; as well as minimizing twist and weather helm, it helps to keep the forestay straight for good pointing ability. If you need to feather during the gusts, ease the sheets (genoa first, if it's a large one) or let off the traveller still further. In the northern hemisphere, gust cells normally cause the wind to veer as it strengthens, and to back in the lull; so the apparent wind's change of direction is likely to be much greater on starboard tack than on port. (Antipodeans, please read port for starboard; your wind *backs* in a gust.) Since the apparent wind tends to draw aft in a gust, playing the traveller is a quicker and more effective way, in most boats, of dumping the excess power than easing either of the sheets, which is liable to produce a bag of sail that increases the heeling force. As boatspeed increases and pulls the wind forward again, or as the puff passes, it is easier to pull back the traveller to its previous position than to heave in metres of sheet and judge the trim all over again. But for this a long traveller track is essential. If your boat doesn't have one, try

doing both at once – letting down the traveller as well as easing the mainsheet just enough to twist off the leech and spill some wind, without making the sail too full bellied. Some skippers prefer to do this anyway, even with a long track. Despite the extra handful of string, they find it the fastest procedure of all. Incidentally, neither of these methods applies to racing dinghy cats, with their comparatively short lengths of sheet and hair trigger responses, the favoured procedure being to leave the traveller positioned as near amidships as the average wind strength allows, continually pumping the mainsheet to regulate the power and the angle of heel.

Reaching

The cockpit geometry of some cruising boats restricts them to a short mainsheet track. Once the wind angle has opened sufficiently to take the boom beyond the end of its track, it must be held down with the vang, which is mechanically a less efficient way of doing it, although fortunately the further you head off the wind, the less critical the sail shape becomes and the less meaningful the antics of the telltales. (With a long enough track, there's no need for a vang; but on boats with only a fixed mainsheet anchorage it must of course be used all the time.)

As with monohulls, reaching is the fastest point of sailing, with the apparent wind blowing from between slightly forward to slightly aft of the beam. For the fast multihull, this means that except in very light airs, the true wind will be somewhere out on the quarter and drawn forward by the speed of the boat, which in turn will be noticeably affected by quite small alterations in your heading. Time can often be saved, when the rhumb line course to an objective requires a broad or a quartering reach, by bringing the apparent wind on to the beam so as to increase boatspeed, and partially raising a centreboard until you judge you are making sufficient leeway to compensate for the change in heading. Similarly, when reaching at right angles across a tidal stream with the wind on the opposite side to it, you can hold your speed by lifting a board and using the leeway to maintain course, instead of aiming off downwind and slowing the boat.

It also makes an interesting and rewarding experiment with a new boat to sail an acceleration curve, preferably in a light breeze, beginning with a quartering reach, sails trimmed accordingly and a cat's leeward centreboard fully raised. You will probably find the main still drawing powerfully with the boom right out and almost touching the shrouds, so unless you can see the luff collapsing, resist the temptation to sheet in at this stage. Oversheeting the main is a common mistake when reaching, stalling the sail, losing power,

Fig 9.3 When reaching in heavy weather resist any temptation to luff in a squall. Centrifugal force could capsize the boat over the heavily loaded leeward hull.

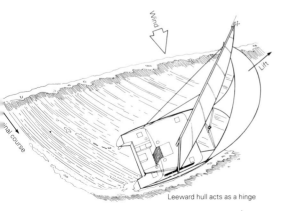

Leeward hull acts as a hinge

and increasing both weather helm and heeling. A rotating mast should be squared off to 80–90° to optimize the airflow, and had you intended staying on this heading, you would slacken off the clew outhaul as well.

The jib should also be freed well off, and unless your boat has a second sheet track for the headsail further outboard, you can considerably improve the shape of the sail by rigging a barber hauler, comprising a line to a snatch block on the sheet, or hooked to the clew and running via a block on the hull or float back to the cockpit. A barber hauler can also be used instead of the vang to hold down the boom when running or reaching, but make sure you can release it easily.

As the boat accelerates and the apparent wind increases and swings towards the beam, sheet in to maintain the trim; speed will continue to build and you keep on sheeting in until you are tramping along at or near top speed on a close reach, with the wind just forward of the beam. Such is the overall increase in the apparent wind during this manoeuvre that if you were to begin it in a moderate breeze of, let's say, 12 knots of true wind (Force 4), you would probably feel the need to reef by the time you were close reaching. With experience, of course, you might have done so before you started it. On a multihull it always pays to take reefs early; it is easy enough to shake them out if you find they are not needed.

In strong winds, with the sails developing maximum power and the boat at top speed, close reaching is also the point of sailing with the highest risk of capsize. However, you are unlikely to approach the stability limit, provided you are suitably reefed and have retracted a cat's lee centreboard – and partially raised the windward one as well (the only one, in the case of most tris) if the conditions should become worrying. If the boat should then become temporarily overpowered in a squall and you want to ease her through it by altering course, it is *absolutely vital* to resist the keelboat sailor's natural instinct to luff the boat. This cannot be emphasized too strongly. Because by doing so you would add considerable centrifugal force to the sideways pressure of the sails, and the combined capsizing moment could be enough to take her over, especially if while luffing you were to bring the boat broadside on to a heavy breaking sea. Instead, you should immediately bear away, so as to sail the boat back under the mast head, and run off downwind until the gust has passed. Similarly, if you are hard on the wind and becoming overpressed, bear away. Sail pressure should ease automatically as the rig stalls, but for safety's sake pay out plenty of sheet or traveller line as quickly as you can, and power up again – or take another reef – when you've taken stock of the situation. Only when you are already pinching up with sails feathering in a squall is it preferable to luff – and then only gently – because bearing off on to a reach takes longer, sail power will increase dramatically, and the boat will accelerate just when you want to slow down.

Running

Because of its freedom from rolling, the multihull gives you a steady and relaxing ride downwind, without the continual large helm corrections needed on a keelboat. Its boom and mainsail leech are not swaying about under constant threat of being caught by the wind on the wrong side, followed by an unintentional gybe. If it is a light boat it is also, because of its low drag, sailing at possibly three-quarters of the true windspeed, so there's relatively little airflow across the deck and gybing in a gentle breeze is just a matter of grabbing the mainsheet tackle and heaving the boom over.

In really strong winds there are, however, a couple of inherent dangers in this serene state of affairs. Under open sea conditions, when the waves themselves can sometimes be travelling at anything up to 10–15 knots, their speed is effectively added to the speed of the boat as she is picked up and carried along on the crest. The apparent wind can then actually swing *ahead* and back the sails into an unexpected gybe, so avoid this by rigging a preventer. The other potential hazard is present if you intend altering course on to a reach; because as you do so – for example when rounding a buoy – the apparent windspeed can jump from 5 knots to 35 knots in a few seconds as the boat accelerates through the turn, and you may suddenly find you are carrying far too much sail for the good of your health, adding considerably to the risks of capsizing while luffing in strong winds. Always try to anticipate such changes in the strength of the apparent wind – an instrument with a true windspeed readout makes this much easier – and shorten sail before arriving at the mark; or safer still in strong winds, drop the main before you begin the run and set a spinnaker which you can douse or let fly whenever you want to.

Spinnaker handling

The multihull's wide sheeting platform makes spinnaker handling much easier than on a monohull by avoiding the need for a pole, one

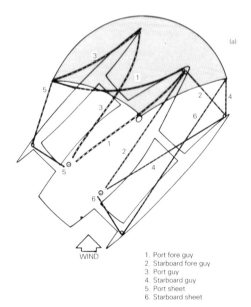

1. Port fore guy
2. Starboard fore guy
3. Port guy
4. Starboard guy
5. Port sheet
6. Starboard sheet

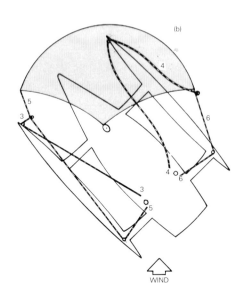

Fig 9.4 *Spinnaker controls. (a) Layout of sheets and guys for poleless spinnaker handling on a trimaran; arrangement on a cat is similar. The fore guys can be replaced by a bowsprit prodder to steady the windward clew. (b) Simplified poleless control layout.*

be positioned to suit the apparent wind direction. A hinged bowsprit or 'prodder' is also fitted on most racing boats to push the tack out ahead of the forestay, so as to give even better control on a tight reach. And if you don't mind the added complication, two more lines can be rigged as fore-guys, running from the clews to central blocks on the deck or crossbeam ahead of the forestay, to enable either clew to be hauled inboard. An excellent alternative is to attach each guy to a barber hauling block running on its respective sheet, so that by pulling in the guyline on the windward side, the sheet is carried down towards the weather bow to act as the guy. This set-up provides a good range of adjustments.

The object is to keep the two clews level with one another, with the line of an imaginary pole between the windward clew and the mast at right angles to the wind. Trimming consists of constantly playing the leeward sheet, freeing it until the leading edge of the sail starts to curl and collapse, hardening quickly to refill it, easing it until the sail is once more on the verge of breaking, and again hardening until it's firm. This is the trim for maximum drive; oversheet and you lose power, as with any other sail. Gybing is just a matter of letting go one guy, pulling in the other, and retrimming the sheets. A nylon squeezer tube or plastics spiral, in which the sail is stowed, hoisted and lowered, makes setting and dowsing relatively quick and easy, and eliminates the possibility of a spinnaker wrap while hoisting.

On a fast multihull, the spinnaker itself should be cut much flatter than a monohull's, to operate over a wider range of windspeeds without collapsing. Depending on the seastate, it can safely be carried on a run by a light, fast boat – but not by a slow cruiser or

clew of the sail being flown instead from each hull or float. The sheets are led back to the cockpit in the usual way via a block on each quarter, and guys are rigged through blocks on each bow, these four lines allowing the sail to in heavy seas – in winds as high as 25 knots or so (Force 6) because of the low apparent windspeed; but you should restrict its use on other points of sailing to reasonably light weather, or risk blowing it out. A flat spinnaker can usually be flown until the wind comes 10–15° forward of the beam. Sailing beyond this calls for an asymmetric cruising chute. They are easy to handle and some of them, depending on how they are cut, remain stable on headings as close as 10° apparent. Though less efficient than a true spinnaker on a run, it makes an extremely useful multi-purpose sail. Having only the one clew, when gybing this has to be pulled round ahead of the forestay and across to the other side, but surprisingly it will continue to function 'back-to-front' until there is an opportunity to reverse it. Cruising chutes are nominally designed to be used with either one sheet or two, and a central tack strop which can be paid out to fly the kite as high as necessary for its stability, but the four- or six-line arrangement gives much better control – at the expense of rather a lot of extra string.

Downwind tacking

The quickest way to reach a downwind objective in light airs, except with the fastest boats, is to sail directly towards it, because any speed gained by aiming off is often more than offset by the extra distance travelled. But downwind tacking begins to pay off – depending on the design of the boat and the sails, and assuming, of course, that you have enough sea room – in winds of Force 3 to 4, say around 10 knots in the average cruiser, less than half that in a featherweight racer or dinghy cat. This is because when sailing dead downwind, the

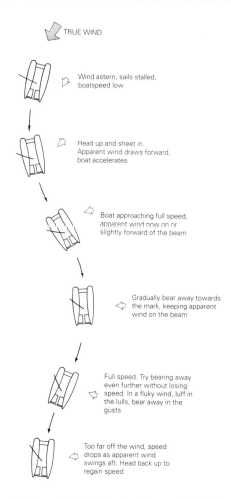

TRUE WIND

Wind astern, sails stalled, boatspeed low

Head up and sheet in. Apparent wind draws forward, boat accelerates

Boat approaching full speed, apparent wind now on or slightly forward of the beam

Gradually bear away towards the mark, keeping apparent wind on the beam

Full speed. Try bearing away even further without losing speed. In a fluky wind, luff in the lulls, bear away in the gusts

Too far off the wind, speed drops as apparent wind swings aft. Head back up to regain speed

Fig 9.5 *Downwind helming in a fast multihull. For best speed in a good breeze, it pays to sail an acceleration curve, followed by a freeing curve. The snaking course is less pronounced the slower the boat or the lighter the wind.*

mainsail – and to a lesser extent the jib – is dead too, completely stalled and developing only the drag of its profile in the direction of travel. The boat is simply being blown along like a flat silhouette, square to the wind and unable to reach the apparent windspeed by its own forward movement. To do this, each sail must be made to generate lift by allowing the wind to blow across both its sides – in other words, by turning the boat on to a reach, first on one gybe and then on the other, without straying too far off the direct rhumb line course.

The faster the boat, the further the apparent wind may with advantage be brought forward. For dinghy cats and other racers, this usually means a beam reach, but on a slower boat this would almost certainly take you too far off course for the more modest speed increase to compensate for the extra distance sailed. If you can find a pair of suitable marks, or can lay them using danbuoys, try sailing a series of short downwind legs against a stopwatch, first on the rhumb line and then tacking through compass angles varying from 20° up to about 80°, to see the effect and determine the best tactics with your particular boat. Better still, calculate the VMG on each heading, or use a meter (explanation later).

Downwind tacking can also be used to take you into a more favourable position – to cheat the tide, for example. The amount of aim-off and the resultant tacking angle will vary with wind strength and boatspeed, and just to complicate matters you should actually sail a snaking course between tacks, starting with an acceleration curve as you luff away from the rhumb line to gain speed, followed by a freeing curve as you bear away towards the mark as much as you can without significantly losing speed. Perfecting this technique calls for a lot of practice and cruising folk mostly don't bother with it; it's hard work for somewhat limited rewards. But if you are racing or are otherwise in a hurry with a reasonably fast boat, it's well worth persevering with it, because even when you don't get it quite right, you can still gain several valuable seconds on even a short downwind leg. Upwind, VMG has an even more important part to play.

Velocity Made Good (VMG)

As the term implies, VMG is the boat's speed made good towards an objective – speed through the water, that is, not allowing for any tidal stream or leeway. When this lies to windward, VMG indicates how fast you are sailing towards the eye of the wind; and conversely when the objective is downwind, how fast you are moving away from the wind. In the latter case, when sailing dead downwind, VMG and boatspeed naturally have the same value. On all other points of sailing, VMG equals

Fig 9.6 *Velocity Made Good (VMG). Progress towards the objective counts for more than sheer boatspeed through the water. These diagrams show the VMG to windward recorded on the author's trimaran in 15 knots of true wind.*

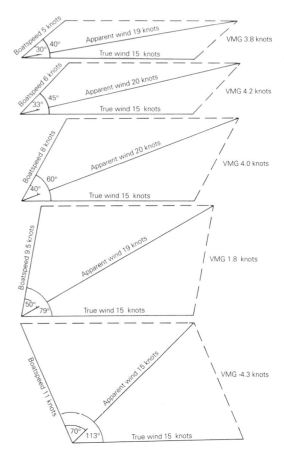

boatspeed times the cosine of the angle sailed towards the true wind (or away from it, when the true wind is aft of the beam). Its value can either be calculated at the chart table, or more easily read directly off an electronic instrument, which automatically computes it on inputs from the log and masthead wind unit, the object being to sail at maximum VMG, if navigational considerations allow.

For an example of how VMG might vary with your heading, suppose you are helming a typical cruising micro (the figures that follow were in fact recorded on the author's own boat). The sea is calm, the true wind a steady 15 knots, and you have pinched up to windward as close as you reasonably can, so that the sails are only just driving. The apparent wind angle is 30°, true wind 40°, your boatspeed a mere 5 knots and your wake shows that you are probably making quite a bit of leeway; VMG works out at 3.8 knots. You try bearing away 3°, the true wind frees to 45°, your wake straightens, speed immediately picks up to 6 knots and VMG to 4.2 knots. So far, so good. You come further off the wind to 40° apparent and the speed jumps to 8 knots; but the true wind is now at 60° and the VMG has eased back to 4 knots. Next, you try 50° apparent and soon you are up to 9.5 knots. The boat really seems to have come alive, but the true wind is round to 79° and the VMG needle has slunk back to 1.8 knots. Finally you free off to 70° and you are slicing along at 11 knots – surely this must be what multihull sailing is all about. But the boat is now heading at 113° to the true wind, with the result that VMG reads *minus* 4.3 knots: you are actually travelling *away* from the mark.

Sailing downwind, the story is different. Boatspeed increases as soon as the heading is altered to bring the wind off the stern, but to a much greater extent than in the initial part of the upwind case, because of the large and immediate gain in the efficiency of the sails. VMG also rises until the optimum off-wind angle is reached – typically some 30°–40° off the true wind, depending on wind strength and your boatspeed, with the apparent wind more or less abeam. In practice, once the heading for best VMG has been established, the boat should be tacked downwind, sea room permitting, in a series of gybes through twice the optimum VMG angle.

In either circumstance, the increase in VMG indicates the extent to which the extra distance is justified by the increased speed through the water. To windward, the balance between sailing free and fast, or closer to the wind and slower, is a delicate one. The latter tactic usually pays off in smooth water, while the former is necessary to keep the boat moving in a seaway. Downwind, the trade-off in increased mileage for a faster passage, or a reduced time to the next mark, is clearly beneficial. It is also, from a design standpoint, an interesting measure of the overall efficiency of the hull and its rig, which can be expressed as the ratio of VMG to true boatspeed. And always remember, if you don't mind using the engine, that you can improve the VMG upwind or down, by motor-sailing.

Reefing

Furling the jib or genoa is child's play with roller reefing. Just ease the sheet until the sail begins to flutter, then start pulling in the furling line from the drum, while continuing to pay out the sheet just fast enough to maintain some tension in it. This is essential in order to achieve a tidy roll of sail instead of a loose, baggy bundle. When you have reduced sail sufficiently, cleat off the furling line, move the sheet fairlead forward to maintain the correct lead to the clew (see p. 110), and sheet in again. Incidentally, when you've rolled the sail up completely, it's always a good idea to put a lashing round it before leaving the boat, otherwise if the furling line should come adrift for any reason, the sail can unroll and flog itself to pieces.

Reefing the mainsail is easy too on a multihull, because it provides a reasonably level and stable working platform, and on a catamaran an exceptionally wide and secure one as well. Assuming your boat is fitted with a slab reefing system, the normal reefing sequence is as follows:

1. Let off the vang (if fitted) or ease the sheet, and head up, so that the sail is no longer drawing.
2. Set up the topping lift, or the lazyjacks, to support the boom, or in the case of a micro, just lay it on the deck.
3. Ease the halyard, pull the luff down far enough to hook on its reef cringle, and re-tension the halyard.
4. Haul the clew cringle down on to the boom with the reefing pendant.
5. Ease away the topping list, re-tension the vang, and sheet in.

In order to lose as little boatspeed as possible, the first two items can be omitted, although it's sometimes hard work. The sequence begins instead by easing the halyard (try standing on it; it makes a very effective brake) and clawing the luff down by hand with the sail still sheeted in – it may be necessary to head up slightly to relieve some of the tension on the slides or boltrope. Then proceed as before, but ease the sheet at the same time as

you haul in the clew pendant, and harden in again as soon as the clew is down on the boom.

To shake out a reef, you simply follow the opposite sequence, making sure you free off the clew reefing pendant before releasing the luff and retensioning the halyard, otherwise you risk damaging the sail.

The alternative system of roller reefing around the boom is even simpler to operate and gives a neat stow, but the resulting shape of the reefed sail is seldom as good as that achieved with slabs. The advantages of both systems can be combined, however, by rolling down the sail until the reef cringles are reached, locking the furling handle, and using the slab procedure as before. The vang must of course be replaced by a barber hauler for offwind working if the mainsheet track is not long enough.

Reefing on the run can be difficult, but it's worth trying as an alternative to rounding up into the wind, especially if you've left things a bit late and are carrying too much sail. Even with the low apparent windspeed, there will almost certainly be too much pressure of wind on the sail to be able to lower it with the boom squared out, so first sheet it in tight and bring it amidships with the traveller. Windspeed across the deck will increase dramatically as the boat slows down, and the helmsman must respond quickly to any tendency to broach. Much of the friction will now have gone from the luff, and it should be possible to pull the sail down – all the way, if you want a breather; you can always reef it and raise it after you have come head to wind.

If the sail still refuses to move sufficiently, your only other option is to keep the boom amidships and slow the boat still further by furling or dropping the jib. Then come slowly round on to the wind, letting fly the traveller control line as you do so – and the mainsheet too if need be – so as to keep the speed down.

Neither of these tactics is to be recommended, but it is only too easy to be lulled into a false sense of security by the ease with which these boats can run, and to be fooled by the seeming absence of much wind. In doing so, you overlook the multihuller's number one safety maxim: reef early.

Strong wind sailing

Busting along in half a gale can be loads of fun. Most of us enjoy sailing in rough weather once in a while, so long as it doesn't last too long. But the sea is not a playground. It demands increasing alertness and concentration the more conditions deteriorate, and mistakes become potentially more costly, especially in coastal waters. Here the seas in strong winds always seem more savage than out on the deep ocean, becoming shorter and steeper as the waves roll in and start to feel bottom at 30–40m, beginning to topple as the water shoals further, and finally breaking as the depth decreases to about twice wave height. In shallow water, an uneven or steeply shelving seabed can also cause some evil overfalls and eddies, and patches of white water in any races. When the stream turns against the wind in tidal waters, a three knot current can double the wave height, and a quiet stretch of sea can be whipped up in minutes into marching ranks of whitecaps. Cross-seas can superimpose themselves following a windshift, or from the backwash off a headland, and high ground will often cause turbulence to windward of it, and gusting in its lee. Combine these sometimes nasty conditions with the constant presence of commercial shipping traffic, and one can understand why blue water yachtsmen usually regard their departure and approach to land as the most taxing parts of their voyages.

Nevertheless, up to Force 5 or so, small boat sailing can certainly be fun, although there will inevitably come a time when, as the man said as he stood on the harbour wall, 'I'd rather be here, wishing I was out there, than be out there wishing I was back here.' If you have any doubts about your capabilities or those of your crew, and there's dirty weather about, don't go; but if you are already out in a strong breeze and a rapid deterioration is forecast, you can use your speed to seek shelter. A fast multihull stands a good chance of being able to outrun a storm; and if it is ever caught out in survival conditions, it will more than likely live through them, given competent handling, such is the seaworthiness and structural integrity of most modern designs. But even in everyday strong winds and in anything of a seaway, certain techniques need to be understood and practised in order to get the best out of the boat, and to avoid breaking gear and frightening the crew (and yourself), or risking capsize. Bear in mind that a rise in the wind strength from, say, 15 knots to 30 (Force 4 to Force 7) will quadruple both the pressure acting on the sails – from 4 to 16kg/m² (0.8 to 3.2lb/ft²) – and the typical wave height from around a foot to nearly four feet (0.3 to 1.2m).

STEERING TO WINDWARD

To repeat the golden rule, if you are beating and beginning to worry about the way the boat is handling – and certainly before you even think of bearing away on to a reach – reef and slow down. Butting into a head sea at four

Fig 9.7 *Sailing too slowly to windward in rough seas is to risk stalling on top of a large wave, sliding backwards and sideways down its face, and possibly even capsizing.*

knots is much kinder to the boat and its crew than slamming into it at eight. But be sure you leave enough sail up to maintain full control.

In winds approaching gale force, a near bullet-proof combination of sails consists of a heavyweight storm jib, set if necessary on a portable forestay, and either your deeply reefed main or preferably a storm trisail in place of it. This is smaller than the reefed main – say a quarter of the size of the full sail – made of very heavy cloth, and loose footed. It is secured in the luff groove in the usual way (or in a second track, leaving the main *in situ*) and it has its own sheets which are passed either side of the boom (which is lashed down out of the way) via snatch blocks to the genoa winches. It is also a good idea to have storm sails made from a fluorescent orange cloth, so that they can easily be seen among the white wave crests.

Another element of the golden rule is to keep the boat moving decisively ahead with plenty of steerage way, for as long as you have sail up. The prudent use of speed is all part of seamanship. Sail too slowly, or too close to the wind, and the next big wave may stop you dead in the water (unlike a heavy displacement boat, which is more likely to have the momentum to drive through it) or knock you off on to a reach, which is the last thing you want with your centreboards down and sails pinned in. If it were to happen, the boat would start to heel and accelerate, and the problem would be to get her back close hauled without hitting another breaker. Try to keep the speed down by feathering the sails while you look for a gap in the seas, and the moment you spot one, power up and go for it, luffing through it as gently as you can on to your former heading.

Another danger in sailing too slowly to

windward in rough or confused seas is of stalling on top of a wave and sliding backwards and sideways down its face, which not only puts a very heavy strain on the rudders, even enough to break them, but as the bows pay off there is an increased risk of capsize. If you are determined, or obliged by navigational constraints to continue thrashing to windward, be sure to keep plenty of way on and steer a wriggly course, easing the boat as cleanly as you can through each wave by luffing slightly up its face and bearing away sharply as you approach the crest so as to pick up speed again down its back.

Tacking in the rough stuff must obviously be done very carefully to avoid stalling in the middle of the manoeuvre. Bear away before a wave, luff on to it, and go about immediately behind it. If you stall, reverse the helm and hold it very firmly, because the force on the rudders will be considerable during the sternboard; if the tiller were yanked out of your hand, it might be impossible to pull it back and you would lose control.

OFF THE WIND IN HEAVY WEATHER

Sailing a reaching course in breaking seas is difficult and potentially hazardous, because you become vulnerable to wave crests slamming into the boat from abeam and trying to throw her on to her downhill side, with the added risk of structural damage. The centreboard(s) must, of course, be fully retracted to allow her to surf sideways without tripping, crew weight must be positioned as far as possible up on the weather quarter, and a course adroitly steered to avoid the largest waves by luffing (gently, remember) to let one pass ahead and running away from the next one. It can be a somewhat nerve-racking ex-perience, and one that leaves very little margin for error. The sooner you are able to bring the wind and waves well aft of the beam, the better; and the sooner the fun starts.

Running off is also the surest and safest way of slowing the boat under these conditions, 'slow' being a strictly relative term, because you'll still be moving fast. In fact you will have more than enough power to do this without the mainsail, which has a tendency to skew the boat into a broach, so it will be best to hand it before you turn downwind, and to run under jib alone. It's easy on the nerves, and instantly adjustable if you have it on a roller. At the same time you have the option of sailing much faster still, if you have got your breath back and are feeling adventurous again, by hopping on to the front of a wave and surfing.

To do this, you first have to catch your wave by luffing and accelerating to match its speed before settling on it. As the wind draws forward with increasing boatspeed, you progressively bear away again on a freeing curve, adjusting your speed with the helm so as to remain on the wave for as long as you can, or wish to. Do not ever, by the way, be tempted by the seemingly moderate windspeed to fly a spinnaker in really wild weather, because if you were accidentally to run slap into the back of the next steep wave the sudden deceleration, combined with the high level leverage and momentum of the full spinnaker, could easily pitchpole the boat bodily over its bows before you could let fly its halyard or sheets (fig. 4.1). Ocean racing skippers often risk it, and they haven't always got away with it.

Survival tactics

It is unlikely that you will ever be called upon to cope with survival conditions. Given the choice, few of us like to stray far from shelter when dirty weather is forecast, and more often than not we are given the options of discretion and valour. Nevertheless it makes sense to include some suitable tactics in your repertoire in case you are caught out one day in wild weather, dearly wishing you were somewhere else.

The first thing to try, if you have a storm trisail or can set a very small amount of mainsail, is to heave to by sheeting it in hard, and with the traveller down to leeward, lowering a *very* small amount of centreboard (windward side in a cat) and lashing the helm so that the boat is moving slowly to weather at an angle of about 60° to the wind and waves. Some boats can make safe and steady progress like this, others are unpredictable and need constant helm corrections.

If you reach the stage when there's too much wind for this tactic, or you find it isn't working very well, one option is to take off all the remaining sail and lie a-hull with the boards fully raised. Most boats will then drift more or less beam on, surfing sideways with the breaking crests; but a few may not behave so well. To do this would be to invite capsize with a small narrow-beamed cat, whose weather hull would be liable to be lifted high enough by a big wave for it to be blown over the leeward one before it could start to surf; and a tri with low-buoyancy floats is even more unsuited to lying a-hull, because the downhill float will readily dig in and trip the boat. The modern broad-beamed cat, however, or tri with high-buoyancy floats will usually lie a-hull under most conditions in comparative safety.

Another sound strategy, provided there is sufficient sea room, is to continue running dead downwind, the slowest point of sailing, with only the storm jib set, or only the merest scrap of headsail unfurled. In either case, the sail is best held flat amidships using both sheets, so as to minimize the drive and to act as a vane to keep the boat's head downwind. If this results in your moving too fast and in danger of surfing, which might leave you with little or no rudder control in the aerated water flowing forward under the boat – or there is a need to reduce leeway because of the presence of land – you can slow the boat by taking off all sail and trailing a long bight of rope with one end attached to each stern or float.

If this still doesn't put the brakes on sufficiently, resort to towing a sea anchor comprised of one or more motor tyres (without which it is said no long distance sailor puts to sea) weighted down with several metres of chain, or use one of the commercially available parachute or metal drogues, including a swivel in the line to prevent the whole lot from winding itself up into an ineffective bunch. If you haven't any such items aboard, the boat's bower anchor will offer a fair amount of drag through the water. Again, take advantage of the multihull's width by streaming the drogue on a strong bridle, at least 50m long for preference, secured to the stern mooring cleats and backed to other rugged strong-points such as the bow cleats, or even to the base of the mast – or led through heavy snatch blocks on the sterns to the primary winches. The bridle will exert a powerful straightening force to hold the boat end on to the seas – or angled off them, if she rides more easily like that –

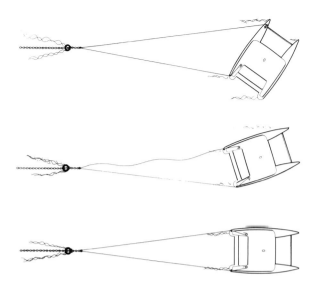

instead of allowing her to slew broadside as can happen with a monohull, and the relative lengths of the bridle warps can be adjusted to steer her straight following a windshift. Aim to reduce speed to 2–3 knots, but don't try to take all way off, as a breaking sea could poop you. An alternative which suits some boats is to make fast the bridle to the ends of the weather hull or float, again suitably backed, and to adjust them so that she is riding at a broad angle to the waves without too many of them jumping aboard to pound the superstructure.

The further alternative of lying to a drogue rigged from the bows so as to take the waves head on, or at a shallow angle, is generally not favoured by those who have tried it, because of the likelihood of damage to the rudders when the bows lift and the boat is hurled backwards on to her sterns, and the danger of diagonal bows-over-quarter capsize despite the bridle's restraining influence; both have happened. But a parachute anchor large enough effectively to stop the vessel from making any sternway – which means a minimum of 3–4m diameter for a small boat and several times

Fig 9.8 *Lying to a sea anchor. (top) Rigged to the windward hull. (centre and bottom) Secured to the sterns, where bridle exerts a powerful straightening force that tends to keep the boat end on to the waves.*

that size for a large one – has helped many a long distance sailor to survive.

Opinions are divided as to which is the preferred type of boat in these conditions, the cat with enormous reserves of buoyancy in its lee hull, or the still wider tri with its greater static stability, but with rather less buoyancy to leeward. It probably comes down to a matter of luck, and the combination of the particular design characteristics with the wind and wave patterns at the time.

The safest course with any multihull, in the view of most of the experienced sailors who have tried it all ways, is to head off downwind under bare poles, streaming warps or dragging a drogue, keeping your fingers crossed for enough sea room.

Whatever action you take, there's always the chance, however remote, of meeting 'the ultimate wave', and the only certain way of avoiding that is to stay at home. Fortunately for the majority of amateur sailors, the possibility never arises. But if the worst should happen and your boat is capsized, stay with it for as long as it floats. For sure you should carry a liferaft on offshore voyages, together with drysuits and a grab bag of essentials, but *never* make the mistake of getting into it until you are convinced your vessel is going to sink – which with modern designs is so unlikely as to be well-nigh impossible. Life on or inside an upturned hull will be miserably damp and uncomfortable, to say the least, even with a survival compartment. But it will be sheltered and, except in some of the smaller boats without much inverted airspace, far less dangerous than clinging for any length of time to the slippery, waveswept bottoms of the hulls, or being tossed around at the mercy of the weather in a tiny raft.

Discretion or valour? The ultimate discretion would probably be to sell your boat and take up golf. Yet there's equally little point in being brave and scaring yourself and your crew witless. Certainly, anyone who puts to sea and is not in some measure frightened of it must be totally lacking in imagination. Indeed most of us do it as much for the challenge of coping with an alien environment as for any other reason, and we take a certain pride in the self-reliance that the sea demands. Nevertheless, our kind of sailing is supposed to be fun, not an ordeal. Most multihulls have enormous reserves of stability. Just be careful you don't call on them unnecessarily. Prudence is, after all, one of the most essential ingredients of seamanship. So relax and enjoy yourself – and take care.

APPENDIX 1

Recommended reading

MAGAZINES

Multihull International, 2 Please's Passage, Totnes, Devon TQ9 5QN, UK.

Multihulls, 421 Hancock Street, Quincy (Boston) MA 02171, USA.

Multicoques Magazine, 16 Centre commercial du Nautisme, 83400 Hyères, France.

BOOKS

Sailing Theory and Practice, C. A. Marchaj (Adlard Coles, London).

Seaworthiness: The Forgotten Factor, C. A. Marchaj (Adlard Coles, London).

Small Boat Sails, Jeremy Howard-Williams, (Adlard Coles, London).

The Best of Sail Trim, edited by Charles Mason (Adlard Coles, London).

The Gougeon Brothers on Boat Construction (Gougeon Bros. Inc., P.O. Box X908, Bay City, Michigan 48707, USA).

Moxie, Phil Weld (available from *Multihull International*).

Multihulls Offshore, Rob James (Macmillan, London).

Canoes of Oceania, A. C. Haddon & J. Hornell (Bishop Museum Press, Honolulu).

Two Girls, Two Catamarans, James Wharram (available from James Wharram, Greenbank Road, Devoran, Truro, Cornwall TR3 6PJ, UK).

Multihull clubs and organisations

GREAT BRITAIN

Amateur Yacht Research Society, R. Michael Ellison, Pengelly House, Wilcove, Torpoint, Cornwall P11 2PG

Catalac Owners Assn, Mary Lack, Flagstaff House, Mudeford, Christchurch, Dorset

Cruising Assn, Ivory House, St Katharine Dock, London E1 9AT

Heavenly Twins Assn, Mary Challis, Tideway, Prinsted, Emsworth, Hants

Hirondelle Assn, John Edwards, P.O. Box 256, Camberley, Surrey

International Yacht Racing Union (IYRU), Simon Forbes, 60 Knightsbridge, London SW1X 7JX

Iroquois Owners Assn, Stuart Fisher, Huntswood, St Helena's Lane, Streat, Nr Hassocks, Sussex BN6 8SD

Multihull Offshore Cruising & Racing Assn (MOCRA), Janice Uttley, 1 Ward Crescent, Emsworth, Hants PO10 7RR

Polynesian Catamarans Assn, Ms Sandy Turner, Foss Quay, Millbrook, Torpoint, Cornwall PL10 1EN

Prout Catamaran Owners Assn, Tony Williams, 9 Chestwood Close, Billericay, Essex CM12 0PB

Royal Yachting Assn (RYA), RYA House, Romsey Road, Eastleigh, Hants SO5 4YA

Telstar Owners Assn, Dave Howell, 1 Roman Reach, Caerleon, Gwent

AUSTRALIA

Cairns Yacht Club, John Croucher, P.O. Box 279, 4 Esplanade, Cairns, Queensland 4870

Multihull Yacht Assn of New South Wales, David Bishop, Box 4820, GPO Sydney 2001

Multihull Yacht Club of Victoria (MYCV), A.J. Considine, P/L, 437 St Kilda Road, Melbourne, Victoria 3004

Queensland Multihull Yacht Club, Ian Kelshaw, P.O. Box 4, East Brisbane, Queensland 4169

Trailertri Assn of Queensland, Margaret Finegan, 189 Collingwood Road, Wellington Point, Queensland 4160

Trailertri Club of South Australia, Jacob Baden, 28 Kandahar Crescent, Colonel Light Gardens, SA 5042

Trailertri-Tramp Assn of New South Wales, Chris Nelson, 62 Coonong Road, Gymea Bay, NSW 2227

BRAZIL

Associacoa Brasileira de Multicascos de Oceano, Sergio Chermont, Rua Barata Ribeiro 807/604, Copacabana, Rio de Janeiro CEP 22051

Multiforme-Brasil, C.P.111580, R. Fernando de Norhonha 285, 28900 Cabo Frio RJ

CANADA

Atlantic Multihull Assn (AMA), John Culjak, P.O. Box 322, Armdale, NS B3L IJ7

British Columbia Multihull Society (BCMS), Len Chambers, P.O. Box 2751, Vancouver BC V6B 3X2

Kingston Catamaran Club, Brian Dash, 163 Chelsea Road, Kingston, Ontario K7M 3Y9

Lake Ontario Multihull Racing Assn (LOMRA), Jacqui Webb, 45 Loggers Run, Unit 8, Barrie, Ontario L4N 6W3

Polynesian Catamaran Assn, Roly Heubsch, 214 Glebemount Avenue, Toronto, Ontario M4K 3P1

Toronto Multihull Cruising Club (TMCC), Flo Rutland, 188 Gough Avenue, Toronto, Ontario M4K 3P1

Western Multihull Assn (WMA), P. Vaissade, 9043 Collingwood, Vancouver, BC U6R 3K7

DENMARK

Danske Flerskrogssejler (DF), Jannik Cortssen, Snekkeled 30, Munkebo, DK-5330

FRANCE

Assn of International Competitors on Oceanic Multihulls (ACIMO), 220 rue de Rivoli, 75001 Paris

Fédération Française de Voile, Michel Barbier, 55 Avenue Kleber, 75784 Paris Cedex 16

Formule 28 Assn, Gilles Abeloos, BP40, 60 Avenue de Paris, 95290 l'Isle-Adam

Les Glenans Sailing Assn, Quai Louis Bleriot, 75781 Paris Cedex 16

International Formula 40 Council, 55 Avenue Kleber, 75784 Paris Cedex 16

Rhone-Alpes Multicoques Sailing Assn, B.P.9, route du Port, 74410 St Lorioz

Union Nationales des Multicoques (UNM), John Jeuffrain, 2 rue de la Gare, 27400 Louviers

HOLLAND

Catamaran en Trimaran Club Nederland, W. Basle, Reigerstraat 6, 1452 XR Ilpendam

International Micro Multihull Class Assn (IMCA), Alexander Verheus, Overtoom 166-1, 1054 HP Amsterdam

IRELAND

Irish Multihull Assn, Ken Burke, 17 Harbour Road, Skerries

ITALY

Assn Italiana Proprietari Multiscafi, Alberto Rapi, C. so Porta Romana 17, 20122 Milano

NEW ZEALAND

Auckland Multihull Sailing Assn (AMSA), Duncan Stuart, P.O. Box 3337, Auckland

NORWAY

Norsk Flerskrog Seilklubb (NFS), Anders Amble, P.O. Box 102, Sentrum, 0104 Oslo

Viken Flerskrogseilere, Anders Amble, Haraasveien 1b, 0283 Oslo

SWEDEN

Sveriges Catamaran och Trimaran Seglare (SCTS), Dag Sjogenbo, Eckbachavagen 5, Saltsjo-Boo 13200

Vaestustens Flerskorvs Seglare (VFS), Bengt Hellqvist, Grinnekullegatan 10, S-41747 Goteborg

UNITED STATES

Amateur Yacht Research Society (AYRS), Michael Badham, Rt 2, Box 180, Bath, ME 04530

Chesapeake Cruising Multihull Assn (CCMA), Herb Butler, 3906 Calawassee Road, Edgewater, MD 21037

Columbia Multihull Society (CMS), Bernard Kobliha, P.O. Box 915, Beaverton, OR 97075

Florida Multihulls Assn, Joan Gregory, 1414 Von Pfister Street, Key West, FL 33040

Florida Offshore Multihull Assn (FOMA), Doug Fricke, P.O. Box 13293, St Petersburg, FL 33733

Formula 500 Assn, Alan O'Driscoll, Star Route 3, La Honda, CA 94020

Galveston Bay Multihull Assn (GBMA), Frank Tuma, 18619 Upper Bay Road, Houston, TX 77058

Gemini Owners Assn (GOA), Pat or Jim Godfrey, 3122 Bryant Lane, Webster, TX 77598

Great Lakes Multihull Assn (GLMA), R. VandenBosche, 1328 West Barry 3rd, Chicago, IL 60657

New England Multihull Assn (NEMA), Debbie Druan, 89 Cochituate Road, Framingham, MA 01701

Northwest Multihull Assn (NWMA), Lin Santer, P.O. Box 70413, Ballard Station, Seattle, WA 98107

Ocean Racing Catamaran Assn (ORCA), A. Victor Stern, 279 Ravenna Drive, Long Beach, CA 90803

Pacific Multihull Assn (PMA), Peter Jongblood, 1312 West 37th Street, San Pedro, CA 90731

Performance Cruising Multihull Assn, P.O. Box 381, Mayo, MD 21160

San Francisco Bay Area Multihull Assn (BAMA), Lynn K. Therriault, 6127 Plymouth Avenue, Richmond, CA 94805

Sea Wind Assn, Ed Diehl, 11999 49th Street North, Unit 103, Clearwater, FL 34622

Telstar Trimaran Owners Assn, 27150 Moody Court, Los Altos Hills, CA 94022

Trailerable Multihull Assn, Wayne Evans, 87 Maplewood Drive, Athens, OH 45701

Trailertri Assn, Ian Farrier, P.O. Box 7362, Los Altos Hills, CA 92012

U.S. Formula 40 Class Assn, Cameron C. Lewis, P.O. Box 1370, Newport RI 02840

U.S. Yacht Racing Union (USYRU), Lee Parks, P.O. Box 209, Newport, RI 02830

Viking Multihull Sail Club, Doug Kayner, 2023 Norfolk, Ann Arbor, MI 48103

WEST GERMANY

Multihull Deutschland, Heinrich Wolper, Parkallee 227, 2800 Bremen

---

Compiled with the assistance of *Multihulls* magazine.

INDEX